Road Biking
Northern New England

A Guide to the Greatest Bike Rides in Vermont,
New Hampshire, and Maine

To buy books in quantity for corporate use
or incentives, call **(800) 962–0973**
or e-mail **premiums@GlobePequot.com.**

FALCONGUIDES®

Photos by Sandy Duling unless otherwise indicated.
Maps by Tim Kissel © Morris Book Publishing, LLC

Library of Congress Cataloging-in-Publication Data

Duling, Sandy.
   Road biking northern New England: A guide to the
greatest bike rides in Vermont, New Hampshire, and
Maine/Sandy Duling
        p. cm.
     ISBN 978-0-7627-3897-7
   1. Bicycle touring–Maine–Guidebooks. 2. Bicycle
touring–New Hampshire–Guidebooks. 3. Bicycle touring–Vermont—Guidebooks. 4. New England–Guidebooks.
I. Title.

GV1045.5.M2D85 2008

796.630974–dc22
                            2008005976
Printed in the United States of America
10 9 8 7 6 5 4 3 2 1

Contents

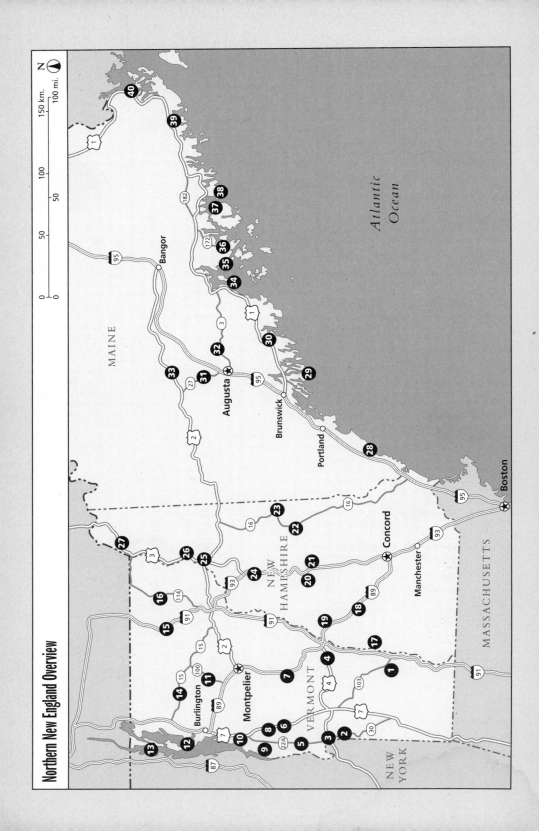

Northern New England Overview

Preface

It would have been easy to identify forty rides in any one of the three northern New England states. From a large pool of potential choices, I've tried to select a few of the best in each state. Routes were chosen based on scenic interest, volume of traffic, safety, length, and terrain. Sadly, I had to exclude a number of otherwise lovely rides because of volume of traffic or inadequacy of road shoulders. Other selection criteria were points of interest and possible stops. Just about every ride has an interesting stop or two. Some have many such stops. Casual cyclists will want to take in all the sights. Serious cyclists will skip most of the stops and concentrate on fine pedaling.

Thanks to all the friends and family who made trip suggestions, pedaled with me, patiently posed for photographs, provided bed and breakfast, and enthusiastically joined in the fun of this project: Alec Duling, Amanda Duling, Andy Duling, Elizabeth Mann, Jane Pawling, Glenn Deruchie, Ginny Thompson, Joe Thompson, Suzanne Gallagher, Mary Hamilton, Pat Max, Becky Lamey, Susan Buzzell, Peter Spitzform, and the owners and employees of all the bike shops I visited. Special thanks to Debbie Robinson, who tirelessly and with infinite good humor made sure we got the details right on the Maine rides. And, of course, thanks to my husband, Ennis Duling, for years of support and encouragement, for lots of help with the photography, and for being such a fine biking companion.

And finally, thanks to the owners and employees of northern New England's general stores. This book is dedicated to you. Research on almost every ride reminded me of the vital role these little stores play in the community life of rural New England. May you flourish.

Introduction

The best way to see Vermont, New Hampshire, and Maine is by bike. Automobile-bound visitors may cover more miles, but they miss many of the smells, tastes, and historical details that cyclists are certain to discover. And the details are everywhere, from a Civil War–era fort on the Maine coast to tiny eighteenth-century cemeteries and the remains of stone walls on forested hillsides.

The three northern New England states have many similarities, but each has a unique character—a character in large part shaped by its terrain. Vermont has its Champlain Valley and Connecticut Valley dairy farms, New Hampshire its rugged White Mountains and lakes, and Maine, of course, has its coast. Rides were selected for this collection to take advantage of each state's special terrain and character.

Working on this book was a real pleasure. I knew it would be fun, but it was even more rewarding than I anticipated. My passion for biking has taken me, over the years, to many parts of northern New England, but here was an excuse to test-ride new routes in unexplored territories. If, from the experience of these rides, I were to draw a single conclusion, it would be this: The beauty and variety of northern New England scenery is surpassed only by the energy and individuality of its people. There was the seventy-year-old woman at Lake Bomoseen (Vermont) who was out for a 20-mile ramble. And there was the young man in the donut shop near Damariscotta (Maine), happily making his way through a mountain of donuts and a large coffee during a pause in his pedal from Virginia to Bar Harbor. Northern New England bikers all seem to embody the qualities that characterize the inhabitants of these states: a quirky individuality, tough-mindedness, concern for the environment, and a sense of adventure. And just as memorable are the nonbikers I met in my travels—who may, in fact, be bikers but whom I happened to meet in other capacities: those stalwart keepers of the general stores, who patiently dish out ice cream, directions, and local news; town clerks, who know the name of every local road, path, and pothole; state park employees and volunteers; truck drivers; tractor and hay wagon drivers; librarians; anglers; kids on playgrounds; town road crews. They all waved, moved over, pondered directions, or lent a hand. It's my hope that readers of this collection of rides will have as much fun enjoying northern New England's scenery and people as I've had.

Safety

Wear a helmet. Most people who do a significant amount of biking will, eventually, take a tumble. Mine occurred while working on a previous bike book. My helmet broke, dispersing the blow, and I walked away from the fall. Without the helmet, what was a very minor accident would have resulted—at best—in a head injury. The helmets now available are designed to be lightweight, easily adjustable, and provide good ventilation. If you haven't bought a new helmet in the last few years, it's probably time for an update.

Ride single file and stay to the right. A surprising number of visiting cyclists are so delighted with the rural aspect of northern New England roads that they assume there is no traffic at all. They're sometimes found riding two or even three abreast down the center of the road. Remember that what looks like a quaint country road to the visitor is, in fact, the main route between towns, to work, or to the big city for local folks.

Be sure your bike is in good working order. Check brakes, cables, and tires regularly.

Carry water and at least a small snack. Biking is strenuous exercise, and, especially in summer, it doesn't take long to become dehydrated. Clear and pristine as New England streams may appear, do not drink water from them without first treating it.

Be visible. The bright biking jerseys cyclists wear are more than a fashion statement—they're safer than duller-colored shirts. Don't set out until daylight in the morning and stop riding before dusk. Be predictable: signal your intentions before turning. Drivers aren't necessarily accustomed to having bicycles on the road, and even when you think you're in plain sight, they may not notice you. Pedal defensively. Watch especially carefully for cars backing out of parking areas.

Equipment

All rides in this collection are well suited to touring or road bikes. I've done them all on a road bike with 28mm tires, and my biking companions have often had skinnier tires. A few rides use short sections of unpaved road, but none that aren't suitable for even the skinniest tires. Road and touring bikes are definitely the best bet for the longer rides. Hybrid bikes would also be fine for shorter routes.

Other than bike, helmet, and a water bottle, little additional equipment is absolutely necessary. A cyclocomputer or a GPS unit will allow you to make best use of the Miles and Directions section for each ride. A few simple tools for repair are a good idea: a mini pump, a spare tube, a couple of tire irons. Without these, a flat could mean a long walk. Tools are especially important on some of the longer, more remote routes, where it could be 10, 20, or even 30 miles to the next town. The possible need for extra clothing should always be considered. Northern New England weather is notoriously changeable, and it's wise to carry at least a windbreaker. In spring and fall—and even in the summer—low temperatures, cold rain, and a stiff wind can combine to cause hypothermia. Pay attention to weather forecasts, and pack accordingly.

Most cyclists have something in which to carry an assortment of the above-mentioned items, plus car keys, money, food, and perhaps a camera. A backpack is usually a poor choice for biking. It's often uncomfortable, and it raises the rider's

Pedaling around Hollywood's "Golden Pond" on the Squam Lake Cruise

center of gravity. Small wedge packs that fit under the bike seat hold a surprisingly large amount, and are often all that's needed. Slightly larger packs that attach to the handlebars are also popular. For overnights, you'll want a rack and panniers, or perhaps smaller "saddle bags."

Other Sources of Information

Local bike shops and cycling clubs (often with headquarters at a local bike shop) are the best source of information on local rides. Many have Web sites that have been included in the additional information following each ride description in this collection.

The Adventure Cycling Association is a trusted source of maps and cycling advice. Section 11 of their TransAmerica Northern Tier Route crosses all three northern New England states.

State departments of transportation and local chambers of commerce are often surprisingly helpful. The Maine Department of Transportation has published *Explore Maine by Bike: 25 Loop Bicycle Tours,* available from the Maine Department of Transportation or online at www.exploremaine.org/bike/bike_tours.html. Most of the loops are quite long, but they generally offer a couple of alternatives for shorter trips as well. The New Hampshire Department of Transportation has produced a series of regional bicycle maps, available from the New Hampshire Department of Transportation, regional tourist information centers, or online at www.nhbikeped.com. These are not tours; the maps attempt to indicate the safest and most scenic cycling roads in a section of the state.

Touring near Mt. Mansfield, the highest point in Vermont

How to Use This Guide

Directions, turns, and points of interest are indicated by mileage from the beginning of the ride. I've aimed for accuracy to the tenth of a mile. Although the directions will be good guides for anyone, the mileage indicators will be most useful for riders who have a cyclocomputer. Cyclocomputers are quite inexpensive—less than $20 for one with lots of fancy functions. Remember, however, that cyclocomputers are not uniformly accurate. If it hasn't been correctly calibrated, if tire pressure varies, or you're carrying an unusually heavy load, readings can be off. And remember that the cyclocomputer records every little detour to check out a view or buy a candy bar. Having a cyclocomputer along doesn't mean you don't have to read maps. Some serious touring cyclists carry GPS units. Although more accurate than cyclocomputers, the same caution about little detours applies, and they have their own quirks: They need to "see" the sky, so a particularly shady road may cause them to gloss minor twists and turns, and record inaccurate distances.

Each chapter includes brief additional information about local places to find food, accommodations, attractions and events, bike shops, and additional sources of local information. I have included only highlights here, and have tried to limit listings to sites that seem likely to be stable. Businesses come and go, phone numbers and Web addresses change, and we all have our own ideas of what constitutes an "attraction." These listings are merely suggestions for putting together your own biking adventure. Please notify the publisher of name changes, errors, and additional attractions that should be included.

Some biking guidebooks (including some in this series) have a separate listing of restrooms for each ride. I have occasionally mentioned restrooms in the text and in the Miles and Directions sections. But most rides in this collection are in very rural areas. General stores (not "convenience stores") are still the norm in much of northern New England. The typical general store has its own septic system, which simply won't support a public restroom. Occasionally, a general store will allow a cyclist to use their toilet, but they can't permit me to publish the availability of a restroom in their store. A prominent northern New England bicycle touring company clearly explains to their riders that public restrooms are not generally available, and that cyclists should plan to use the "green door" restroom. (We may not have many convenience stores, but we have lots of forests.)

A map is provided for each ride. Note that the maps are not on a uniform scale throughout the book, and so cannot be used for purposes of comparison. In addition to the map and directions provided here, it's wise to use a more detailed topographic map such as those in the DeLorme atlases. I actually rip pages out of my DeLorme atlases so I can carry only the necessary map(s) on my rides. After the ride, I slide the pages back in the book. (For those of us who love books, it's hard to make that first tear. But you get used to doing it, and it doesn't really diminish the usefulness of the atlas. If you get too much flack from the rest of the family, buy them another copy.)

Having the contour lines on the DeLorme maps can be especially important. This isn't Connecticut or Rhode Island, where you can be sure it's all reasonably flat. Rides included here range from quite flat (southern coastal Maine and the Champlain Valley) to downright mountainous (Franconia and Dixville Notches). I've tried to take terrain into account when assigning ride categories. So a shorter ride with steeper terrain might be placed in a more difficult category. Conversely, a longer ride with flat terrain and little traffic might go in an easier category.

Rides range from 10 to almost 100 miles, with a majority in the shorter range. In order to help with planning, the rides have been assigned one of four designations, based on length and level of difficulty. A cautionary note: Assessing "difficulty" is a very subjective thing. What seems a mountain to one rider may be a modest hill to another, and vice versa. Although the four categories of rides will offer general assistance, it's important to read ride descriptions and consult a map with contour lines when making ride selections.

Rambles are the easiest and shortest rides in the book, accessible to almost all riders and easily completed in one day. They are less than 35 miles long and are generally on easier terrain.

Cruises are intermediate in difficulty and distance. They are generally 25 to 50 miles long and may include some moderate climbs. Cruises will generally be completed easily by an experienced rider in one day, but inexperienced or out-of-shape riders might want to take two days with an overnight stop.

Challenges are more difficult, designed especially for experienced riders in good condition. They are usually 40 to 60 miles long and may include some steep climbs. Again, experienced riders will probably complete them in a day, but casual riders may want to take two days.

Classics are long and hard. They are over 60 miles and may include steep climbs and high-speed downhills. Even fit and experienced riders may want to take two days. These rides are not recommended for less fit and experienced riders unless they are done in shorter stages.

Map Legend

Limited Access Freeway	═══════════	
U.S. Highway/ Featured U.S. Highway	▭▭▭▭▭ / ▬▬▬▬▬	
State Highway/ Featured State Highway	────── / ━━━━━━	
County or Local Road/ Featured Road	────── / ━━━━━━	
Bike Route/ Featured Bike Route	·········· / ■■■■■■■■	

Capital	⊛	Small Park or Forest	♠
Town	○	Historic Site	🏛
Interstate Highway	89	Museum	🏛
U.S. Highway	1	University	🎓
State Highway	16	Church	⛪
Point of Interest	▫	Airport	✈
Building or Structure	■	Picnic Area	🌲
Campground	▲	Ski Area	⛷
Starting Point	❶	Mountain	▲
Mileage Marker	↗ 10.0	Boat Launch	🚤
Directional Arrow	→	Bridge	≍
Reservoir or Lake	⬭	Cemetery	⚰
River or Creek	～	Wildlife Area	🦅
Large Park/Forest	////////	Information	❷
State/Country Border	─··─··─	Lighthouse	🗼

Vermont

According to the 2000 census, Vermont is the most rural of the fifty states. In other words, of all the states, Vermont has the greatest percentage of people living in rural areas. From a biker's point of view, that means lots of back roads with relatively sparse traffic. Add a wonderful variety of scenery, terrain that varies from flat to mountainous, historic sites, swimming holes, and a population staunchly committed to an environmental ethic, and you've got the setting for terrific biking.

Farm country near Pawlet, Vermont PHOTO BY ENNIS DULING

The Green Mountains are Vermont's backbone. The Taconic Mountains and Lake Champlain mark the state's western boundary, and the Connecticut River forms much of the eastern border. Note that a number of rides in this collection are clustered in the west-central part of the state, in the relatively flat and fertile Champlain Valley. Pedaling is easy here, and dairy farm scenery is straight out of *Vermont Life*. The eastern margin of the state, along the Connecticut River, is also known for dairy farming, but the floodplain is narrower here than in the Champlain Valley.

The central part of the state offers a different kind of scenery. Large portions are part of the Green Mountain National Forest. The occasional farms here will be smaller "hillside farms," and logging is likely to be more important than livestock. This is where Vermont's famous ski areas are located. There are fewer rides in the center of the state. The reason isn't so much an avoidance of steep terrain (although some readers may applaud that logic). The reason is simply that there are fewer roads. A cautionary note: Because of the Green Mountains, there are a limited number of east-west roads across Vermont. Most are heavily traveled truck routes with narrow shoulders. If you plan a long-distance adventure that includes an east-west Vermont crossing, get advice from the Adventure Cycling Association or from local cyclists or bike shops.

One further note: Vermont's rural roads and scenic countryside are great, but they're just half of the pleasure of Vermont biking. You've missed the other half if you don't meet the people. Stop at the general stores, public libraries, roadside stands, and farmers' markets. Calvin Coolidge—a true Vermonter—summed it up in a speech he delivered in Bennington in 1928.

I love Vermont because of her hills and valleys, her scenery and invigorating climate, but most of all, because of her indomitable people. . . . If the spirit of liberty should vanish in other parts of the union, and support of our institutions should languish, it could all be replenished from the generous store held by the people of this brave little state of Vermont.

1 Grafton Ramble

This is a hilly ride through Vermont's history. Begin at the Grafton historic restoration and pedal to Athens—or what remains of Athens. It's all back roads and great scenery.

Start: Parking area next to the Information Building and adjacent to the Windham Foundation Building, in Grafton.
Length: 17.5 miles.

Terrain: Hilly.
Traffic and hazards: Traffic will be light. There is a short section (1 mile) of unpaved road that shouldn't be a problem for road bikes.

Getting there: From the Brattleboro area, take Interstate 91 north to exit 5. Get on Vermont Highway 5 North and proceed about 2 miles to the junction with Vermont Highway 121. Turn left off VT 5 onto VT 121 West. Continue on VT 121 about 12 miles to Grafton. In the center of Grafton, turn left off Main Street (VT 121) onto Townshend Road. Proceed 0.2 mile south on Townshend Road to the Information Building and municipal parking area on the left.

Grafton, our starting point, is a village that requires a little explanation. Grafton is perhaps best described as a miniature Williamsburg: Vermont's version of an historic restoration. In the early part of the nineteenth century, Grafton was a thriving town with a population of almost 1,500 people and about 10,000 sheep. By the mid-nineteenth century the Vermont wool industry began suffering from strong competition. Many Vermonters moved westward, and Grafton, like other Vermont towns, began a general decline. By the 1940s Grafton's population was a mere 393 people, and most of its buildings had deteriorated badly. In 1963 rescue arrived in the form of the Windham Foundation, a philanthropic organization whose first purpose is "to restore buildings and economic vitality in the village of Grafton." Today the Windham Foundation owns about half the buildings and a number of the businesses in town, including the renowned Old Tavern and the Grafton Village Cheese Company. The restorations are beautiful, and you'll note that Grafton attracts plenty of visitors. The Information Building and the adjacent Windham Foundation Center Building are both worth a stop.

It's downhill for the first 4 miles. VT 121 follows Saxton's River closely, paralleling its every twist and turn. Roads like this remind you that today's New England highways are built along what once were footpaths through the wilderness. Over the centuries they've been widened and the surfaces greatly improved, but we're still following that original route, which stuck close to the river.

After the turn onto Vermont Highway 35, it's a gentle uphill for a little over a mile. After the fork at 5.5 miles, prepare for a climb. For the next few miles you'll be pedaling through an area that once was much more populated than it is today. You'll pass overgrown pastures, remnants of foundations, and stone walls in what are now mature forests. Notice the handsome brick meeting house on the right at 6.5 miles. It was built in 1817, when Athens was thriving and sheep raising was big

Taking a break at the Grafton General Store

business. The ascent is a little over 2 miles, including a mix of steeper and quite gradual sections. The short dirt stretch shouldn't be a problem, but it may provide an opportunity to stretch your legs and walk a bit. You're at the top of the climb at about 8 miles. Then it's a long downhill.

Watch carefully for the right turn at 11.0 miles. You could be descending pretty fast at this point, and the turn is immediately after a bend. You'll be turning onto Townshend Road, but it's unmarked here. (Note that it's the first paved right after the fork at 5.5 miles.) Then it's a serious uphill again for a little over a mile. The climb levels off gradually, then you begin the long gradual descent back to Grafton.

Townshend Road is a wonderful biking road. It's hard to beat 5 miles of gradual descent along a sparsely traveled road with terrific scenery. Once again, the road follows the river very closely. This stream is the South Branch of Saxton's River. It's everything a mountain stream should be: a torrent in the spring, a great place to cool off in summer, an invitation to photograph its collection of colors in the fall.

Plan to stop at the Grafton Village Cheese Company on the right at 17.1 miles. They have a viewing window on the processing areas, and, after more than 17 miles, the free samples are a treat. The parking area in Grafton is less than half a mile away, so buying a brick of cheese to carry home won't be a hardship.

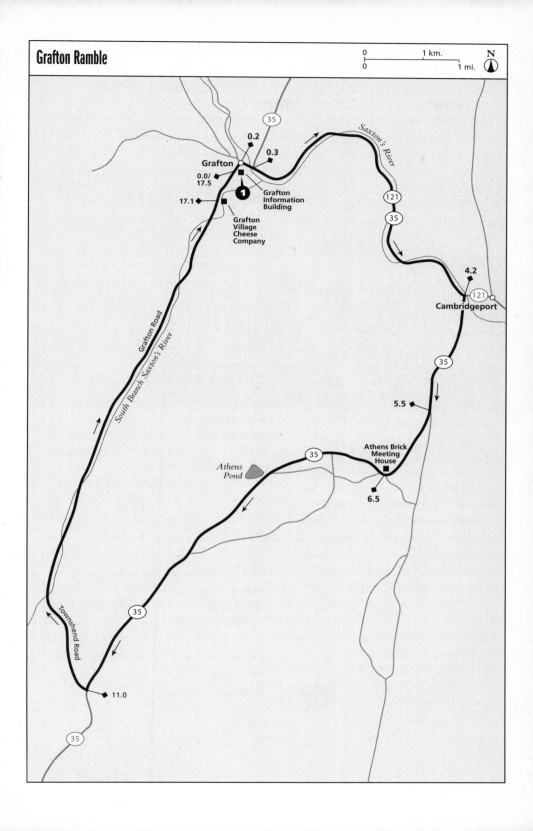

Grafton Ramble

0 — 1 km.
0 — 1 mi.

N

35

0.2

0.3

Grafton

0.0/
17.5

1 Grafton
Information
Building

17.1

Grafton
Village
Cheese
Company

Saxton's River

121

35

4.2

121

Cambridgeport

35

5.5

Grafton Road

South Branch Saxton's River

Athens
Pond

35

Athens Brick
Meeting
House

6.5

35

11.0

Townshend Road

35

35

Miles and Directions

0.0 Turn right (north) out of the Grafton Information Building parking area onto Townshend Road, heading toward Grafton's Main Street.

0.2 Junction with Main Street. Turn right (east) onto Main Street (VT 121).

0.3 Cross bridge, pass junction with VT 35 north to left. Continue east on VT 121.

4.2 Turn right off VT 121 and go south on VT 35.

5.5 Road forks. Bear right, continuing on VT 35, and following signs for Townshend. Begin climb.

6.1 Road surface turns to dirt.

6.5 Athens Brick Meeting House on right.

7.1 Road surface returns to asphalt.

7.7 Athens Pond to the right.

8.2 Approximate top of the watershed. Begin descent.

11.0 Turn right (north) off VT 35 onto Townshend Road. Begin ascent.

12.3 Begin gradual descent to Grafton.

17.1 Grafton Village Cheese Company is on right.

17.5 Arrive back at the parking area.

Local Information

Historic Grafton Information Center, 56 Townshend Road, Grafton, VT; (802) 843-2255; www.sover.net/~Grafton.

Local Events/Attractions

Grafton Village Cheese Company, 533 Townshend Road, Grafton, VT; (800) 472-3866 or (802) 843-2210; www.graftonvillagecheese .com. Watch cheese-making, try samples, buy cheese to take home.

Food

Grafton Grocery Market, 162 Main Street, Grafton, VT; (802) 843-1196.
Daniels House Gift Shop & Café, 56 Townshend Road, Grafton, VT; (802) 843-2255. Located behind the Old Tavern.

Accommodations

The Old Tavern, 92 Main Street, Grafton, VT; (800) 843-1801; www.old-tavern.com. Elegant lodging and dining.

Happy Trails Motel, 321 Route 103, Ludlow, VT; (802) 228-8888 or (800) 228-9984; www.happytrails.com. Located about 0.5 mile east of Ludlow, which is a tourist destination about 20 miles north of Grafton and home of Okemo Mountain Ski Resort. Ludlow offers the widest selection of lodging in the area.
Best Western Colonial Motel, 93 Main Street, Ludlow, VT; (802) 228-8188; www.best western.com.

Bike Shops

West Hill Shop, 49 Brickyard Lane, Putney, VT; (802) 387-5718 or (866) 663-0443; www.westhillshop.com. Active center for biking and cross-country skiing.
Mountain Cycology, 5 Lamere Avenue, Ludlow, VT; (802) 228-2722.

Map

DeLorme: Vermont Atlas & Gazetteer: Page 26.

2 Taconic Valleys Classic

At 96.3 miles, it's not exactly a century—but mighty close. This is a good choice for serious cyclists who want a single-day century ride where terrain isn't too difficult. For those who prefer a more leisurely pace, this is a lovely two-day ride with an overnight in the Arlington area and possibilities for a delightful variety of stops. Riders determined to do a century will have to take a final victory lap around Poultney to make up the remaining 3.7 miles, or take a short side-trip along the way.

Start: Corner of College and Main Streets in Poultney, at the entrance to Green Mountain College.
Length: 96.3 miles.
Terrain: Gently rolling; a few significant climbs, but the route sticks primarily to the valleys of the Taconics.
Traffic and hazards: Avoiding traffic was a major factor in the design of this ride. In order to link the beautiful series of back roads that are used, however, a few connectors on more heavily traveled roads were necessary. Be especially careful on the very short sections of Vermont Highway 7A (0.1 mile in Arlington) and of New York Highway 22 (0.9 mile in Salem). The section of Vermont Highway 30 by Lake St. Catherine is narrow and winding, and can be quite busy during summer.

Getting there: From Rutland, proceed west on U.S. Highway 4 to exit 4. Turn left off the exit ramp and follow VT 30 south about 7 miles to the traffic light in Poultney. Turn right at the traffic light onto Main Street, heading west. Proceed about 0.3 mile to the end of Main Street and the entrance to Green Mountain College. For overnight parking, stop in the Administration Building at the college. They're happy to have cyclists leave a car overnight, but they'd like to know you're there. For a single-day ride, park anywhere along Main Street in Poultney.

The Taconic Mountains form the western boundary of Vermont from the Massachusetts border to Lake Champlain. They provide a stunning background for much of this ride. In Arlington the route follows the Battenkill River through a deep cut in the Taconics and makes a loop into New York State.

From Poultney, head east to East Poultney and on to Middletown Springs. Riders taking a leisurely approach might want to stop at Mineral Springs Park, to the left after the turn onto Vermont Highway 133. VT 133 from Middletown Springs south to Pawlet is one of the finest biking roads in the state. Traffic is sparse, hills are gently rolling, and views of the Taconics are superb. Working farms alternate with beautifully restored colonial homes.

Everyone—even the most serious century riders—should plan to stop in Pawlet. Those on the leisurely schedule may decide to visit the craft shops in Pawlet. *Everybody* should stop in Mach's General Store. If you've ever wondered about the "general" in "general store," Mach's will illustrate. From hardware to deli sandwiches, they've got it. Don't leave without seeing the river through the hole in the floor (head through the hardware and toward the coolers at the rear).

From Pawlet, take VT 30 south. This is the valley of the Mettawee River, and those are the Taconics to either side. VT 30 here is flat and straight, with at least a small shoulder. The scenery is quintessential Vermont, but keep an eye on the road as VT 30 carries more traffic than you've seen so far on the ride.

At 26.3 miles, turn right off VT 30 onto Vermont Highway 315 West, then make an immediate left onto Dorset West Road. Dorset West Road parallels VT 30 but is much quieter. Traffic is light as you pedal through upscale residential areas of Dorset. At about 28 miles, notice the golf course on your left. That's the Dorset Field Club. Built in 1886 it's a contender for the title of oldest golf course in the United States.

At 31.2 miles the route returns to VT 30, but only for a half mile. Then turn right onto another West Road. Again it parallels VT 30, now taking you past some of Manchester's estates. The tallest of the mountains to the right is Mount Equinox (3,840 feet). Notice the swaths created by avalanches and rock slides. After a long gradual downhill, West Road ends at a junction with VT 7A. This is Manchester Village, and that's the Equinox Hotel to the right. During the nineteenth century, the Equinox was a vacation destination for a variety of notables, including the Lincoln family. Today the hotel is regularly included in directories of exclusive hotels and spas. Equinox Village Shops, on the corner of Union and VT 7A, is a mini mall of craft shops, with a restroom.

Manchester Village is the old town. The commercial center is Manchester Center, about 1.5 miles to the north. A side-trip into Manchester Center is possible but not advised. VT 7A here is dangerous. If riders are intent on a detour into Manchester Center, the best plan is to use the sidewalk that stretches the whole way. (Yield to pedestrians.)

Union Street takes you downhill a little farther, to the bottom of the valley created by the Battenkill River. The Chiselville Covered Bridge, at 44.5 miles, spans Roaring Branch, a tributary of the Battenkill. A sign on the bridge warns of a ONE DOLLAR FINE FOR DRIVING FASTER THAN A WALK ON THIS BRIDGE. Clearly, there are local drivers willing to risk that dollar. It's one lane, so stop, take a photo, then be sure the coast is clear before pedaling through.

The stop sign at 46.4 miles signals the junction with VT 7A. The Arlington area has several motels, inns, B&Bs, and restaurants, in a variety of price ranges. It's a good halfway point for riders who are doing the route as a two-day trip. For those just rolling through, the Stewart's convenience store on the right, immediately after the turn onto VT 7A North, has the usual snacks and restroom. If using one of the motels or restaurants along VT 7A, exercise extreme caution getting there and back. VT 7A carries a lot of traffic, so stay right and be visible.

The route turns off VT 7A almost immediately and follows the Battenkill as it cuts through the Taconics toward New York. This is a particularly beautiful section of the trip. The valley is very narrow, so Vermont Highway 313 is close to the river. There are several fishing/swimming pull-offs, an official beach at the Arlington Covered Bridge, and a large picnic area just after the Vermont/New York border. The

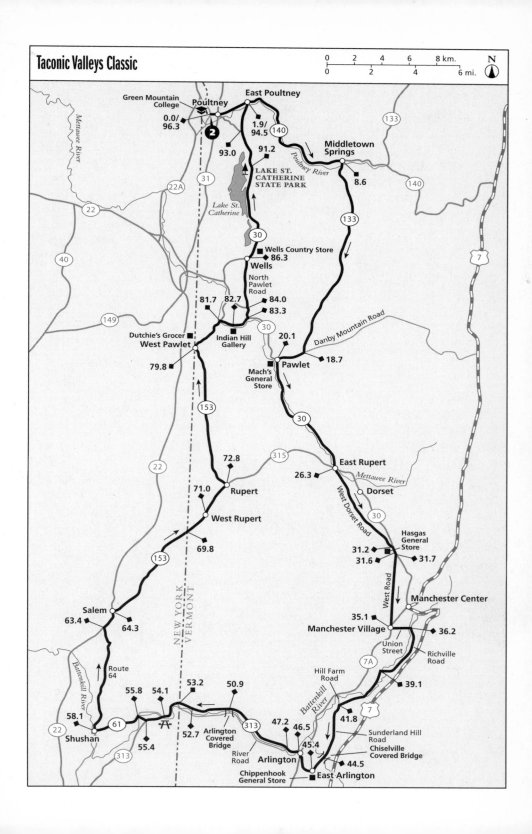

Taconic Valleys Classic

0   2   4   6   8 km.
0   2   4   6 mi.

N

Mettawee River

Green Mountain College
Poultney
0.0/ 96.3
2
1.9/ 94.5
East Poultney
140
133
93.0
91.2
Poultney River
Middletown Springs
8.6
140
LAKE ST. CATHERINE STATE PARK
22A
31
Lake St. Catherine
22
133
30
40
Wells Country Store
86.3
Wells
North Pawlet Road
81.7   **82.7**   **84.0**
83.3
149
7
Dutchie's Grocer
West Pawlet
Indian Hill Gallery
30
20.1
Danby Mountain Road
18.7
79.8
Pawlet
Mach's General Store
153
30
22
72.8
315
East Rupert
26.3
Mettawee River
Dorset
71.0
Rupert
West Dorset Road
30
West Rupert
69.8
Hasgas General Store
31.2   **31.7**
31.6
153
West Road
Manchester Center
NEW YORK
VERMONT
Salem
63.4   **64.3**
35.1
Manchester Village
36.2
Union Street
7A
Richville Road
Hill Farm Road
39.1
Route 64
53.2   **50.9**
Battenkill River
55.8   **54.1**
41.8
7
58.1
61
47.2
46.5
Sunderland Hill Road
22
Arlington Covered Bridge
313
Chiselville Covered Bridge
Shushan
52.7
River Road
45.4
55.4
Arlington
44.5
313
Chippenhook General Store
East Arlington
Battenkill River

Battenkill is a renowned trout fishing stream and is also a popular canoe and tubing river. So it can be busy from dawn to dusk in spring and summer. VT 313 has some traffic, and shoulders are not substantial until you reach the New York border. Those taking a more leisurely trip may want to make a left off VT 313 at 47.2 miles onto River Road. River Road parallels VT 313, on the south side of the river. It's about the same mileage, but is a dirt road. It has almost no traffic and the same great scenery. Its surface is hard-packed dirt that's suitable for skinny tires as long as riders are willing to slow the pace. River Road rejoins VT 313 at 52.7 miles.

As you cross the border into New York, VT 313 becomes New York Highway 313 and improves, as shoulders now become the size of another lane. Hooray for New York State taxpayers.

New York Highway 61 is a rolling, meandering road that takes you into Shushan, New York. If you're ready for a break, continue straight instead of making the right turn onto New York Highway 64 in Shushan. Yushak's Meat, Groceries, Deli is on the left. Continue a very short distance and turn left onto Adams Lane, following signs for Georgi Museum and Park. The park has a picnic area along the Battenkill, which has gotten a lot bigger since you saw it last.

Get fluids in Shushan, as the uphill out of Shushan on NY 64 may be a little daunting—especially if you're doing the ride in one day. NY 64 is another magnificent biking road: sparse traffic, beautiful farms, more views of the Taconics. At about 62.0 miles, begin a wild downhill to Salem, New York. Use your brakes, then exercise extreme caution as you turn right onto NY 22. The turn onto NY 22 is at the outskirts of the town of Salem. The speed limit is 30 here, but don't assume drivers know that. NY 22 is a major road with heavy traffic and not much shoulder. The good news is that you'll turn off NY 22 in less than a mile.

Salem is the largest town you'll pass through on the trip. There's the ever handy Stewart's on the corner, opposite the turn onto New York Highway 153. Next door to Stewart's is Steininger's, a café renowned for its chocolates, coffee, desserts, and lunches. Their Raspberries Linderhoff (puff pastry, ice cream, hot fudge, and raspberries) is sinfully delicious and will definitely supply enough calories for the return to Poultney.

NY 153 represents another terrific 15 miles of biking. It parallels an abandoned railroad line, a sure sign that this is the flattest, most direct route from Salem, New York, to West Pawlet, Vermont. The good news for bikers is that although this may have been an important route in the nineteenth century, not many people seem interested in traveling between those two places today. Be sure to bear left with NY 153 in Rupert. (Continuing straight would take you over Rupert Mountain. If you're tempted to do this, find a topo map and take a careful look at the contour lines!)

West Pawlet, where five roads come together, is a little confusing. Be sure to bear right (east) onto Vermont Highway 153, following signs for Wells. Leaving West Pawlet, you'll pass through old slag heaps and active slate quarries. Slate is still an important industry in this part of the Taconics. Notice the Welsh family names, perhaps on mailboxes. Many residents are descendants of Welshmen who came to the area in the late nineteenth century to work in the quarries.

The route makes a right off VT 153 onto River Road, at 81.7 miles. Indian Hill Gallery (on the right at 82.7 miles) is a photo gallery and workshop. It's the kind of gallery you'd be pleased to find in Boston or Paris. But here it is, in a field by the Mettawee River, open on weekends and ready to welcome cyclists.

The Wells Country Store is a friendly stop, with ice cream, deli, restroom, and picnic area. The route from Wells north to Poultney is on VT 30, along the east shore of Lake St. Catherine. Be careful next to the lake, where the road is narrow and where, in summer, there will be more traffic. A swim at Lake St. Catherine State Park might be a pleasant way to end the trip.

Miles and Directions

0.0 Intersection of College and Main Streets (entrance to Green Mountain College) in Poultney. Proceed east on Poultney's Main Street.

0.3 Traffic light at intersection of Main Street (also Vermont Highway 140) and VT 30. Continue straight on VT 140 East.

1.9 East Poultney. East Poultney General Store is on right. Continue straight on VT 140 East.

8.6 Middletown Springs. Stop sign at intersection of VT 140 and VT 133 South. Turn right onto VT 133 South.

18.7 VT 133 makes sharp right. (Danby Mountain Road to left.) Bear right (west), following signs for Pawlet.

20.1 Stop sign at junction with VT 30 in Pawlet. Turn left onto VT 30 South. Mach's General Store is across the intersection.

26.3 Turn right off VT 30 onto VT 315 West, then make an immediate left onto Dorset West Road, heading south.

31.2 Junction with VT 30. Turn right onto VT 30 South.

31.6 Hasgas General Store on right.

31.7 Turn right off VT 30 onto West Road, heading south.

35.1 Stop sign. Turn right onto VT 7A South, then make an immediate left onto Union Street, heading east.

36.2 Stop sign. Union Street ends. Turn right onto Richville Road (unmarked here), heading south.

39.1 Stop sign at junction with River Road. Turn left onto River Road, heading south.

41.8 Hill Farm Road to right. Continue straight on Sunderland Hill Road.

44.5 Chiselville Covered Bridge. One lane. Exercise caution.

45.4 Chippenhook General Store on left.

46.4 Junction with VT 7A. Turn right onto VT 7A North. Stewart's convenience store on right.

46.5 Turn left off VT 7A onto VT 313 West.

47.2 River Road to left. **Option:** Turn left onto River Road to take dirt road route on south side of the Battenkill River.

50.9 Arlington Covered Bridge, park, swimming, and picnic area on left.

52.7 River Road (to left) rejoins VT 313. Continue west on VT 313.

53.2 Cross border into New York State. Shoulders widen.

54.1 Battenkill Public Access on left. Canoe launch and picnic area.

55.4 Turn right off NY 313 onto NY 61, following signs for Shushan.

55.8 Stop sign. Turn left, continuing on NY 61 North.

58.1 Town of Shushan. Yushak's Grocery is ahead on left. Turn right off NY 61 onto NY 64 North.

62.0 Begin steep downhill.

63.4 Stop sign at junction with NY 22. Turn right onto NY 22 North.

64.3 Traffic light in Salem. Stewart's convenience store on corner, Steininger's Café next to Stewart's. Turn right off NY 22 onto NY 153 North (also called East Broadway here.)

69.8 Cross border into Vermont.

71.0 West Rupert. Sherman's store on left. Continue straight on VT 153 North.

72.8 VT 153 makes a sharp left. Continue on VT 153 North, following signs for Pawlet.

79.8 West Pawlet. Five-road intersection. Take the second right, continuing on VT 153 North. Dutchie's Store is across the intersection.

81.7 Turn right off VT 153 onto River Road, heading east.

82.7 Indian Hill Gallery is on the right.

83.3 Stop sign at junction with VT 30. Turn left onto VT 30 North.

84.0 Turn right off VT 30 onto North Pawlet Road, heading north.

86.3 Stop sign at junction with VT 30 in Wells. Wells Country Store on right. Turn right onto VT 30 North.

91.2 Lake St. Catherine State Park on left. Swimming and picnic areas.

93.0 Bear right off VT 30 onto Thrall Road, still heading north and following signs for East Poultney.

94.5 East Poultney. Junction with VT 140. East Poultney General Store on right. Turn left onto VT 140 West, heading back to Poultney.

96.0 Traffic light in Poultney. Continue straight on Main Street.

96.3 Return to intersection of Main and College Streets (entrance to Green Mountain College).

Local Information

Poultney Area Chamber of Commerce, P.O. Box 151, Poultney, VT 05764; (802) 287-2010; www.poultneyvt.com.

Manchester and the Mountains Chamber of Commerce, 5046 Main Street, Suite 1, Manchester Center, VT; (802) 362-2100 or (800) 362-4144; www.manchestervermont.net.

Local Events/Attractions

Indian Hill Gallery of Fine Photography, 671 River Road, Wells, VT; (802) 325-2274.

Equinox Resort and Spa, 3567 Main Street, Manchester, VT; (802) 362-4700; http://equinox.rockresorts.com.

Hildene (The Lincoln Family Home), c/o Friends of Hildene, P.O. Box 377, Manchester, VT 05254; (802) 362-1788.

Vermont Lakes Region Cycling Weekend, (802) 287-9190; www.cyclingvermont.org. Annual event sponsored by the Poultney Rotary Club. Mid-July.

Food

Perry's Main Street Eatery, 16 Main Street, Poultney, VT; (802) 287-5188.
Large portions of homemade favorites.
Tot's Diner, 84 Main Street, Poultney, VT; (802) 287-2213. Breakfast and lunch. A local favorite.
Mach's General Store, 18 School Street, Pawlet, VT; (802) 325-3405.
Hasgas General Store, 69 VT 30, Dorset, VT; (802) 362-4250.
Chippenhook General Store, 13 Old Mill Road, East Arlington, VT; (802) 375-8389.
Yushak's Supermarket, 3 Main Street #A, Shushan, NY 12873; (518) 854-7519.
Steininger's Restaurant and Chocolate Shop, 191 South Main Street, Salem, NY 12865; (518) 854-3830; www.steiningers.com.
Dutchie's Grocer, 1 Railroad Street, West Pawlet, VT; (802) 645-0069.
Stewart's Shops in Poultney and Arlington, VT and in Salem, NY. Stewart's are the favorite full-service convenience stores of locals in southwestern Vermont and neighboring New York. Stewart's has good coffee and the usual staples. Many people consider Stewart's ice cream the equal of pricier premium brands.

Wells Country Store, 150 Main Street (VT 30), Wells, VT; (802) 645-0332.

Accommodations

Cutleaf Maples Motel, 3420 VT 7A, Arlington, VT; (802) 375-2725.
Country Willows B&B, 332 East Arlington Road, Arlington, VT; (802) 375-0019 or (800) 796-2585; www.countrywillows.com. An elegant country inn on the route.
Birdhouse Inn B&B, 1430 East Main Street, P.O. Box 646, East Poultney, VT 05741; (802) 287-2405; www.birdhouseinnvt.com.
Holly Hill Inn, 82 East Main Street, Poultney, VT; (802) 287-5250; www.thehollyhillinn.com.
Lake St. Catherine State Park Campground, 3034 VT 30 S, Poultney, VT; (802) 287-9158; www.vtstateparks.com/htm/catherine.cfm. Open Memorial Day through Labor Day.

Bike Shops

Battenkill Sports Bicycle Shop, 1240 Depot Street, Manchester, VT; (802) 362-2734 or (800) 340-2734; www.battenkillsports.com.

Maps

DeLorme: Vermont Atlas & Gazetteer: Pages 24, 25, 28, 29.
DeLorme: New York Atlas & Gazetteer: Page 81.

3 Bomoseen Ramble

This ride makes a nice introduction to cycling in western Vermont: not too long and not too difficult but lots of scenery and lots of history.

Start: Parking area at the west end of the town green in Fair Haven.
Length: 12.0 miles.
Terrain: Rolling hills.

Traffic and hazards: No shoulders on most roads. Summer traffic along Lake Bomoseen necessitates extra care.

Getting there: From Rutland, proceed about 16 miles west on U.S. Highway 4 to exit 2. Turn left off the exit ramp onto Vermont Highway 22A, following signs for Fair Haven. Go south less than a mile to the intersection with Vermont Highway 4A. Bear right (west) onto VT 4A, which is Fair Haven's Main Street. The town green will be on your right. Continue to the west (far) end of the town green and park in the public lot.

Fair Haven is a typical Vermont community, with a lively history and an impressive town green. Slate quarrying was, and still is, an important industry here. Start noticing the handsome slate roofs, and keep looking for them as you tour the area. On Fridays in summer, the town green becomes a traditional farmers' market—fresh produce, baked goods, crafts, and a pleasant way to begin or end a ride.

Creek Road takes you north along the western edge of Lake Bomoseen, with cottages to your left and water to your right. There's some controversy over the origin of the lake's name. It sounds like a variation on an Indian name, but some feel certain that Samuel de Champlain called it "Bombazon," the name of a silky cloth that the lake's smooth surface resembled. In any case, local residents like to point out that Bomoseen is the largest lake entirely within the boundaries of Vermont. Summer cottages will be occupied, and there will be traffic during July and August, but you won't see much activity on or around the lake during the rest of the year. The Edward F. Kehoe boat launch, at 4.7 miles, is a good place to stop for a break and to admire the view. Notice the island to the north. That's Neshobe Island, formerly owned by Alexander Woollcott, who vacationed there with an assortment of zany celebrity friends, including the Marx Brothers.

Continue on the paved road as it continues up the lakeshore and then veers west, away from the water. At 6.7 miles you'll come to the entrance to Bomoseen State Park (beach, bathhouses, concession stand). If you're not ready for an official beach stop but would like a quick dip or a rest by the water, continue about 50 yards to a dirt road to the right. Another 50 yards on that dirt road brings you to the boat launch on Glen Lake. People picnic and swim from the shore to the right of the boat launch. During midweek, even on the hottest days, it's often remarkably empty. As you leave Glen Lake (same way you came in), notice the remains of a slate milling

Lake Bomoseen PHOTO BY ENNIS DULING

factory and foundations of the cottages where factory workers lived. This area was once the town of West Castleton, and the center of a thriving slate business.

Get back on the paved road, and almost immediately on the right (at 6.9 miles), look for an impressive rock formation—an overturned syncline. It's a classic example of folded layers, and geology classes from near and far seem delighted with it. You'll continue along the shore of Glen Lake for a bit and then climb a short hill. At about 7.5 miles you'll pass a large working slate quarry. All along this road you'll see slag heaps (piles of discarded slate) to your right. Most are from quarries that are long closed. At about 10 miles you'll begin to see views of the Adirondacks to the west. A wonderful panorama any time of year, it's spectacular on a clear day in the fall. The final miles of the trip are a pleasant descent back to Fair Haven.

Miles and Directions

0.0 Public parking lot at west end of town green. Turn right onto Main Street (VT 4A/22A).

0.1 Turn left off Main Street onto River Street.

1.9 Stop sign. Turn left onto Blissville Road.

2.7 Intersection with VT 4A. Turn left onto VT 4A, then make an immediate right onto Creek Road.

2.8 Harbor View General Store on the left.

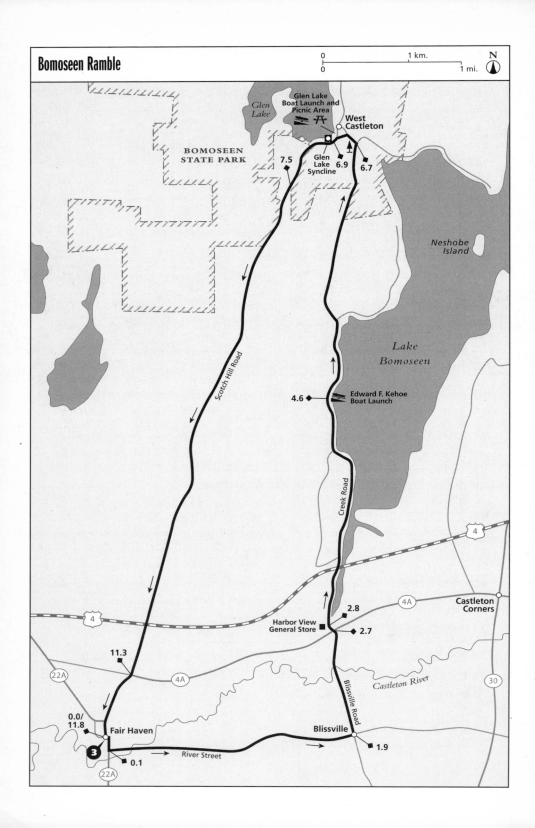

Bomoseen Ramble

0 1 km.
0 1 mi.

N

Glen Lake

Glen Lake
Boat Launch and
Picnic Area

West
Castleton

BOMOSEEN
STATE PARK

7.5

Glen
Lake
Syncline

6.9

6.7

*Neshobe
Island*

*Lake
Bomoseen*

Scotch Hill Road

4.6

Edward F. Kehoe
Boat Launch

Creek Road

4

2.8

4A

Castleton
Corners

Harbor View
General Store

2.7

11.3

22A

4A

Castleton River

30

Blissville Road

0.0/
11.8

Fair Haven

Blissville

1.9

3

0.1

River Street

22A

4.6	Edward F. Kehoe boat launch.
6.7	Entrance to Bomoseen State Park.
6.7	Entrance to Glen Lake boat launch.
6.9	Glen Lake syncline (rock formation) on right.
7.5	Working slate quarry.
11.3	Intersection with VT 4A. Turn right onto VT 4A, heading southwest.
11.8	Back to parking lot.

Local Information

Fair Haven Area Chamber of Commerce, P.O. Box 206, Fair Haven, VT 05743; (802) 265-8600; www.fairhavenchamber.com.

Rutland Region Chamber of Commerce, 256 Main Street, Rutland, VT; (802) 773-2747 or (800) 756-8880; www.rutlandvermont.com.

Local Events/Attractions

Bomoseen State Park, 22 Cedar Mountain Road, Fair Haven, VT; (802) 265-4242; www.vtstateparks.com/htm/bomoseen.cfm. Open Memorial Day through Labor Day. Swimming, picnicking, hiking.

Rutland Ethnic Festival, annually, late July. Sponsored by the Downtown Rutland Partnership, 103 Wales Street, Rutland, VT; (802) 773-9380; www.rutlanddowntown.com/ethnic .html. Street vendors, sidewalk sales, ethnic foods and music, and more.

Vermont Lakes Region Cycling Weekend, (802) 287-9190; www.cyclingvermont.org. Annual event sponsored by the Poultney Rotary Club. Mid-July. Includes rides in the Poultney and Fair Haven areas.

Food

Fair Haven Inn Restaurant, 5 Adams Street, Fair Haven, VT; (802) 265-4907; www.fairhaveninn.com. A local favorite for special occasions. Specializes in Greek dishes.

Wooden Soldier Restaurant, 31 Main Street, Fair Haven, VT; (802) 265-7985. Good diner food.

Harbor View General Store, 33 Creek Road, Hydeville, VT; (802) 265-8884.

Accommodations

The best selection of motels will be in Rutland, about 16 miles east of Fair Haven. See the Rutland Region Chamber of Commerce Web site for listings.

Haven Guest House Bed & Breakfast, 1 Fourth Street, Fair Haven, VT; (802) 265-8882; www.havenguesthousevt.com.

Bomoseen State Park Campground, 22 Cedar Mountain Road, Fair Haven, VT; (802) 265-4242; www.vtstateparks.com/htm/bomoseen .cfm. Open Memorial Day through Labor Day.

Lake St. Catherine State Park Campground, 3034 Vermont Highway 30 S, Poultney, VT; (802) 287-9158; www.vtstateparks.com/htm /catherine.cfm. Open Memorial Day through Labor Day.

Bike Shops

Great Outdoors Trading Company, 219 Woodstock Avenue, Rutland, VT; (802) 775-9989.

Green Mountain Cyclery, 133 Strongs Avenue, Rutland, VT; (802) 775-0869.

Sports Peddler, 158 North Main Street, Rutland, VT; (802) 775-0101.

Map

DeLorme: Vermont Atlas & Gazetteer: Page 28.

4 Quechee Watershed Cruise

This ride crosses the watershed between the Ottauquechee River and the White River, and then crosses back again to the Ottauquechee. That means up, down, up, down, with lots of picture-postcard scenery the whole way. If not the easiest ride in this collection, it certainly ranks with the prettiest.

Start: Village Green parking area, on the south side of Quechee Main Street, about 0.2 mile west of the covered bridge.
Length: 25.6 miles.
Terrain: Two serious climbs and descents.
Traffic and hazards: The route uses secondary roads, where traffic should be light. A cautionary note: On a road map, it appears that U.S. Highway 4 between Woodstock and Quechee might be a sensible alternative route. It isn't. US 4 is very busy. The stretch between Woodstock and Quechee is narrow and winding, has no shoulders, and is particularly dangerous. If you make a side-trip to Woodstock, come back to the intersection by the Billings Farm to make the return trip to Quechee. Don't take US 4. There is a short flat stretch (2.2 miles) of dirt road along the Ottauquechee River that shouldn't be a problem for skinny tires.

Getting there: From Rutland, take US 4 East about 38 miles to a blinking light at a four-way intersection. Turn left off US 4 and immediately cross a reproduction covered bridge over the Ottauquechee River. Bear left after the bridge and proceed 0.2 mile to the Village Green parking area on the left. Park there.

From points south, take Interstate 91 north to exit 10 and the junction with Interstate 89. Proceed north on I-89 about 3 miles to exit 1. Get on US 4 West and proceed 3.7 miles (crossing Quechee Gorge) to a blinking light at a four-way intersection. Turn right off US 4 and immediately cross a reproduction covered bridge over the Ottauquechee River. Bear left after the bridge and proceed 0.2 mile to the Village Green parking area on the left. Park there.

Quechee, our starting point, represents the upscale end of Vermont's social and economic spectrum. Formerly a small New England mill town whose woolen industry harnessed the Ottauquechee River, Quechee is now known for its expensive condo communities, golf courses, and specialty shops. One new industry has forged a link with the town's past: The Simon Pearce Glass Works, which produces handblown glassware, is located in an old mill and uses the Quechee waterfall for hydropower.

Although not terribly long, this ride boasts a couple of real climbs and exciting descents. There won't be a store for almost 16 miles, so bring water and perhaps a snack. The first 2.5 miles will be gradually uphill, to the top of the watershed between the Ottauquechee River and the White River. Then it's downhill, with some steep hairpin turns, to the White River. Our route parallels the White for about a mile, with plenty of spots for a river stop, then heads west and begins the second crossing of the watershed.

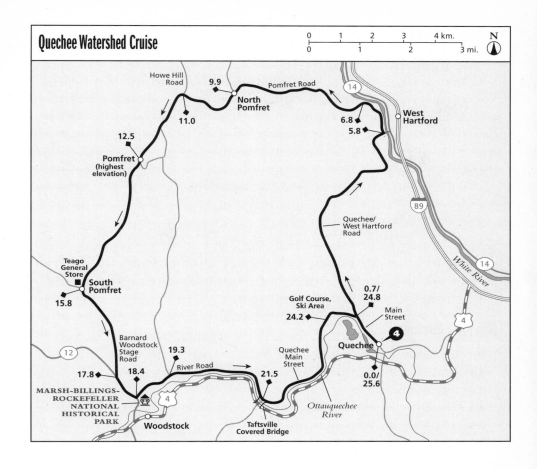

Quechee Watershed Cruise

Howe Hill Road
9.9
North Pomfret
Pomfret Road
14
11.0
West Hartford
6.8
5.8
12.5
Pomfret (highest elevation)
89
Quechee/ West Hartford Road
White River
14
Teago General Store
South Pomfret
15.8
Golf Course, Ski Area
24.2
0.7/ 24.8
Main Street
4
Quechee
4
Barnard Woodstock Stage Road
19.3
River Road
Quechee Main Street
21.5
0.0/ 25.6
12
17.8
18.4
MARSH-BILLINGS-ROCKEFELLER NATIONAL HISTORICAL PARK
4
Woodstock
Taftsville Covered Bridge
Ottauquechee River

0   1   2   3   4 km.
0   1   2   3 mi.
N

    The 5-mile stretch from the White River to Pomfret is a long, gradual uphill. Downshift, relax, and enjoy the climb. The road crosses Mill Brook several times, scenery is quintessential *Vermont Life,* and traffic is very sparse. Take a breather in North Pomfret, where there's a post office and a classic New England white church. Sadly the general store—like many in the state—closed recently. You won't really be to the top of the watershed until you reach Pomfret, in a couple more miles. Watch for signs at about 11.0 miles. Howe Hill Road, which would take you back down to the White River, is to the right. Be sure to bear left onto Pomfret Road. (A mistake here would mean doing that climb again!)

    At about 12.5 miles you're at the top of the watershed, and the pace will accelerate. It's time to stop admiring the scenery, shift gears, and concentrate on the descent to the Ottauquechee River. The first 3 miles are the steepest (steeper than the section coming up from the White River). Use caution and use your brakes. The fastest part of the descent ends in South Pomfret, at a junction with the Barnard

Woodstock Stage Road. The Teago General Store is on the corner, and there's a town park across the road, in case it's time for a snack.

As you make a left off Vermont Highway 12 at 18.4 miles, you'll pass the entrance to the Billings Farm and Museum and the Marsh–Billings–Rockefeller National Historical Park. Billings is a working farm that preserves the heritage of the nineteenth-century Vermont family farm. The Marsh of the Marsh–Billings–Rockefeller National Park was George Perkins Marsh, one of America's earliest environmentalists. The park is dedicated to interpreting the history of conservation in America and promoting sustainable environmental practices today.

For those interested in a side-trip, the town of Woodstock (exquisitely restored homes, many stores, lots of traffic) is just ahead on VT 12. Bear right with VT 12 instead of taking the left at 18.4 miles.

The road along the north bank of the Ottauquechee is very close to the river for most of this section of the ride. There are a number of side roads to the left. Just stay on River Road, next to the river, and you won't go wrong. On a hot day, you'll probably see canoes, swimmers, and kids leaping from a rope swing into a swimming hole. You may want to cool off, too.

Miles and Directions

0.0 Turn left (west) out of Village Green parking area.

0.7 Road forks. Bear right (north) onto Quechee/West Hartford Road. Begin climb.

2.5 Begin descent.

5.8 Turn left (west) onto Pomfret Road, immediately before bridge over White River.

6.8 Road swings away from river; begin uphill.

9.9 Village of North Pomfret. Continue straight on Pomfret Road.

11.0 Howe Hill Road to the right. Continue straight on Pomfret Road.

12.5 Pomfret Center School on left, Town Hall on right. Begin descent.

15.8 Stop sign at junction with Barnard Woodstock Stage Road (unmarked here). Teago General Store on right. Turn left onto Barnard Woodstock Stage Road, heading south.

17.8 Stop sign at junction with VT 12. Turn left onto VT 12, still heading south.

18.4 Road forks. Turn left (east) off VT 12 onto River Road (unmarked here). Entrance to Billings Farm and Museum and to Marsh-Billings-Rockefeller National Historical Park is immediately on the right.

19.3 Road surface changes to dirt.

21.5 Stop sign at junction with Quechee Main Street. Dam and Taftsville Covered Bridge to the right. Turn left onto Quechee Main Street. Road surface returns to asphalt.

24.2 Ski area to the left, golf course to the right.

24.8 Quechee/West Hartford Road to the left. Continue straight on Quechee Main Street.

25.6 Back to parking area.

Local Information

Quechee Chamber of Commerce, 15 Main Street, Quechee, VT; (802) 295-7900; www.vtliving.com/towns/quechee.
Woodstock Chamber of Commerce, 18 Central Street, Woodstock, VT; (802) 457-3555 or (888) 496-6378; www.woodstockvt.com.
Quechee Gorge Visitor Center, 6054 Woodstock Road (US 4), White River Junction, VT; (802) 295-6852.

Local Events/Attractions

Billings Farm & Museum, P.O. Box 489, Woodstock, VT 05091; (802) 457-2355; www.billingsfarm.org. A working farm and museum dedicated to Vermont's rural heritage.
Marsh-Billings-Rockefeller National Historical Park, 54 Elm Street, Woodstock, VT; (802) 457-3368; www.nps.gov/mabi. Tours of restored homes, interpretive hiking trails, a conservation study institute.
Simon Pearce Mill, 1760 Quechee Main Street, Quechee, VT; (802) 295-2711; http://SimonPearce.com. Watch glassblowing.
Quechee Balloon Festival & Crafts Fair. Annually on Father's Day weekend (mid-June). See the Quechee Chamber of Commerce Web site (www.vtliving.com/towns/quechee) for details.

Food

Village Green Deli, 1 Village Green, Quechee, VT; (802) 295-2786.
Teago General Store, 2035 Barnard Stage Road, South Pomfret, VT; (802) 457-1626.
Simon Pearce Mill, 1760 Quechee Main Street, Quechee, VT; (802) 295-2711; http://SimonPearce.com.
There are also restaurants, delis, bakeries, etc. in Woodstock.

Accommodations

Web sites for the Quechee and Woodstock Chambers of Commerce are the best bet for finding accommodations.
The Quality Inn at Quechee Gorge, 5817 Woodstock Road (US 4), Quechee, VT; (802) 295-7600 or (800) 732-4376; www.quality innquechee.com.

Bike Shops

Woodstock Sports, 30 Central Street, Woodstock, VT; (802) 457-1568; www.woodstock sports.com.
Omer and Bob's Sport Shop, 7 Allen Street, Hanover, NH 03755; (603) 643-3525; www .omerandbobs.com.

Map

DeLorme: Vermont Atlas & Gazetteer: Pages 31, 35.

5 Orwell/Lake Champlain Ramble

This part of the state is open and rolling. For those who combine their love of biking with an interest in colonial history, this is a perfect ride. The trip as written takes you to the shore of Lake Champlain, where Ethan Allen and the Green Mountain Boys launched an attack on Fort Ticonderoga. There are options for extending the ride to two separate colonial era forts: Mount Independence and Fort Ticonderoga.

Start: Parking area adjacent to Orwell school and town offices.
Length: 19.7 miles.
Terrain: Gently rolling, open.

Traffic and hazards: Minimal traffic on most roads. There may be small spurts of traffic on Vermont Highway 74, when the ferry docks and unloads.

Getting there: Proceed west from Rutland on U.S. Highway 4. Take exit 2 off US 4 onto Vermont Highway 22A, heading north. Continue north on VT 22A about 15 miles to the intersection with Vermont Highway 73. Turn right (east) onto VT 73, reaching Orwell in 0.3 mile. Park to the left, off VT 73, in front of the Orwell school and town offices.

During this ride you'll pass through some of Vermont's most prosperous farmlands. This is the Champlain Valley, where dairy farming is still a dominant way of life.

The first optional side-trip is at 0.6 mile. To visit Mount Independence, continue straight here on Chipman Point Road (following signs for Mount Independence), instead of bearing right on VT 73. The Mount Independence State Historic Site is about 5 miles ahead. This was a large fort built by Americans during the Revolution. It's directly opposite Fort Ticonderoga (built during the French and Indian War) and was linked to Ticonderoga by a floating bridge in 1776. Today the only building at Mount Independence is the visitor center, but well-marked trails lead to the sites of former fortifications and barracks.

Back on the regular route: At about the point when you begin to see views of Lake Champlain, look for Norton's Gallery on your left. Even if you're not in the market for a piece of wooden sculpture, this is a fun stop.

The second optional side-trip—to Fort Ticonderoga—is highly recommended. The ferry ride is short (six minutes), and it's about 1 mile from the ferry landing on the New York side to the fort. Fort Ticonderoga, which has a long and colorful history, is now privately owned and carefully restored. A trip across the lake and up the drive to the fort provides a rare opportunity to see and feel the historical significance of this area.

Even if you don't wish to cross the lake, plan to stop at Larrabee's Point. A ferry crossing has been here since 1759. In 1775 Ethan Allen crossed the lake just north of this spot on his way to capture Fort Ticonderoga. In what was to be the first

Clarence investigating a bike PHOTO BY ENNIS DULING

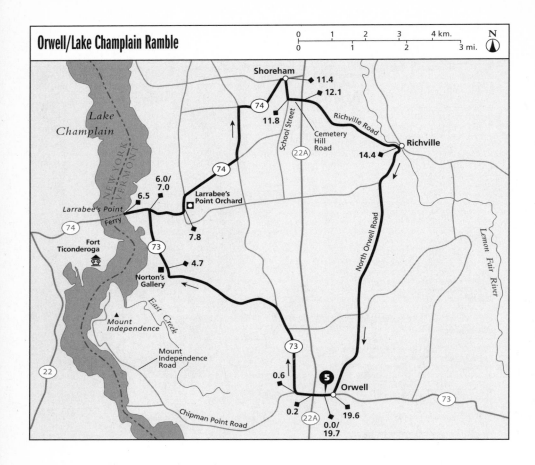

Orwell/Lake Champlain Ramble

0   1   2   3   4 km.   N
0   1   2   3 mi.

offensive action of the American Revolution, he demanded the British surrender, "In the name of the Great Jehovah and the Continental Congress."

For those more interested in rocks than history, a few minutes of walking north along the shoreline will be rewarded with as many fossils as you can carry. Be conservative—there's still some pedaling ahead.

Backtrack on VT 74, passing the junction with VT 73, and continuing east. At 7.8 miles, pass Larrabee's Point Orchard, a handy stop during apple season. VT 74 makes some turns, and several dirt roads join it; you won't go astray if you stay on the paved road. Watch for the turn off VT 74 at 11.4 miles, and then the turn onto Cemetery Hill Road at 11.8 miles. You're making this little jag in order to avoid pedaling on VT 22A, a major north/south truck route.

Richville Road is hilly, with one particularly exhilarating descent. The right turn off Richville Road marks the beginning of a particularly fine stretch of biking, all the way back to Orwell. Views for the final 5 miles are superb. Those are the Green Mountains to your left, and the Adirondacks to your right. Cars are rare, the road is straight, and it's easy pedaling. Relax, enjoying the farms and the sweeping vistas unique to this part of the state. Again, there will be a few intersections with dirt roads. Continue straight on the asphalt, and you can't go wrong.

Miles and Directions

0.0 Parking area in front of Orwell school and town offices. Turn right, heading west on VT 73.

0.2 Cross VT 22A, continuing on VT 73.

0.6 Road forks. Bear right, continuing on VT 73. **Option:** Continue straight on Chipman Point Road for side-trip to Mount Independence. When Chipman Point Road turns left, stay straight on Mount Independence Road.

4.7 Norton's Gallery on left.

6.0 Junction with VT 74. Turn left onto VT 74, heading west.

6.5 Road ends. **Option:** Take ferry across to New York. Turn around and retrace VT 74 to junction with VT 73.

7.0 Pass junction with VT 73. Continue straight on VT 74.

7.8 Pass Larrabee's Point Orchard.

11.4 Turn right off VT 74 onto School Street, heading south.

11.8 Turn left off School Street onto Cemetery Hill Road, heading east.

12.1 Stop sign at four-way intersection. Cross VT 22A onto Richville Road, continuing east and following signs for Shoreham Center.

14.4 Turn right (south) off Richville Road onto North Orwell Road. This turn is immediately before a bridge.

19.6 Junction with VT 73. Turn right onto VT 73, heading west.

19.7 Back to parking area.

Local Information

Brandon Chamber of Commerce, 16 Mount Pleasant Drive, Brandon, VT; (802) 247-6401; www.brandon.org.

Local Events/Attractions

Mount Independence State Historic Site, Mount Independence Road, Orwell, VT; (802) 948-2000; www.historicvermont.org/ mountindependence. Open late May through mid-October.

Norton's Gallery, P.O. Box 201, VT 73, Shoreham, VT 05770; (802) 948-2552; www.nortonsgallery.com. Delightful wooden sculptures, indoors and out. They welcome bikers and have a restroom.

Fort Ticonderoga, P.O. Box 390, Ticonderoga, NY 12883; (518) 585-2821; www.fort ticonderoga.org. Open early May through late

October. Special events throughout the season, including reenactments, encampments, fife and drum performances, bagpiping, and more. Restaurant and snack bar.

Fort Ticonderoga Ferry, (802) 897-7999 or www.middlebury.net/tiferry. Operates early May through late October in all but the most severe weather.

Food

Unless you make the side-trip across the lake to Fort Ticonderoga, where there's a snack bar/restaurant, there won't be opportunities to buy food along this route. General stores at the ferry landing and in Shoreham have recently closed. So it's wise to stock up in Orwell before you pedal off.

Buxton's Store, 499 Main Street, Orwell, VT; (802) 948-2112.

Accommodations

Brandon, about 13 miles east of Orwell, is home to a variety of country inns and B&Bs. See the Brandon Chamber of Commerce Web site for a list.

Brandon Motor Lodge, Vermont Highway 7, Brandon, VT; (802) 247-9594 or (800) 675-7614; www.brandonmotorlodge.com. Good choice for those on a budget.

Bike Shop

The Bike Center, 74 Main Street, Middlebury, VT; (802) 388-6666; www.bikecentermid.com.

Map

DeLorme: Vermont Atlas & Gazetteer: Page 32.

6 East Middlebury Ramble

Pleasant back roads, rolling hills, and a happy mix of classic and unusual Vermont scenery make this ride a real favorite. And there's a swimming beach, a haunted house, and the famous Waybury Inn along the way.

Start: Gravel rest area/fishing parking area on Three Mile Bridge Road, west of U.S. Highway 7.
Length: 16.0 miles..
Terrain: Gently rolling to hilly.
Traffic and hazards: Traffic will be light for most of the ride, and moderate on the mile of Vermont Highway 125. Exercise caution crossing U.S. Highway 7, which is very busy. Bring bug repellent if riding in summer and planning to stop. This area is famous for a thriving population of mosquitoes. They aren't interested in moving targets, but if you stop, they'll find you fast. There is one short section (0.4 mile) of unpaved road that shouldn't be a problem for road bikes.

Getting there: Middlebury is on US 7, in the west-central part of the state, about halfway between Rutland and Burlington. From Middlebury, proceed about 4 miles south on US 7. Pass a left turn for VT 125 and Vermont Highway 116. About 0.2 mile later, pass another left turn for VT 125 and VT 116. About 0.2 mile after that second left, turn right off US 7 onto Three Mile Bridge Road, following the sign for a rest area. The rest area is a gravel pull-off immediately on the left. Park here.

The first few miles are a lovely, gently rolling pedal through picturesque farm country. The barns, silos, cows, and corn are just what you'd expect. But Shard Villa, on the right at 3.0 miles, comes as a bit of a surprise. In his *Green Mountain Ghosts, Ghouls & Unsolved Mysteries* (1994), Joe Citro describes Shard Villa as an "Italianate-Gothic–Second-Empire hodgepodge of Victorian architecture." Citro considers it one of Vermont's notable haunted houses. Columbus Smith, its builder, apparently went mad after the deaths of his two children. His will directed that the house become a home for the elderly, and subsequent residents have told assorted tales of

Shard Villa

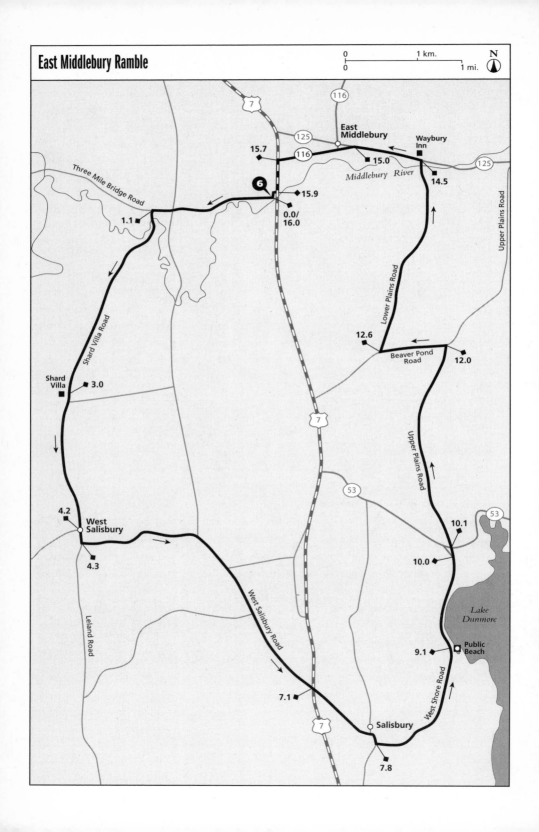

East Middlebury Ramble

0 1 km.
0 1 mi.

N

ghosts and mysterious happenings. Looking at the house, and the mausoleum on its grounds, it's not hard to believe those tales.

At 4.3 miles, be sure to bear left onto West Salisbury Road. Prepare for some slightly bigger hills and more classic Vermont scenery.

Shortly after crossing US 7, at 7.1 miles, you'll be in the village of Salisbury: a school, a church, but no general store. If you're looking for a cold soda, keep pedaling (uphill, but not for long) to the boat launch and public beach on Lake Dunmore. There is a small admission fee to swim, but the snack bar is open to everyone.

Upper Plains Road, north from Lake Dunmore, is a fine, easy pedal. Don't miss the turn onto Beaver Pond Road at 12.0 miles. Beaver Pond Road is a short stretch of hard-packed dirt road (less than a half mile) that connects Upper Plains Road with Lower Plains Road. Turn right (north) onto Lower Plains Road, and it's pretty much downhill for the rest of the ride.

Notice the Waybury Inn on the right, immediately after you make the turn onto VT 125. It may look familiar. A view of its exterior greeted viewers of the old *Newhart* TV show each week. Filming of the show took place elsewhere, but most of America figured that Bob handled the predicaments of his eccentric guests and neighbors right here in this classic Vermont inn in East Middlebury.

From the Waybury Inn it's a short 1.5 miles back to the parking area.

Miles and Directions

0.0 Turn left out of the rest area onto Three Mile Bridge Road, heading west.

1.1 Dirt road straight ahead. Stay on paved road, which swings sharply left.

1.2 Cross bridge over Middlebury River.

3.0 Shard Villa on right. Columbus Smith Road (dirt) on left. Continue straight.

4.2 West Salisbury Road to right. Continue straight on Shard Villa Road.

4.3 Leland Road straight ahead. Bear left (east) onto West Salisbury Road.

7.1 Junction with US 7. Cross US 7, following signs for Lake Dunmore.

7.8 Road forks. Bear left on West Shore Road, following signs for Lake Dunmore.

8.4 Rogers Road to right. Continue straight on West Shore Road.

9.1 Boat launch and public beach on Lake Dunmore.

10.0 Road forks. Bear right, staying on West Shore Road.

10.1 Stop sign at a four-way intersection. Proceed straight (north) onto Upper Plains Road.

12.0 Turn left (west) off Upper Plains Road onto Beaver Pond Road.

12.2 Road surface turns to dirt.

12.6 Turn right (north) off Beaver Pond Road onto Lower Plains Road. Road surface returns to asphalt.

14.4 Cross bridge over Middlebury River.

14.5 Junction with VT 125. Turn left onto VT 125, heading west. The Waybury Inn is on VT 125, immediately on the right.

15.0 Road forks. Bear left onto VT 116.

15.7 Stop sign at junction with US 7. Turn left onto US 7, heading south.

15.9 Turn right off US 7 onto Three Mile Bridge Road.

16.0 Return to parking area.

Local Information

Addison County Chamber of Commerce, 2 Court Street, Middlebury, VT; (802) 388-7951 or (800) 733-8376; www.midvermont.com.

Local Events/Attractions

Addison County Fair & Field Days, P.O. Box 745, Middlebury, VT 05753; (802) 545-2557; www.addisoncountyfielddays.com. A real agricultural fair. One of the Vermont Chamber of Commerce's "Top 10 Summer Events."

University of Vermont Morgan Horse Farm, 74 Battell Drive, Weybridge, VT; (802) 388-2011; www.uvm.edu/morgan.

Frog Hollow Vermont State Craft Center, 1 Mill Street, Middlebury, VT; (802) 388-3177; www.froghollow.org.

Food

Middlebury has many restaurants, delis, a bakery, etc. The following are south of Middlebury, a short distance north of the ride's start.

Rosie's Restaurant, 886 US 7 South, Middlebury, VT; (802) 388-7052. A local favorite.

A & W All-American Food, 1557 US 7 South, Middlebury, VT; (802) 388-2876. A 1950s-style A & W drive-in, with waitstaff on roller blades and real root beer.

Accommodations

The best options are in the college town of Middlebury, a short distance north of the ride. See the Addison County Chamber of Commerce Web site for a comprehensive list.

Courtyard by Marriott Middlebury, 309 Court Street (US 7 South), Middlebury, VT; (802) 388-7600; www.middleburycourtyard.com.

Waybury Inn, P.O. Box 27, 457 East Main Street, East Middlebury, VT 05740; (802) 388-4015 or (800) 348-1810; www.waybury inn.com.

Branbury State Park Campground, 3570 Lake Dunmore Road (Vermont Highway 53), Salisbury, VT; www.vtstateparks.com/htm/branbury .cfm. Open Memorial Day through Columbus Day.

Kampersville Campground, P.O. Box 56, Salisbury, VT 05769; (802) 352-4501 or (877) 250-2568; www.kampersville.com. Just off the route, at the north end of Lake Dunmore.

Bike Shop

The Bike Center, 74 Main Street, Middlebury, VT; (802) 388-6666; www.bikecentermid.com.

Map

DeLorme: Vermont Atlas & Gazetteer: Page 33.

7 Northfield Challenge

Racers will love doing it fast. Traffic is light on both Vermont Highways 12A and 12, much of it is relatively flat, and there are opportunities to use the big gears. The fastest cyclists will manage it in a couple of hours. Weekend riders will take a more leisurely approach and will enjoy a halfway break to explore the town of Northfield.

Start: Shaw's Shopping Plaza, on VT 12 south of Randolph.
Length: 41.4 miles.
Terrain: VT 12A from Randolph north to Northfield is surprisingly flat. There's one long climb and a steep descent on VT 12, on the return from Northfield.
Traffic and hazards: The only notable traffic will be in the towns of Randolph and Northfield.

Getting there: Take exit 4 off Interstate 89 and get on Vermont Highway 66 West, following signs for Randolph (not Randolph Center, which is to the east). Proceed about 2.7 miles, to the intersection with VT 12 and VT 12A. Turn left onto VT 12 South, cross a bridge over the river, and continue south through Randolph. The Shaw's Shopping Plaza is on the left, 1 mile south of the bridge.

A glance at a Vermont map indicates that this ride is smack in the middle of the state. It's well-known that the Green Mountains form the state's backbone, so it would be logical to assume this is going to be a tough ride with some difficult climbs. Not so. In fact, you'll be surprised how flat the first 22 miles are. There is a long (about 5.5-mile) climb as you head south from Northfield. But it's one of those climbs that never seems terribly steep, and it's punctuated by level stretches. The reward for reaching the top is a long, winding descent back to Randolph.

Take another look at the Vermont map, and you'll note that I-89 parallels VT 12A and VT 12, with exits at both Randolph and Northfield—both ends of our loop. This is good news for bikers: Through traffic—and especially through truck traffic—will take the interstate. Even local commuters are likely to hop on the interstate for the trip between Randolph and Northfield. Traffic on VT 12A and VT 12 is going to be light.

For almost the entire length of VT 12A, you'll be following the Third Branch of the White River. VT 12A is remarkably flat because it follows the river so closely. Notice that the railroad takes advantage of the valley created by the Third Branch, too. The railroad, the river, and fine rural scenery will be nearly constant between Randolph and Northfield. The Roxbury Country Store (the only opportunity for refills and snacks between Randolph and Northfield) is conveniently located at 15.9 miles.

Serious cyclists intent on speed will probably want to skip the tour of Northfield. Everybody else will enjoy seeing Norwich University and stopping at the Vermont Chocolatiers in downtown Northfield. Norwich University is a military

Village of East Braintree

school, so don't be surprised by lots of uniforms on the streets of Northfield. Other than the Red Kettle Restaurant, just south of Northfield, there are no stores or restaurants on VT 12 until you return to Randolph. Be sure you've got fluids before starting the climb out of Northfield.

The boat launch on Baker Pond is a pleasant rest stop. Immediately after Baker Pond, notice the left onto Vermont Highway 65. Although a numbered route and a thick red line on the map, it's actually a dirt road. If you made a left here, you'd come to the entrance to Allis State Park (camping, picnic area, a fire tower with amazing views) in about a mile.

Reach the highest elevation of the ride at about 30.8 miles, and prepare for a long plunge down the other side.

East Braintree, at 35.0 miles, is about as picturesque a Vermont village as you'll find. Alas, the general store has closed, a victim of easy travel to bigger places. You may have noticed other Braintrees earlier in the ride: You went through West Braintree and past the Braintree School as you headed north on VT 12A. If you've got fatter tires—and a lot of energy left—you can make a detour here to visit the third village in the town of Braintree: Braintree Hill, in the middle of the loop. The name says it all. It's a dirt road, and low gears will come in handy.

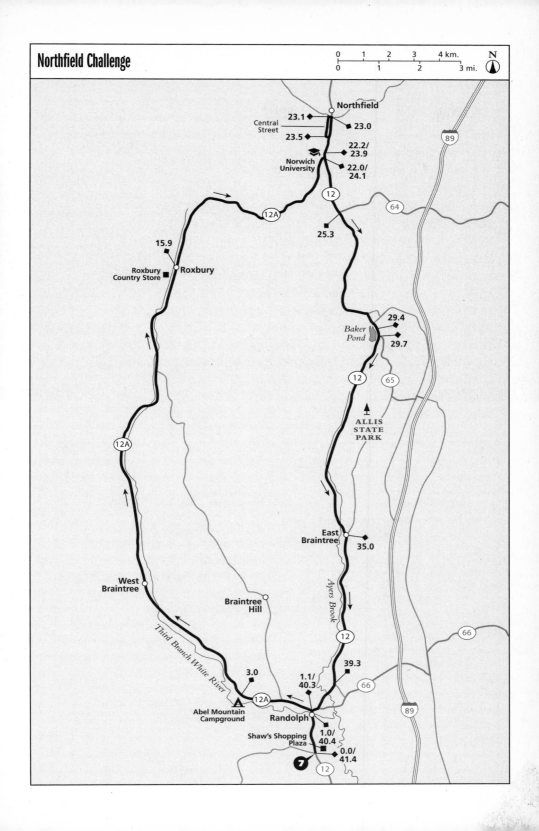

Northfield Challenge

0 1 2 3 4 km.
0 1 2 3 mi.

N

Northfield
23.1 ◆
23.0 ■

Central
Street
23.5 ◆

22.2/
23.9
Norwich
University
22.0/
24.1

12

25.3

12A

15.9 ■
Roxbury
Country Store
Roxbury

*Baker
Pond*
29.4 ◆

29.7 ◆

12 65

**ALLIS
STATE
PARK**

12A

**East
Braintree**
35.0 ◆

Ayers Brook

64

89

66

**West
Braintree**

**Braintree
Hill**

Third Branch White River

12

3.0 ■

1.1/
40.3

39.3

66

89

Abel Mountain
Campground

12A

Randolph

Shaw's Shopping
Plaza

1.0/
40.4 ■

0.0/
41.4 ◆

7

12

After East Braintree, continue a gentle descent along Ayers Brook, through farm country and fine views, back to Randolph.

Miles and Directions

0.0 Exit shopping plaza parking lot onto VT 12, heading north toward Randolph.

1.0 Cross bridge over Third Branch of the White River, in Randolph.

1.1 Intersection with VT 12A. Bear left onto VT 12A North.

3.0 Abel Mountain Campground on left.

15.9 Village of Roxbury. Roxbury Country Store on left. Continue straight on VT 12A North.

22.0 Junction with VT 12. Turn left onto VT 12 North and enter town of Northfield.

22.2 Norwich University to the left. Continue straight on VT 12 North.

23.0 Center of Northfield. Pass town green on left, then turn left off VT 12 onto Depot Street.

23.1 Bear left at end of Depot Street, cross Wall Street onto Central Street, heading south.

23.4 Central Street bears left. Stay on Central Street.

23.5 Junction with VT 12. Turn right onto VT 12 South.

24.1 Road forks. Bear left, staying on VT 12 South.

25.3 Vermont Highway 64 to the left. Continue straight on VT 12 South.

29.4 Baker Pond boat access to the right. Continue straight on VT 12 South.

29.7 VT 65 to left. Continue straight on VT 12 South.

35.0 Hamlet of East Braintree. Continue straight on VT 12 South.

39.3 Windover Road to the left. Bear right, continuing on VT 12 South.

40.1 Junction with VT 66. Turn right onto VT 66 West.

40.3 Junction with VT 12A. Bear left, continuing on VT 12 South and entering town of Randolph.

41.4 Return to parking area south of Randolph.

Local Information
Central Vermont Chamber of Commerce, P.O. Box 336, Barre, VT 05641; (802) 229-4619; www.central-vt.com.

Local Events/Attractions
Allis State Park, 284 Allis State Park Road, Randolph, VT; (802) 276-3175; www.vtstate parks.com/htm/allis.cfm.

Food
Defelices Sandwich Shop & Café, 7 South Main Street, Northfield, VT; (802) 485-4700. **Vermont Chocolatiers,** 14 East Street, P.O. Box 333, Northfield, VT 05663; (802) 485-5181; www.vermontchocolatiers.com. A mouthwatering stop. You've got many miles to go, so relish those calories.

The Common Café, 12 Depot Square, Northfield, VT; (802) 485-4011. **Red Kettle Family Restaurant,** 165 VT 12 South, Northfield, VT; (802) 485-4336. A local favorite. **Patrick's Place Restaurant,** 2 Merchants Row, Randolph, VT; (802) 728-6062.

Accommodations
See the Central Vermont Chamber of Commerce for a list of lodging options. **The Northfield Inn,** 228 Highland Avenue, Northfield, VT; (802) 485-8558; www.thenorthfieldinn.com. **Allis State Park Campground,** 284 Allis State Park Road, Randolph, VT; (802) 276-3175; www.vtstateparks.com/htm/allis.cfm. Small

campground. Open Memorial Day through Labor Day.

Abel Mountain Campground, 354 Mobile Acres Road #6F, Braintree, VT; (802) 728-5548; www.abelmountaincampground.com

Bike Shops

Onion River Sports, 20 Langdon Street, Montpelier, VT; (802) 229-9409; www.onionriver.com.

Bicycle Express Ltd., 3 Stallion Inn Stock Farm Road, Randolph, VT; (802) 728-5568.

Green Mountain Bicycles, 105 North Main Street, Rochester, VT; (802) 767-4464; www.greenmountainbikes.com.

Map

DeLorme: Vermont Atlas & Gazetteer: Pages 34, 40.

8 Otter Creek Cruise

Otter Creek is a key player on this ride. Once known as "The Indian Road," it's the longest river in Vermont and was a major south/north travel route for Indians, and for colonists, too, when roads were little more than muddy paths. Its floodplain forms much of the rich farmland you'll pass through, where farmers still occasionally find Indian artifacts. Minimal traffic, rolling hills, and grand views of both the Green Mountains and the Adirondacks combine to make this ride a contender for the best of Vermont cycling.

Start: The public parking area at the end of Bakery Lane in Middlebury, next to Otter Creek and Mister Ups restaurant. Most parking areas in Middlebury impose time limits (and local police do check). This area doesn't have limits, and it even offers an overnight parking section. Mileage begins at the back of the parking area, next to Otter Creek.
Length: 29.0 miles.
Terrain: Rolling hills.

Traffic and hazards: The only significant traffic will be in the towns of Middlebury and Vergennes. Walk bikes over the pedestrian bridge in Middlebury. Otter Creek floods regularly in the spring, occasionally forcing the closing of nearby roads. It's wise to call ahead if planning this trip in April, to be sure all roads are open. Phone (802) 388-4919 for state police in Middlebury.

Getting there: Middlebury is on U.S. Highway 7, in the west-central part of the state, about halfway between Rutland and Burlington. From the north, turn right off US 7 and onto Vermont Highway 30 (Middlebury's Main Street). Proceed about 0.2 mile south on Main Street, crossing Otter Creek. Turn left onto Bakery Lane, following signs for the public parking area.

The earthy smell of aerated water, as you cross the pedestrian bridge over Otter Creek, will set the tone for this ride. The Middlebury Falls will be the first of three waterfalls on the trip, and Otter Creek, although only occasionally visible, will be a nearby companion the whole way.

The Pulp Mill Covered Bridge, at 1.2 miles, is thought to be one of the oldest covered bridges in Vermont. It's unusual in being a two-lane bridge of three spans,

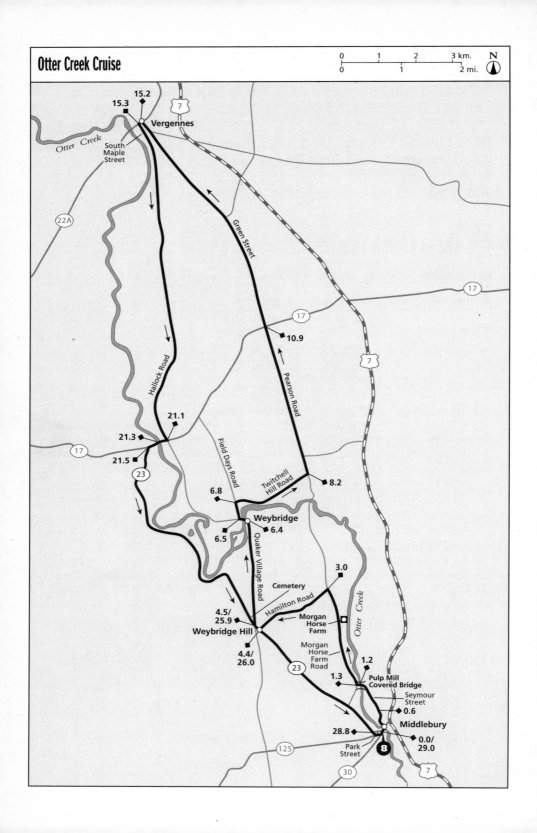

Otter Creek Cruise

0   1   2   3 km.
0   1   2 mi.

N

7

Otter Creek

15.2
15.3
Vergennes

South
Maple
Street

22A

Green Street

17

7

10.9

Hallock Road

Pearson Road

21.1
21.3
21.5

17

23

Field Days Road

Twitchell Hill Road

6.8

8.2

6.5

Weybridge

6.4

Quaker Village Road

3.0

Cemetery

Hamilton Road

Otter Creek

4.5/
25.9
Weybridge Hill

Morgan
Horse
Farm

4.4/
26.0

23

Morgan
Horse
Farm
Road

1.2

1.3

Pulp Mill
Covered Bridge

Seymour
Street

0.6

28.8

Middlebury

0.0/
29.0

8

Park
Street

125

30

7

one of only two such bridges in the United States in regular use. You'll bear right after the bridge and will want to stop to look at the falls—the second of the trip.

The University of Vermont's Morgan Horse Farm is at 2.5 miles, on the right. It's dedicated to breeding, training, and selling the descendents of the stallion Justin Morgan received in payment for a debt in 1790. The main barn is on the right, with pastures on the left. In spring and summer there are sure to be mothers and foals in the pasture. (Watch the poison ivy if you approach the fence for a closer look.)

Come to a stop at 4.4 miles, in the tiny village of Weybridge Hill. Visitors frequently remark that Vermont seems to have at least two or three, often more, towns with essentially the same name (Weybridge, Weybridge Hill, Middlebury, East Middlebury). It can be a source of confusion, particularly as locals often seem to have their own versions as well as the official designations. And this is a particularly confusing intersection, so pay attention to road signs and directions.

Stop on the bridge over Otter Creek in Weybridge to look at the Weybridge Dam. Water coming over the dam is actually higher than the road, and during spring runoff you're likely to get a little wet from the spray. Accounts of early explorers and settlers describe Otter Creek's abundant fish and wildlife, including beavers and otters (hence the name). Although not as plentiful as they once were, otters are still seen. Even if you're not lucky enough to spot an otter, you might see an "otter slide" (path where they've enjoyed sliding into the water) on a muddy bank.

The right turn off Quaker Village Road at 6.5 miles is onto Field Days Road. Our route turns off Field Days Road very soon, but if you were to continue straight, you'd come upon the reason for the name: the large fairgrounds that are the site of the Addison County Field Days in mid-August. If you happen to be doing this ride then, it's worth a detour.

The rest of the trip to Vergennes is simply beautiful Vermont biking: quiet roads and Champlain Valley farms against the backdrop of the Green Mountains in the distance.

Vergennes is a likely refueling stop. Buy a soda and sandwich, and picnic on the town green directly across the intersection with Vermont Highway 22A. Then head south again. Now the fine views will be of the Adirondack Mountains to the west. The prosperous farmland is the floodplain of Otter Creek to your right. If you're looking for it, you'll catch occasional glimpses of the creek. Immediately after the turn onto Vermont Highway 17, cross Otter Creek, then continue south on Vermont Highway 23, another delightful biking road.

At about 25.5 miles, begin the only real climb of the trip. Now you'll know why that village is called Weybridge Hill. You'll recognize the intersection at 26.0 miles (you're seeing the cemetery from the other side), but this time you'll stay on VT 23, heading south. A couple more miles of gently rolling hills, and you're back in Middlebury.

If time permits, plan to check out some of Middlebury's shops and museums. Otter Creek Brewery and the Frog Hollow Craft Center are examples of fun places to visit.

Miles and Directions

0.0 From the parking area next to Otter Creek, return to Main Street.

0.1 Cross to the west side of Main Street, cross the little park with the cannon, and turn right onto Park Street.

0.2 Junction of Park Street and Mill Street. Turn left onto Mill Street, then make an immediate right off Mill Street to cross the footbridge over Otter Creek.

0.3 After crossing the footbridge, you'll be in the parking area for the "Marble Works." Bear left by the Noonie Deli. This is Maple Street (unmarked here).

0.6 Stop sign at end of Maple Street. Turn left onto Seymour Street, heading north.

1.2 Bear left off Seymour Street and cross Pulp Mill Covered Bridge.

1.3 After crossing bridge, bear right onto Morgan Horse Farm Road, heading north.

2.5 University of Vermont Morgan Horse Farm on right.

3.0 Turn left (west) off Morgan Horse Farm Road onto Hamilton Road.

4.4 Stop sign at junction with VT 23 in Weybridge Hill. Turn right onto VT 23 North.

4.5 Bear right off VT 23 onto Quaker Village Road, heading north. The cemetery will be on your left.

6.4 Bridge over Otter Creek in Weybridge. Dam and hydroelectric plant on north side of bridge.

6.5 Turn right off Quaker Village Road onto Field Days Road, heading north.

6.8 Turn right off Field Days Road onto Twitchell Hill Road, heading east.

8.2 Junction with Pearson Road. Turn left onto Pearson Road, heading north.

10.9 Stop sign at the bottom of a hill, at the intersection with VT 17. Continue straight across VT 17 onto Green Street (unmarked here). Be careful here: VT 17 carries a lot of traffic.

15.2 Stop sign at junction with VT 22A. Turn left onto VT 22A South.

15.3 Turn left onto South Maple Street, heading south.

21.1 Junction with VT 17. Turn right onto VT 17 West.

21.3 Bridge across Otter Creek.

21.5 Turn left off VT 17 onto VT 23 South, also called Weybridge Road, following signs for Middlebury.

26.0 Village of Weybridge Hill. Continue south on VT 23. (Watch signs here, as VT 23 bears left.)

28.8 Junction with Vermont Highway 125. Turn left onto VT 125 East.

28.9 Junction with VT 30. Cross VT 30 onto Bakery Lane (a few yards on VT 30 North, then an immediate right onto Bakery Lane).

29.0 Return to parking area.

Local Information

Addison County Chamber of Commerce, 2 Court Street, Middlebury, VT; (802) 388-7951 or (800) 733-8376; www.midvermont.com.

Local Events/Attractions

Addison County Fair & Field Days, P.O. Box 745, Middlebury, VT 05753; (802) 545-2557; www.addisoncountyfielddays.com. A real agricultural fair. One of the Vermont Chamber of Commerce's "Top 10 Summer Events."

Frog Hollow Vermont State Craft Center, 1 Mill Street, Middlebury, VT; (802) 388-3177; www.froghollow.org.
University of Vermont Morgan Horse Farm, 74 Battell Drive, Weybridge, VT; (802) 388-2011; www.uvm.edu/morgan.

Food

Otter Creek Bakery, 14 College Street, Middlebury, VT; (802) 388-3371; www.ottercreek bakery.com. Pastries, deli sandwiches, and a restroom.
Mister Ups, 2 Bakery Lane, Middlebury, VT; (802) 388-6724. Next to the ride's start. Nice views of the river and good food.
3 Squares Cafe, 221 Main Street, Vergennes, VT; (802) 877-2772. European-style deli and cafe.

Accommodations

The Addison County Chamber of Commerce Web site is the best place to look for lodging. Middlebury is a college town, and there are lots of options.
Courtyard by Marriott Middlebury, 309 Court Street (US 7 South), Middlebury, VT; (802) 388-7600; www.middleburycourtyard.com.

Bike Shop

The Bike Center, 74 Main Street, Middlebury, VT; (802) 388-6666; www.bikecentermid.com.

Map

DeLorme: Vermont Atlas & Gazetteer: Pages 32, 33, 38.

9 Champlain Valley Cruise

This is the Champlain Valley, characterized by flat, fertile farmland and long vistas in all directions. This is an easy 36 miles and is especially recommended for people who are ready to move up from "rambles" to an easy "cruise." It's also possible to shorten the ride if time doesn't permit the whole route. See the map for obvious cross roads. Parts of the route follow the Lake Champlain Bikeway.

Start: Dead Creek Wildlife Area public access parking lot, on the north side of Vermont Highway 17, in the town of Addison. Alternative parking is possible at any of the bird-watching pull-offs along VT 17 east of the Dead Creek Wildlife Area.
Length: 36.0 miles.

Terrain: Mostly flat, with a few gentle hills.
Traffic and hazards: Traffic will be very light on most roads. Moderate traffic on the short stretches of VT 17 and Vermont Highway 125. There are two short sections of unpaved road (each a little over a mile). Neither should be a problem for road bikes.

Getting there: From the Burlington area, take U.S. Highway 7 south to the intersection with Vermont Highway 22A, just north of Vergennes. Turn right onto VT 22A and proceed about 7 miles to the intersection with VT 17. Turn right off VT 22A onto VT 17. Take VT 17 west 2.2 miles to a large parking area on the right, just before a bridge over the creek. This is the Dead Creek Wildlife Area Access area, where there will be ample parking.

This is about as flat as a Vermont bike ride can get. Pick a high gear as you start and, if you wish, leave it there for most of the ride. It's a beautiful trip any time of year,

Champlain Valley farm

but is especially recommended for fall, during the waterfowl migration. Canada geese regularly stop here, and in recent years large flocks of snow geese have adopted the Dead Creek area as a resting point in their migration from the eastern arctic to the southern states. The parking area where the ride begins is part of the Dead Creek Wildlife Management Area. In October, the peak of the migration, you'll find yourself in the company of lots of bird-watchers. Canada geese tend to arrive earlier in the month, snow geese a little later. If seeing the geese is a goal (and it's a very impressive sight), plan to start the ride early in the morning when they're likely to be feeding and moving from field to field. Winds off the lake can be cold. If you plan a fall trip, bring extra clothing.

The turn off VT 17 onto Jersey Street at 1.7 miles marks the start of your tour of Champlain Valley farms. For the next 6 miles, you'll literally be riding through farms, and tractors and hay wagons are likely to be more plentiful than cars. You can't miss the authentic smells of corn and hay and cows. These are family farms on a much larger, flatter scale than the hillside farms in the central part of the state. Count the silos, and note the size of the herds. While many smaller Vermont farms have failed in recent years, it's heartening to see that those in the Champlain Valley are prospering.

The general store in Panton is a nice stop. Across from the store there's a handy picnic area with long views across the valley to the Green Mountains.

The turn onto Arnold Bay Road means you've reached the northernmost point of the ride and are now heading west toward the lake. The four-way intersection at 10.6 miles offers the opportunity of an optional side-trip for a closer look at Arnold Bay. The bay is so named because this is where Benedict Arnold—an American hero in 1776—burned what was left of his fleet after the Battle of Valcour Island.

After the turn onto Lake Road at 11.2 miles, you'll notice that development along the lake is definitely upscale. Some of those homes can only be called mansions.

The junction with VT 17 is a little disappointing. So far you've probably only encountered a handful of cars and trucks—in addition to assorted farm equipment—along the road. Traffic will increase now for a while, so stay right and stay focused. VT 17 is an east/west truck route, with connections to New York State via the Crown Point Bridge.

The D.A.R. State Park is on the right at 17.9 miles. The shoreline here is rocky. Although there is no official beach at the park, people swim off the rocky shore. The limestones along the lake are good fossil hunting territory.

At the junction with VT 125 at 19.2 miles, historians will want to make another short side-trip to the Chimney Point State Historic Site, adjacent to the Crown Point Bridge. It's a fine little museum that houses displays on the history of the area, from prehistoric to modern times. Even those who don't care to visit the museum are likely to enjoy a stop to admire the views of the lake and Crown Point on the opposite shore. Like Ticonderoga to the south, this area was considered a strategic stronghold during the colonial and revolutionary periods. The ruins of Fort Crown Point are directly across the lake, just north of the bridge. (The side-trip to Fort Crown Point is fascinating but recommended only for experienced cyclists, as the bridge carries a lot of traffic and doesn't have much of a shoulder.)

After the turn off VT 125 onto Lake Street, traffic all but disappears, and you're back to the occasional tractor and farm truck. This is a particularly lovely section of the ride, with smooth pedaling and fine views of farms and lake. It would be easy to miss the turn off Lake Street onto Middle Road at 24.6 miles, as the Lake Champlain Bikeway goes straight here. Our route heads east, with remarkable views of the lake and the Adirondack Mountains behind as you pedal inland. Turn north onto Basin Harbor Road at 26.6 miles, and the views continue, with the lake and the Adirondacks to your left and the Green Mountains to your right. And more farms—all the way back to the parking area at Dead Creek.

Miles and Directions

0.0 Turn right out of parking area at Dead Creek Wildlife Area onto VT 17, heading west.

0.1 Cross bridge over Dead Creek.

1.7 Turn right off VT 17 onto Jersey Street, heading north.

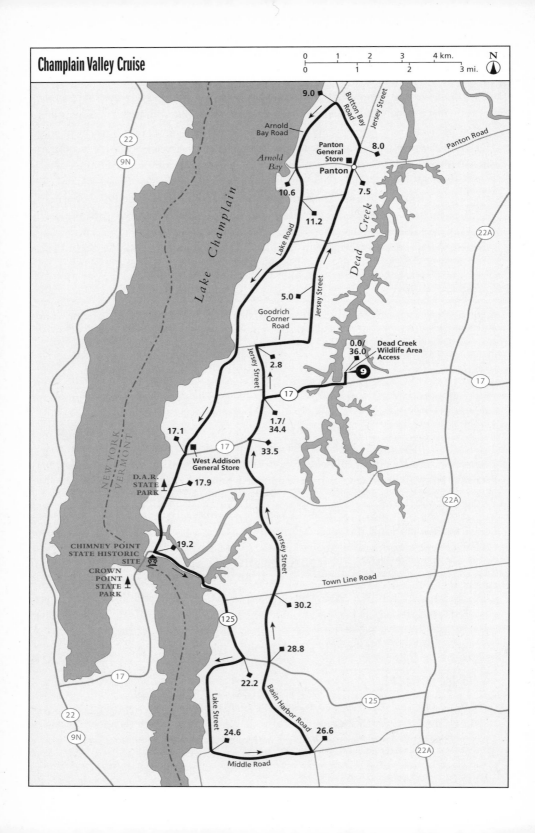

Champlain Valley Cruise

0 1 2 3 4 km.
0 1 2 3 mi.

N

9.0

Button Bay Road

Jersey Street

Arnold Bay Road

8.0

Panton Road

Panton General Store

Arnold Bay

Panton

7.5

10.6

Lake Road

11.2

Dead Creek

Lake Champlain

5.0

Jersey Street

Goodrich Corner Road

0.0/ 36.0

Dead Creek Wildlife Area Access

9

2.8

Jersey Street

17

22A

1.7/ 34.4

17.1

17

33.5

West Addison General Store

NEW YORK
VERMONT

D.A.R. STATE PARK

17.9

CHIMNEY POINT STATE HISTORIC SITE

19.2

Jersey Street

CROWN POINT STATE PARK

22A

Town Line Road

30.2

28.8

125

22.2

125

Lake Street

Basin Harbor Road

24.6

26.6

22A

17

Middle Road

22

9N

22

9N

22

9N

2.8 Junction with Goodrich Corner Road. Turn right onto Goodrich Corner Road, heading east. Road surface turns to dirt almost immediately.

4.2 Road surface returns to pavement.

5.0 Cross into town of Panton. Road is now called Jersey Street again. Continue north on Jersey Street.

7.5 Hamlet of Panton. Panton Road is to the right, and Panton General Store is to the left. Continue straight on Jersey Street.

8.0 Road forks. Bear left off Jersey Street onto Button Bay Road, still heading north and following signs for Lake Champlain Maritime Museum and Button Bay State Park.

9.0 Turn left off Button Bay Road onto Arnold Bay Road (unpaved road surface here).

10.0 Road surface returns to pavement.

10.6 Four-way intersection. **Option:** Turn right onto Adams Ferry Road for close-up view of Arnold Bay. Continue straight on Arnold Bay Road.

11.2 Arnold Bay Road ends. Bear right onto Lake Road, following signs for the Lake Champlain Bikeway.

17.1 Stop sign at junction with VT 17. West Addison General Store is on the left. Bear right onto VT 17, heading south.

17.9 Entrance to D.A.R. State Park on right.

19.2 Intersection with VT 125. The Bridge Restaurant is on the left. Bear left onto VT 125 East. **Option:** Stay on VT 17 for side-trip to the Chimney Point State Historic Site and/or across the bridge to Crown Point, New York. Caution: Heavy traffic, minimal shoulders on bridge.

22.2 Turn right off VT 125 onto Lake Street, heading south.

24.6 Turn left off Lake Street onto Middle Road, leaving the Lake Champlain Bikeway.

26.6 Turn left off Middle Road onto Basin Harbor Road, heading north.

28.8 Stop sign at intersection with VT 125. Continue straight (north) on Basin Harbor Road.

30.2 Four-way intersection where Town Line Road crosses. Continue straight on what is now called Jersey Street.

33.5 Junction with VT 17. Turn right onto VT 17 East.

34.4 Jersey Street is to the left. Bear right, staying on VT 17.

36.0 Return to Dead Creek parking area.

Local Information

Addison County Chamber of Commerce, 2 Court Street, Middlebury, VT; (802) 388-7951 or (800) 733-8376; www.midvermont.com.

Local Events/Attractions

Chimney Point State Historic Site and Museum, 7305 VT 125, Addison, VT; (802) 759-2412; www.historicvermont.org /chimneypoint.

Crown Point State Historic Site, 739 Bridge Road, Crown Point, NY 12928; (518) 597-3666; www.lakechamplain.com/cphistoricsite.

Lake Champlain Bikeways Clearinghouse, c/o Local Motion Trailside Center, 1 Steele Street, #103, Burlington, VT; (802) 652-BIKE; www.lakechamplainbikeways.org. Maps of over 1,300 miles of routes in the Lake Champlain Basin (including areas of Vermont, New York, and Quebec).

Dead Creek Wildlife Area (the starting point for the ride). Information at http://vt.audubon .org/IBADeadCreek.html. Almost 3,000 acres of preserved forest, fields, marsh, and floodplain. Managed by the Vermont Fish and Wildlife Department.

Food

Panton General Store, 3074 Jersey Street, Panton, VT; (802) 475-2431.

West Addison Country Store, 5944 VT 17 W, Addison, VT; (802) 759-2071.

The Bridge Restaurant, junction of VT 125 W and VT 17 E, Addison, VT; (802) 759-2152. Popular with tourists and locals. A good halfway stop.

Accommodations

The best options for lodging are in the college town of Middlebury, about 17 miles to the east. See the Addison County Chamber of Commerce Web site for a comprehensive list.

Courtyard by Marriott Middlebury, 309 Court Street (US 7 South), Middlebury, VT; (802) 388-7600; www.middleburycourtyard.com.

D.A.R. State Park (campground), 6750 VT 17 W, Addison, VT; (802) 759-2354; www.vtstateparks.com/htm/dar.cfm.

Bike Shop

The Bike Center, 74 Main Street, Middlebury, VT; (802) 388-6666; www.bikecentermid.com.

Map

DeLorme: Vermont Atlas & Gazetteer: Page 32, 38.

10 Vergennes/Lake Champlain Maritime Museum Ramble

Many of Vermont's most prosperous farms are in the Champlain Basin, where the soil is fertile and the land is nearly flat. If you've been riding in other parts of the state, you'll be impressed by the scale of the farms here (they're much bigger than Vermont's hillside farms). And you'll be amazed at how flat the terrain is. This is an opportunity to knock the dirt off some of those high gears, which may not get a lot of use elsewhere in the state. The Maritime Museum along Lake Champlain is a rare find. Riders with an interest in Revolutionary history, underwater archaeology, boat construction, or the ecology of the lake will definitely want to plan an extended stop.

Start: Vergennes Falls Park canoe portage and public recreation area. (In spring the park may be flooded. Use parking areas next to the town green in Vergennes as an alternative.)
Length: 14.7 miles.

Terrain: Flat.
Traffic and hazards: Shoulders are minimal to nonexistent, but traffic is light on all roads. Watch out for poison ivy along the banks of Otter Creek.

Getting there: From Burlington, take U.S. Highway 7 south about 20 miles to the intersection with Vermont Highway 22A. Turn right onto VT 22A and proceed about a mile south into the city of Vergennes. In Vergennes, make the first right after the bridge over Otter Creek, onto Canal Street. Bear right again onto Mechanic Street, following signs for Vergennes Falls Park. Park in the parking area at Vergennes Falls Park, a designated canoe portage and public recreation area. (In spring the park may be flooded. Use parking areas next to the town green in Vergennes as an alternative.)

The trip's starting point is a picturesque spot below the Vergennes Falls. Signs tell you that, for Otter Creek paddlers, this is the end of the canoe portage around the falls. For much of the early part of the trip, Otter Creek is close to the road, on the

Gunboat Philadelphia II *at the Lake Champlain Maritime Museum* PHOTO BY ENNIS DULING

Vergennes/Lake Champlain Maritime Museum Ramble

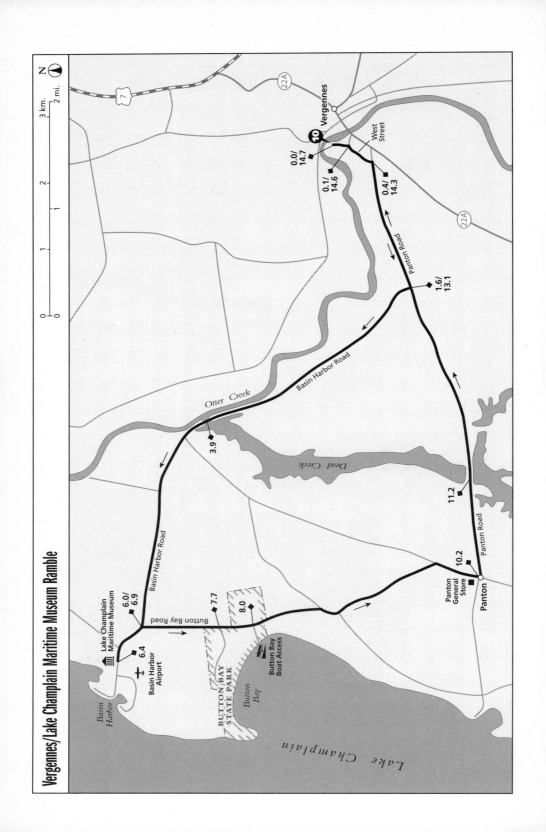

right. The stretch of road at about 3.6 miles is a popular fishing area. Pay attention to where you walk if you decide to take a break along here: The poison ivy looks very healthy.

Dramatic views of the Adirondacks begin at about 0.8 mile and continue for much of the trip. After bearing right at 6.0 miles, the Adirondacks will briefly be to your left and the Green Mountains to your right. Camel's Hump is the most prominent of the Green Mountain peaks seen from here. Samuel de Champlain first called it Le Lion Couchant—the crouching, or resting, lion. It does look more like a sphinx than a camel.

The Lake Champlain Maritime Museum at 6.4 miles is a good rest stop. It's privately owned and has an official policy of being bicycle friendly. Cyclists are welcome to use the picnic areas, water fountain, and restrooms even if not visiting the museum. And many will decide to visit (moderate admission fee). Collections include displays of old boats, from Indian dugouts to ice boats; chronicles of ongoing underwater archaeological projects; a floating replica of *The Philadelphia* (one of Benedict Arnold's gunboats, which fought the British at Valcour Island); boat building demonstrations; and more.

Our route has riders backtrack after the museum stop. However, continuing past the museum for a short distance (0.25 mile or less) takes you on a side-trip to Basin Harbor, a resort community with golf course, restaurant, and a beautiful view of the tiny harbor.

Button Bay State Park at 7.7 miles is another good stop. It offers swimming (pool or lake), picnicking, and fossil hunting along the rocky shore. You may see chunks of fossilized coral reef, fossil sea snails, or the oddly shaped stones—that look a bit like buttons—formed by water percolating through the clay soil of the area (hence "Button Bay").

At 10.2 miles, begin heading east and back toward Vergennes. In another mile, as you cross the bridge over Dead Creek, take a few moments to look for waterfowl and wading birds. Herons are common, and in the fall this area is an important stop for geese migrating along the Champlain flyway.

Miles and Directions

0.0 Exit parking area at Vergennes Falls Park.

0.1 Stop sign at the end of Mechanic Street. Turn left onto Canal Street, then make an immediate right onto West Street.

0.4 Stop sign. Turn right onto Panton Road (unmarked here), heading west.

1.6 Turn right off Panton Road onto Basin Harbor Road.

3.9 Cross bridge over Dead Creek.

6.0 Button Bay Road to the left. Bear right, staying on Basin Harbor Road and following signs for Basin Harbor.

6.4 Entrance to Lake Champlain Maritime Museum on right. Turn around and start retracing route on Basin Harbor Road.

6.9	Road forks. Bear right off Basin Harbor Road onto Button Bay Road, heading south.
7.7	Entrance to Button Bay State Park on right.
8.0	Button Bay Boat Access Area on right.
10.2	Village of Panton. Panton General Store on right. Turn left onto Panton Road, heading east.
11.2	Cross bridge over Dead Creek.
13.1	Basin Harbor Road to left (which completes loop). Continue straight on Panton Road.
14.3	Turn left off Panton Road onto West Street.
14.6	Bear left onto Canal Street, then make an immediate right onto Mechanic Street.
14.7	Back to parking area.

Local Information

Addison County Chamber of Commerce, 2 Court Street, Middlebury, VT; (802) 388-7951 or (800) 733-8376; www.midvermont.com. **Lake Champlain Regional Chamber of Commerce,** 60 Main Street, Suite 100, Burlington, VT; (802) 863-3489 or (877) 686-5253; www.vermont.org.

Local Events/Attractions

Lake Champlain Maritime Museum, 4472 Basin Harbor Road, Vergennes, VT; (802) 475-2022; www.lcmm.org.

Food

Red Mill Restaurant at Basin Harbor Club, 4800 Basin Harbor Road, Vergennes, VT; (802) 475-2317; www.basinharbor.com /redmill.asp. Located just beyond the Maritime Museum, next to the small airport. Open for lunch and dinner.
Panton General Store, 3074 Jersey Street, Panton, VT; (802) 475-2431.
3 Squares Cafe, 221 Main Street, Vergennes, VT; (802) 877-2772. European-style deli and cafe.

Accommodations

The best motel options are probably in Burlington and will be listed on the Lake Champlain Regional Chamber of Commerce Web site. Also see the Addison County Chamber of Commerce site.
Days Inn, 3229 Shelburne Road (US 7), Shelburne, VT; (802) 985-3334 or (800) 329-7466. South of Burlington, it's easy to get to from Vergennes. Clean, convenient, moderately priced. Good breakfast included.
Button Bay State Park Campground, 5 Button Bay State Park Road, Vergennes, VT; (802) 475-2377; www.vtstateparks.com/htm /buttonbay.cfm. Open Memorial Day through Columbus Day.

Bike Shop

The Bike Center, 74 Main Street, Middlebury, VT; (802) 388-6666; www.bikecentermid.com.

Map

DeLorme: Vermont Atlas & Gazetteer: Page 38.

11 Stowe Ramble

This short ride has it all: Stowe's award-winning recreation path, an opportunity for fortune hunters to strike it rich, a haunted covered bridge, and a delightful descent into the village of Stowe.

Start: Recreation path parking area behind the Stowe Community Church.
Length: 10.9 miles.
Terrain: Hilly.

Traffic and hazards: Exercise extra caution on the 0.7-mile portion of the ride on Vermont Highway 100, where traffic can be heavy and the shoulder is narrow.

Getting there: Take exit 10 off Interstate 89, following signs for VT 100 north. Proceed north on VT 100 about 10 miles, passing through Stowe's "Lower Village" and coming to a three-way stop at the junction of VT 100 and Vermont Highway 108 in downtown Stowe. From this intersection, the spire of the Stowe Community Church will be visible directly ahead, on the left off VT 100. Continue on VT 100 to the church. Make a left immediately after the church, following signs for Stowe Recreation Path Parking. Park in the recreation path parking area directly behind the church.

The village of Stowe has thrived on the tourist industry since the nineteenth century, when it was a popular summer resort. Today it's also a center of Vermont's ski industry, and Main Street is crowded with visitors all year long. A majority of Stowe's visitors (and a lot of full-time residents, too) are outdoor types—skiers, hikers, paddlers, and bikers. It isn't surprising that Stowe took a leadership role in establishing a "community created greenway" (its recreation/bike path) that has become a model for similar projects in communities nationwide. Residents of Stowe are proud of their recreation path. They're not just proud of it, they use it—a lot. Don't plan on much speed for the first 3 miles of this trip, as you'll meet or pass all kinds of folks out having fun (walking, running, and pushing baby carriages, as well as pedaling). Plan to relax, enjoying the views, the well-maintained path, and the company.

At 2.9 miles, leave the recreation path and head west on Luce Hill Road. Then watch for the left turn onto Barrows Road. And now you can pick up the pace. Considering its proximity to Vermont's highest peak, this stretch of road is amazingly flat. You'll notice an odd juxtaposition of expensive condos with tennis courts next to trailers and houses that have seen better days. That dichotomy isn't unusual in rural Vermont.

Turn right off VT 100 at 7.1 miles and start uphill on Gold Brook Road. The brook along the side of the road is so named because of the "placer gold" (very tiny nuggets) that has been found here. If you're feeling lucky, and have some idea what to look for, you might want to stop and poke around. Finding gold is unlikely, but most people find enough other pretty rocks to make the remaining climb a little more difficult.

Be sure to stop for a look at the covered bridge on the left at 8.3 miles. Our route continues straight and doesn't actually cross the bridge, but most riders will want to make the very short side-trip over the bridge, just to see if perhaps it feels a little weird. Although this is officially the Gold Brook Covered Bridge, it's usually referred to as "Emily's Bridge" and is widely thought to be haunted. No one has been able to confirm who Emily was or that she actually lived or died in the area. But there are a number of variations on the story of Emily's Bridge. In the most commonly recounted version, Emily hung herself from a rafter of the bridge after her lover failed to meet her there. In another

Visiting "Emily's Bridge"

version she jumped to her death, and in a third she was thrown from her horse on the way to her wedding. In any case, the ghost at Emily's Bridge is reputedly an angry one who slashed at horses in the nineteenth century and at cars as they crossed the bridge in more recent times. In broad daylight it looks like a typical Vermont covered bridge, with a path to a delightful swimming hole on the far side. (Hint for photographers: A little spit on the lens creates a blur on the photo and could serve to enhance the retelling of this ride.)

Miles and Directions

0.0 From parking area behind the church, head west on the Stowe Recreation Path.

2.2 Cross VT 108. (Get off and walk across.) Continue on recreation path.

2.8 Go through underpass under Luce Hill Road.

2.9 Come out of underpass in another recreation path parking area. Exit parking area, leaving the recreation path and making a right onto Luce Hill Road.

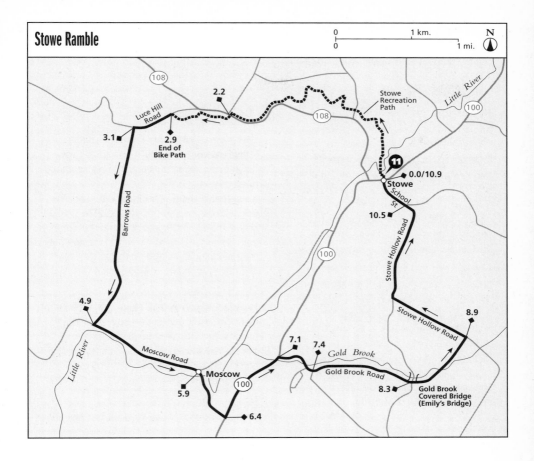

Stowe Ramble

0   1 km.
0   1 mi.

N

3.1   Turn left off Luce Hill Road onto Barrows Road, heading south.

4.9   Junction with Moscow Road (unmarked here). Turn left (east) onto Moscow Road, following signs for VT 100 and I-89.

5.9   Moscow General Store and Deli is on the right. The road forks. Bear right, continuing on Moscow Road.

6.4   Junction with VT 100. Turn left onto VT 100 North.

7.1   Turn right (east) off VT 100 onto Gold Brook Road.

7.4   Four-way intersection. Bear left, continuing on Gold Brook Road, with the brook to the left of the road.

8.3   Four-way intersection. Gold Brook Covered Bridge (Emily's Bridge) is to the left. Continue straight on Gold Brook Road.

8.9   Junction with Stowe Hollow Road. Turn left (northwest) onto Stowe Hollow Road.

10.5   Stop sign at junction with School Street (unmarked here). Turn left onto School Street.

10.8 Junction with Main Street (VT 100). Cross Main Street in front of Stowe Community Church.

10.9 Return to recreation path parking area.

Local Information

Stowe Visitor Information Center, 51 Main Street, Stowe, VT; (877) GO-STOWE; www.gostowe.com.

Local Events/Attractions

Ben and Jerry's, 1281 Waterbury Stowe Road (VT 100), Waterbury, VT; (802) 882-1240 or (866) BJTOURS; www.benjerry.com/our _company/about_us/tours. Tour the ice cream factory and sample the flavors. Located on VT 100, about a mile north of exit 10 off I-89.

Food

Stowe is a resort town, and it has lots of restaurants. Stowe's Web page (www.gostowe .com) contains a comprehensive list.

Main Street Market Deli & Bakery, Old Depot Building, Main Street, Stowe, VT; (802) 253-0077. Has indoor and outdoor seating. Good breakfast prices, daily lunch specials.

Moscow General Store, 539 Moscow Road, Moscow, VT; (802) 253-7363.

Accommodations

Go to www.gostowe.com and click on lodging for the full range of accommodations.

Best Western Waterbury-Stowe, 45 Blush Hill Road, Waterbury, VT; (802) 244-7822; www .bestwesternwaterburystowe.com. Reasonable rates.

Trapp Family Lodge, 700 Trapp Hill Road, P.O. Box 1428, Stowe, VT 05672; (802) 253-8511 or (800) 826-7000; www.trappfamily.com. Best known as a cross-country ski resort, but it's open in summer, too. Yes, these are the Von Trapps of *Sound of Music* fame.

Bike Shops

Mountain Sports & Bike Shop, 580 Mountain Road (VT 108), Stowe, VT; (802) 253-7919. Shop is right off the recreation path.

AJ's Ski and Sports, 350 Mountain Road (VT 108), P.O. Box 1545, Stowe, VT; (802) 253-4593 or (800) 226-6257; www.ajssports.com.

Map

DeLorme: Vermont Atlas & Gazetteer: Page 46.

12 Champlain Islands Classic

Pedal hard for a day, or divide it in two and spend the night. This ride would be a fine introduction to overnight bicycle touring. The scenery is great, pedaling isn't difficult, and there are enough interesting stops to fill a couple of days. The route generally follows the Lake Champlain Bikeway, and there are suggestions for side-trips and extensions.

Start: There are two options: (1) Sand Bar State Park, on U.S Highway 2 just before the causeway to the islands, has swimming and picnic areas. For a two-day trip, this is the best option. They have a special rate for cyclists who want to leave a vehicle. Inquire at the entrance, or ask for a park ranger if the attendant on duty isn't familiar with arrangements for cyclists. (2) There is a public boat launch directly across from Sand Bar State Park, on the south side of US 2. No fee for parking here, there's plenty of space, and it should be fine for a single-day trip. Overnight parking doesn't seem to be prohibited, but it is probably riskier than at the state park.

Length: 74.7 miles.

Terrain: Easy, generally flat pedaling, with some hills in the final 15 to 20 miles.

Traffic and hazards: US 2 on the islands has a paved shoulder and frequent signs encouraging drivers to SHARE THE ROAD. This is a popular cycling area, so most local motorists have become accustomed to bikers. Nevertheless, traffic is significant, especially during summer months. Be especially careful of vehicles pulling boat trailers: Drivers may forget how wide their trailers are.

Getting there: The Champlain Islands are in the northern part of Lake Champlain, between Vermont and New York, and just south of the Canadian border. From the Burlington area, take Interstate 89 north and get off at exit 17, following signs for the Islands. Get on US 2 West and proceed about 4.7 miles to Sand Bar State Park, on the right.

The first stop(s) should be at the ferry landing and the fish hatchery at 7.8 miles, on Vermont Highway 314. The ferry departs for Plattsburgh, New York, every twenty minutes. Taking the ferry to the western side of the lake is one suggestion for a variation on this ride—for a future trip. The Ed Weed Fish Culture Station, 0.2 mile to the east on Bell Hill Road, is for today. This is a state-of-the-art fish hatchery and a fascinating stop—even for folks who thought they weren't particularly interested in fish.

After swinging to the west side of the island, our route rejoins US 2 North at 13.4 miles. Note that the Lake Champlain Bikeway crosses US 2 here, an option for those who don't mind a stretch of dirt road. The bikeway rejoins US 2 just a little north of here. At 15.2 miles, be prepared to stop at the drawbridge if a tall-masted boat happens to be crossing to the other side of the islands. (Note that the bridge surface can be slippery if wet.)

Fishing near Swanton

You've passed through the villages of South Hero and Grand Isle and are heading toward North Hero. The "Heroes" are named in honor of the "Green Mountain Boys"—Revolutionary War heroes who included Ethan and cousin Ebenezer Allen, who was an early island settler. Hero's Welcome General Store and Café, at 18.8 miles, is a recommended stop: good food, a restroom, and a nice lakefront picnic area.

At 24.8 miles, be sure to take the left off US 2 onto Vermont Highway 129. VT 129 is the scenic route north, with spectacular lake views and less traffic. If you're interested in an easy 12-mile side-trip, the circuit of Isle La Motte is recommended. (See the Isle La Motte Ramble for details.)

At 31.9 miles you're back to US 2. People doing the trip in two days will probably want to spend the night somewhere in the Alburgh or Swanton areas. If lodging in the town of Alburgh, make a left onto US 2. Otherwise, turn right onto US 2 East. Another trip, for another day, would be to continue north on US 2, crossing the bridge to Rouses Point, New York, then north into Quebec. Quebec has done a fine job of laying out bicycle routes. You can pick up the Route Verte (see ride information below), just north of the border, and safely pedal all the way to Montreal or points east to loop back into Vermont.

Vermont Highway 78, between Alburgh and Swanton, is a beautiful but heavily traveled section of the trip. The new bridge, completed in summer 2007, is a huge improvement. Nevertheless, this is a major east-west truck route. Stay right, stay focused, and pedal defensively. VT 78 on the Swanton side is flanked by the Missisquoi National Wildlife Refuge. That's the Missisquoi River on your left. Its delta, formed as it flows into Lake Champlain, is home to a variety of waterfowl and other wildlife. Heron sightings are almost guaranteed.

Swanton, on the eastern shore of Lake Champlain, is one of only a few places in Vermont known to be the site of a permanent Indian settlement. The Abenaki village of "Missisasuk" was located here in the early eighteenth century. Excellent fishing and fertile meadows undoubtedly made this an attractive site for the Abenakis and for the French and English settlers who followed. Today Swanton is still the tribal center for Vermont's nearly 3,000 Abenakis, who continue to seek recognition and rights to land lost to the French and English more than 200 years ago.

Make the right turn onto Vermont Highway 36 in Swanton, then head south, perhaps making a stop at the town beach in Swanton (45.0 miles) or the state park in St. Albans (53.7 miles). Stay close to the lake until Melville Landing, a small community south of St. Albans. At Melville Landing, make a left (east) onto Polly Hubbard Road, following the Lake Champlain Bikeway signs. Our route follows the bikeway until the junction with US 2. Watch directions carefully during this portion of the trip. I speak from experience, having made a wrong turn and gotten lost here more than once. In Melville Landing it's time to dust off the lower gears, as there are a few hills on the quiet back roads between here and the end of the ride.

This trip is likely to whet your appetite for more Lake Champlain rides. See information sources below for details. Pay particular attention to the Web site for

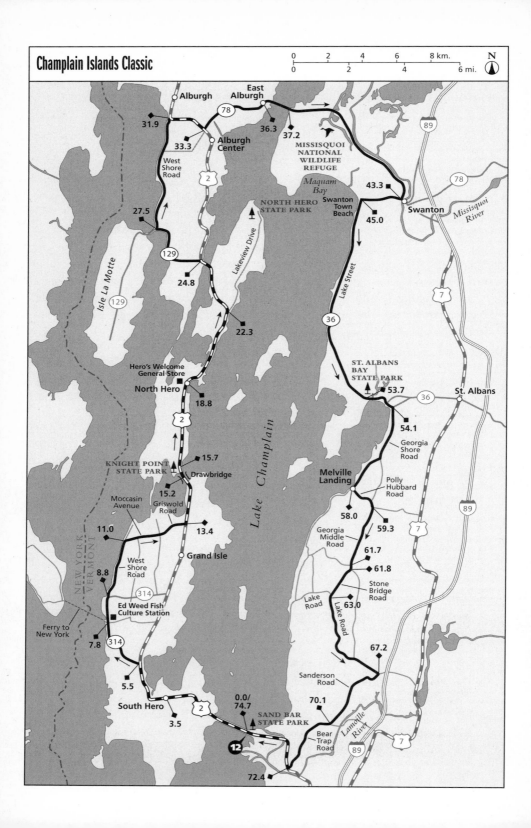

Champlain Islands Classic

0 2 4 6 8 km.
0 2 4 6 mi.

N

Alburgh
East Alburgh
31.9
33.3
Alburgh Center
West Shore Road
36.3
37.2
MISSISSQUOI NATIONAL WILDLIFE REFUGE
89
27.5
129
Maquam Bay
NORTH HERO STATE PARK
Swanton Town Beach
43.3
Swanton
78
45.0
Missisquoi River
24.8
Lakeview Drive
Isle La Motte
129
22.3
Lake Street
7
36
Hero's Welcome General Store
North Hero
18.8
ST. ALBANS BAY STATE PARK
53.7
St. Albans
2
54.1
36
15.7
Georgia Shore Road
KNIGHT POINT STATE PARK
Drawbridge
Melville Landing
Polly Hubbard Road
15.2
Moccasin Avenue
Griswold Road
58.0
59.3
89
11.0
13.4
Georgia Middle Road
7
Grand Isle
61.7
8.8
61.8
West Shore Road
Lake Road
Stone Bridge Road
314
63.0
Ed Weed Fish Culture Station
Lake Road
Ferry to New York
7.8
314
67.2
5.5
Sanderson Road
70.1
South Hero
0.0/ 74.7
Lamoille River
3.5
2
SAND BAR STATE PARK
Bear Trap Road
89
7
12
72.4

Lake Champlain

NEW YORK
VERMONT

Lake Champlain Bikeways and for Local Motion, the Burlington–based organization that is working on connections between the Burlington Bike Path and the islands. The only remaining gap in the connection is between the old Colchester railroad causeway and the southern tip of Grand Isle. During August 2006 and 2007, Local Motion ran a weekend ferry across that gap for cyclists and pedestrians. Contact Local Motion for updates.

Miles and Directions

0.0 Entrance to Sand Bar State Park, or boat launch across the road. Head west on US 2, across the causeway to the islands.

3.5 Allenholm Orchard farmstand is on the left. Good stop in the fall.

5.5 Turn left (west) off US 2 onto VT 314, following signs for ferry to New York State.

7.8 Blinking light at four-way intersection. Ferry to left. Fish hatchery 0.2 mile east on Bell Hill Road, to the right. Continue straight (north) on VT 314.

8.8 VT 314 bears right. Bear left (straight) onto West Shore Road (unmarked here).

11.0 Bear right off West Shore Road onto Moccasin Avenue, heading east and inland.

13.4 At the four-way intersection and junction with US 2, turn left onto US 2 North.

15.2 Cross drawbridge.

15.7 Knight Point State Park on left. Swimming, picnicking. No camping.

18.8 Hero's Welcome General Store is on the left.

20.0 Carry Bay is to the left.

22.3 Lakeview Drive is to the right. This would be the turnoff to North Hero State Park. Continue straight on US 2 North.

24.4 Cross bridge over Alburgh Passage.

24.8 Bear left off US 2 onto VT 129 West.

27.5 Bear right off VT 129 onto West Shore Road (unmarked here), heading north. **Option:** Continue straight on VT 129 for a side-trip to Isle La Motte.

31.9 Junction with US 2. Turn right onto US 2 South.

33.3 At the four-way intersection, turn left off US 2 onto VT 78 East, following signs for Swanton and I-89. The Crossroads Mobil Mart convenience store is on the corner.

36.3 Start across Missisquoi Bay Bridge.

37.2 End of Missisquoi Bay Bridge.

43.3 Stop sign at intersection in Swanton. VT 78 bears left. Continue straight onto VT 36 South.

43.4 Make a sharp right, continuing on VT 36 South (also called Lake Street), following signs for Lake Champlain Bikeway.

45.0 Swanton town beach is on the right.

53.7 St. Albans Bay State Park (beach) is on the right.

54.1 VT 36 turns left toward St. Albans. Continue straight onto Georgia Shore Road, proceeding south along the lakeshore.

58.0 Hamlet of Melville Landing. Turn left (east) off Georgia Shore Road onto Polly Hubbard Road, following signs for the Lake Champlain Bikeway.

59.3 Bear right off Polly Hubbard Road onto Georgia Middle Road (unmarked here), following Lake Champlain Bikeway signs.

61.5 Village of Georgia Plain. Continue straight on Georgia Middle Road.

61.7 Bradley Hill Road is to your right. Continue straight on Georgia Middle Road.

61.8 Road forks. Bear right onto Stone Bridge Road (unmarked here), following Lake Champlain Bikeway signs.

63.0 Road forks. Bear left onto Lake Road (unmarked here), following Lake Champlain Bikeway signs.

67.2 Turn right off Lake Road onto Sanderson Road, following the bikeway.

70.1 Junction with Bear Trap Road. Turn right onto Bear Trap Road, continuing south and west.

72.4 At the junction with US 2, turn right onto US 2 West.

74.7 Return to Sand Bar State Park.

Local Information

Lake Champlain Island Chamber of Commerce, P.O. Box 213, North Hero, VT 05474; (802) 372-8400 or (800) 262-5226; www.champlainislands.com.

Local Events/Attractions

Ed Weed Fish Culture Station, 14 Bell Hill Road, Grand Isle, VT; (802) 372-3171; www.vtfishandwildlife.com/fisheries_ed_weed .cfm. The public is welcome to observe progressive stages in the growth of several varieties of trout and salmon. A self-guided tour takes you by raceways (enormous tanks where juvenile fish are kept), by the stream where salmon migrate, and more.

Grand Isle/Plattsburgh Lake Champlain Ferry, 1268 Gordon's Landing, Grand Isle, VT; c/o Lake Champlain Transportation Company, King Street Dock, Burlington, VT; (802) 864-9804. See www.ferries.com/north_schedule.asp for rates and schedules.

La Route Verte, Vélo Québec, Secrétariat de la Route Verte, 1251 rue Rachel Est., Montréal, Québec, Canada H2J 2J9; (514) 521-8356 or (800) 567-8356; www.routeverte.com/ang. These 3,600 km of bikeways are the best way to explore the province of Quebec.

Lake Champlain Bikeways Clearinghouse, c/o Local Motion Trailside Center, 1 Steele Street, #103, Burlington, VT; (802) 652-BIKE;

www.lakechamplainbikeways.org. Maps of over 1,300 miles of routes in the Lake Champlain Basin (including areas of Vermont, New York, and Quebec).

Food

Hero's Welcome General Store, US 2, North Hero, VT; (802) 372-4161; www.heros welcome.com.

Crossroads Mobil Mart, corner of US 2 and VT 78, Alburgh, VT; (802) 796-3110.

Fish Tales Restaurant, 11 Grand Avenue, Swanton, VT; (802) 868-5800. Good basic food.

Bayside Pavilion, 10 Georgia Shore Road, St. Albans, VT; (802) 524-0909.

Accommodations

Inns and B&Bs are the most prevalent lodging on the Champlain Islands. For more economical motel accommodations, try the major chains outside of Burlington, Swanton, or St. Albans. The Lake Champlain Island Chamber of Commerce is the best source of information on lodging.

La Quinta Inn & Suites in St. Albans is just off the interstate: 813 Fairfax Road, St. Albans, VT; (802) 524-3300; www.vtcomforinns talbans.com.

Thomas Mott Bed & Breakfast, 63 Blue Rock Road, Alburgh, VT; (802) 796-4402 or (800) 348-0843; www.thomas-mott-bb.com. Rates are typical for country inns. Perfect location, just off the route, for people doing a two-day tour.

North Hero State Park Campground, 3803 Lakeview Drive, North Hero, VT; (802) 372-8727; www.vtstateparks.com/htm/northhero.cfm. Open Memorial Day through Labor Day.

Bike Shops

White's Green Mountain Bikes, 1008 Ethan Allen Highway (U.S. Highway 7), Milton, VT; (802) 524-4496.

Old Spokes Home, 322 North Winooski Avenue, Burlington, VT; (802) 863-4475; www.oldspokeshome.com.

North Star Cyclery, 100 Main Street, Burlington, VT; (802) 863-3832.

Map

DeLorme: Vermont Atlas & Gazetteer: Pages 44, 45, 50, 51.

13 Isle La Motte Ramble

This short, flat ramble offers lake views, quiet roads, ancient rocks, and an Old World–style religious shrine.

Start: Parking area at St. Anne's Shrine, along Lake Champlain.
Length: 10.1 miles.
Terrain: Generally flat.
Traffic and hazards: Weekends (especially Sunday) and holidays bring many visitors to the shrine: Watch for cars and pedestrians around the shrine area. There is a short (1.4-mile) section of unpaved road at the southern end of the island. It's hard-packed gravel that shouldn't be a problem for road bikes.

Getting there: From Burlington, take Interstate 89 north to exit 17. Get on U.S. Highway 2 west, following signs for the Lake Champlain Islands. Continue on US 2 northward about 30 miles to South Alburgh. In South Alburgh turn off US 2 onto Vermont Highway 129 West, crossing the bridge to Isle La Motte. About a mile after the bridge, bear right off VT 129 onto Shrine Road, following signs for St. Anne's Shrine. Park in the parking area along the beach, just beyond the shrine.

There is no single image that characterizes all of Vermont. Isle La Motte stands as proof of that. Some visitors to Isle La Motte remark on the feeling of having been transported to an Old World religious site. Many note how strong the French Canadian influence is in this part of the state. There's a lot of evidence that this is still Vermont, but Vermont with a different texture.

Our route begins at St. Anne's Shrine, built on the spot where the first Catholic Mass in Vermont is believed to have been held in 1666. This is also the spot where Samuel de Champlain is thought to have landed in 1609. A statue of Champlain, carved for Montreal's Expo '67, stands on the edge of the island, on the grounds of St. Anne's Shrine. Isle La Motte boasts a population of 400 regular residents and tens of thousands of pilgrims who come to the shrine for relief from suffering and to share the peaceful atmosphere.

Statue of Samuel de Champlain

From the beach next to the shrine, the route heads south along the shore of Lake Champlain. There are cottages and summer homes to the left until about 2.1 miles, when the road passes through a swampy area. This is a beautiful stretch of the ride. With no houses in sight, you can imagine what the Champlain Islands must have been like when Indian hunting and fishing parties camped here. This is a likely area for spotting waterfowl.

You'll need to slow down when the road turns to dirt at 3.4 miles. At about 3.9 miles the Fisk Quarry Preserve, a geologic site, natural area, and state historic site, is on the left. It's worth a stop. Seeing an abandoned marble quarry is interesting, but this one is particularly so. It's part of the Chazy Fossil Reef, and if you look carefully, you'll spot four- to five-hundred-million-year-old fossils underfoot and on the quarry walls. Isle La Motte is one of the nation's only sources of native black marble. Piers of the Brooklyn Bridge came from here. Today just one quarry, on the eastern side of the island, is still in limited use.

Make a second fossil stop by taking a short side trip onto Quarry Road at 5.7 miles. The new Goodsell Ridge Outdoor Museum and Fossil Preserve is on the left about 0.2 mile after the turn.

Come to a four-way intersection at 7.4 miles. This is the tiny village of Isle La Motte. Then watch carefully for the left turn off VT 129 at 9.0 miles. Another mile and you're back to the parking area. On a hot day, the beach across from the shrine will be inviting.

Miles and Directions

0.0 Head south out of the parking area at St. Anne's Shrine on Shrine Road, along the shore.

1.1 Road forks. Bear right, continuing south next to the water on West Shore Road.

3.4 Road surface turns to dirt.

3.9 Fisk Quarry Preserve is to the left.

4.8 Road surface returns to asphalt.

4.9 Road forks. Bear left.

5.7 Optional side trip to Goodsell Ridge Outdoor Museum and Fossil Preserve.

7.4 Four-way intersection in village of Isle La Motte. Continue straight. Sign immediately past intersection indicates that this is VT 129 East.

9.0 Turn left off VT 129 onto Shrine Road.

9.8 Road makes sharp left and descends to the lakeshore.

10.1 Back to parking area.

Local Information

Lake Champlain Island Chamber of Commerce, P.O. Box 213, North Hero, VT 05474; (802) 372-8400 or (800) 262-5226; www.champlainislands.com.

Local Events/Attractions

St. Anne's Shrine, 92 St. Anne's Road, Isle La Motte, VT; (802) 928-3362; www.saintannes shrine.org. Open mid-May through mid-October.
Fisk Quarry Preserve, West Shore Road, Isle La Motte, VT; www.lclt.org/guidefiskquarry.htm. Walking trails and interpretive signs.

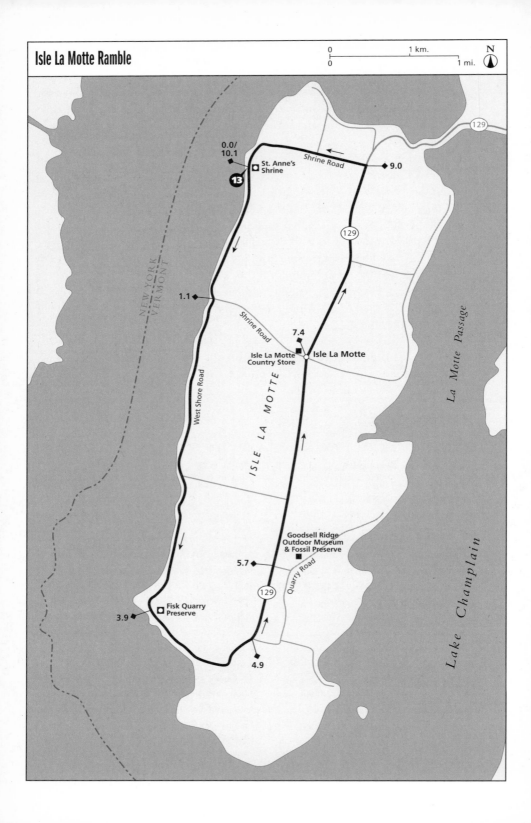

Isle La Motte Ramble

0.0/10.1

St. Anne's Shrine

13

Shrine Road

9.0

129

NEW YORK
VERMONT

1.1

Shrine Road

7.4

Isle La Motte
Country Store

Isle La Motte

WEST SHORE ROAD

ISLE LA MOTTE

La Motte Passage

Goodsell Ridge
Outdoor Museum
& Fossil Preserve

5.7

Quarry Road

129

Lake Champlain

Fisk Quarry
Preserve

3.9

4.9

0   1 km.
0   1 mi.

N

Goodsell Ridge Outdoor Museum and Fossil Preserve, 239 Quarry Road, Isle La Motte, VT. **Lake Champlain Land Trust,** 1 Main Street, Burlington, VT; (802) 862-4150; www.lclt .org/GoodsellUpdate.htm. Recently opened, 81-acre site with a visitor center/museum. Walking paths offer opportunities to view Chazy Reef fossils. Seasonal, variable hours. For more information, contact the Lake Champlain Land Trust (above) or the Lake Champlain Islands Chamber of Commerce (above).

Food

Cafeteria at St. Anne's Shrine, 92 St. Anne's Road, Isle La Motte, VT; (802) 928-3362; www.saintannesshrine.org.
Isle La Motte Country Store, 68 School Street, Isle La Motte, VT; (802) 928-3033. Make a left in the village of Isle La Motte (at 7.4 miles) and it's immediately on your right.

Accommodations

Inns and B&Bs are the most prevalent lodging on the Champlain Islands. For more economical motel accommodations, try the major chains outside of Burlington, Swanton, or St. Albans. The Lake Champlain Island Chamber of Commerce is the best source of information on lodging.
La Quinta Inn & Suites in St. Albans is just off the interstate: 813 Fairfax Road, St. Albans, VT; (802) 524-3300; www.lq.com.

Bike Shops

White's Green Mountain Bikes, 1008 Ethan Allen Highway (U.S. Highway 7), Milton, VT; (802) 524-4496.
Old Spokes Home, 322 North Winooski Avenue, Burlington, VT; (802) 863-4475; www.oldspokeshome.com.
North Star Cyclery, 100 Main Street, Burlington, VT; (802) 863-3832.

Map

DeLorme: Vermont Atlas & Gazetteer: Page 50.

14 Jeffersonville Challenge

When you've completed this one, you'll want to buy one of those T-shirts that proudly proclaims, VERMONT AIN'T FLAT. This definitely isn't a "ramble" or a "cruise," and most will agree that "challenge" is a good word to describe it. It's a good workout for serious bikers. But it's also suitable for casual cyclists, who may want to turn it into a two-day trip, with an overnight stop in Montgomery or Montgomery Center.

Start: Parking area behind the Post Office Building in Jeffersonville. Overnight parking is okay as long as vehicles are behind (not next to) the building. Vehicles left in the paved lot next to the building may be towed.
Length: 54.3 miles.
Terrain: Serious hills with several long climbs and descents.
Traffic and hazards: The most significant traffic will be on Vermont Highway 108, at the beginning of the ride. Traffic on Vermont Highways 118 and 109 will be lighter and will, in fact, be sparse on large portions of VT 118.

Cyclists may be tempted to use Vermont Highway 105 instead of the 2.3 miles of the Missiquoi Valley Rail Trail as the east-west connection at the northern end of the loop. Don't do it. Use the rail trail, which has a hard gravel surface that's fine for road bikes. VT 105 is a major east-west truck route that really isn't suitable for cycling. It doesn't have shoulders, and there's a guardrail along some portions. Riders must use very short sections of VT 105 to get on and off the rail trail and should exercise special caution at those times.

Friendly locals

Getting there: Take exit 18 off Interstate 89 (north of Burlington). Get on U.S. Highway 7 South and proceed about 0.3 mile to a left turn onto Vermont Highway 104A. Follow VT 104A about 4.5 miles, then bear right onto Vermont Highway 104. Stay on VT 104 to the junction with Vermont Highway 15, in about 8.8 miles. Turn left onto VT 15 East. Proceed about 2.9 miles to a right turn onto Church Street, following signs for Jeffersonville. The parking area is on the right about 0.2 mile after the turn off VT 15.

This is a magnificent area of the state for cycling, and it's popular with cycling clubs (including a number of Canadian clubs) and bicycle touring organizations. More than in almost any other part of Vermont, you're likely to encounter groups of fellow cycling enthusiasts. Drivers seem accustomed to bikers and have even been known to offer encouragement to bikers nearing the top of a climb.

The route makes two crossings of the watershed between northern Vermont's two large westerly flowing rivers: the Lamoille and the Missisquoi. There will be fine views of both, as well as stunning mountain scenery. Because the route is challenging, you won't want to carry a lot of extra weight. Fortunately, there are general stores in the regularly spaced villages along the way.

Most of the first 12 miles, to the turn onto Boston Post Road, are a gradual uphill. Bakersfield, at 10.5 miles, is a quaint little town with a handsome town green. Sadly, the old general store opposite the green has closed. But there's a handy convenience store just north of town. There won't be another opportunity to buy food and fluids until East Berkshire, at 23.3 miles.

Boston Post Road will have less traffic and more hills than VT 108. There are some steep short climbs. There's a double reward for those climbs: (1) terrific views of surrounding mountains, farms, and forests and (2) fast descents.

It's important to make the turn, at 20.9 miles, off VT 105 and onto the Missisquoi Valley Rail Trail. (See note above, under "Traffic and hazards.") The entire rail trail is approximately 36 miles long and runs from St. Albans to Richford. Some cyclists consider it too flat to be fun, but it offers lovely views of the Missisquoi River, and it enables a great variety of safe cycling loops in northern Vermont. This route only uses a couple of miles of the rail trail. Make a mental note to revisit it another day.

After the turn onto VT 118 South, begin a very gradual climb to Montgomery, then Montgomery Center. Both are friendly little communities that are home to a variety of outdoor enthusiasts. There are general stores, an ice cream shop, and a couple of bed-and-breakfasts. (See notes below for lodging suggestions if this is a two-day trip.) Be sure to bear right onto VT 118 in Montgomery Center. A left onto Vermont Highway 58 would take you over Hazen's Notch, a very serious climb.

Departure from Montgomery Center signals the start of the longest climb of the trip. It's long, but it isn't terribly steep, and it's not relentless. This will be a close-up view of a largely unspoiled, unsettled part of Vermont. At about 35.2 miles the picnic tables at Avery's Gore Wildlife Management Area offer a nice rest stop. According to Esther Swift, in her surprisingly entertaining *Vermont Place Names,* "gores" are "leftover scraps of land between towns." Gores are typically found at higher elevations: land that nobody considered particularly valuable when town boundaries were being established. Occasional hunting camps are still the most evident settlement along this stretch of road.

After the turn onto VT 109 South, it's a short distance to the top of the watershed. Then it's downhill for the rest of the trip. A year from now, the beautiful ride along VT 109—through Belvidere Center—might be the part of the trip you remember best. The road has an adequate shoulder and very little traffic. It's an exhilarating descent to the banks of the Lamoille.

On return to the parking area, you'll almost certainly want to investigate more biking opportunities in this part of the state. Serious cyclists all eventually decide they need to rise to the challenge of Smugglers Notch, a notoriously difficult climb on a narrow, winding road. Check with the friendly folks at Foot of the Notch Bicycles on Church Street for advice on Smugglers Notch and other routes in the area.

Miles and Directions

- **0.0** Turn right out of the post office parking area onto Church Street, heading east.
- **0.1** Junction with VT 108. VT 108 South is straight ahead. Bear left, on Main Street/VT 108 North.
- **0.4** Intersection with VT 15. Cross VT 15, continuing straight on VT 108 North.
- **0.6** Cross Lamoille River.

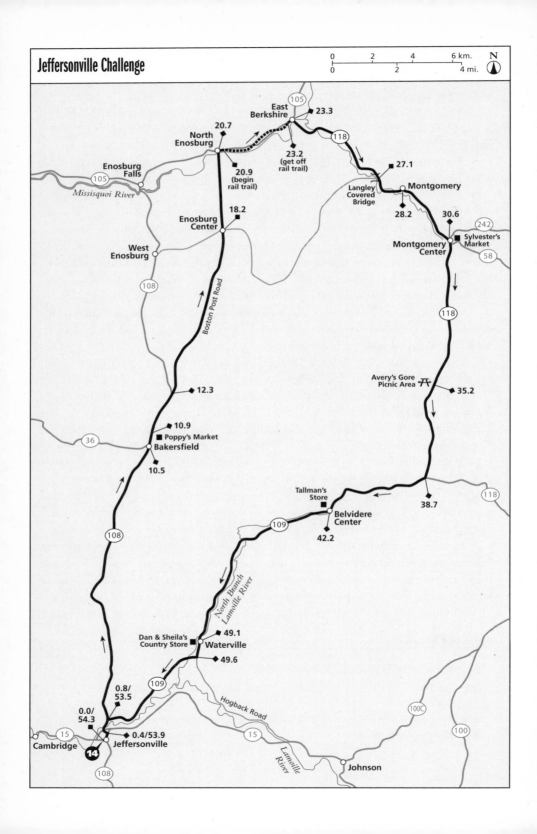

Jeffersonville Challenge

0 2 4 6 km.
0 2 4 mi.

N

Enosburg
Falls

Missisquoi River

105

West
Enosburg

108

Boston Post Road

36

Poppy's Market
Bakersfield

10.9
10.5
12.3

108

North
Enosburg

20.7

20.9
(begin
rail trail)

Enosburg
Center

18.2

East
Berkshire

23.3

105

23.2
(get off
rail trail)

118

27.1

Langley
Covered
Bridge

Montgomery

28.2

30.6

Montgomery
Center

Sylvester's
Market

242

58

118

Avery's Gore
Picnic Area

35.2

38.7

118

Tallman's
Store

109

Belvidere
Center

42.2

North Branch
Lamoille River

Dan & Sheila's
Country Store

49.1

Waterville

49.6

0.8/
53.5

109

0.0/
54.3

Hogback Road

15

100C

100

15

Cambridge

14

0.4/53.9

Jeffersonville

108

Lamoille
River

Johnson

0.8 Road forks. Bear left, continuing on VT 108 North.

10.5 Village of Bakersfield. Continue straight on VT 108 North.

10.9 Paul's Quick Stop on the right.

12.3 Turn right off VT 108 onto Boston Post Road, still heading north and following signs for Bakersfield Country Club.

18.2 Four-way intersection in hamlet of Enosburg Center. Continue straight on Boston Post Road.

20.7 Cross Missisquoi River and come to the junction with VT 105. Turn right onto VT 105 East.

20.9 Rail trail crosses VT 105. Leave VT 105 and continue east on the rail trail.

21.9 Rail trail crosses to northern side of VT 105. Continue heading east on the rail trail.

22.5 Rail trail crosses to southern side of VT 105. Continue heading east on the rail trail.

23.2 Rail trail crosses to northern side of VT 105. Leave the rail trail and get back on VT 105 East.

23.3 Village of East Berkshire and junction with VT 118. Turn right off VT 105 onto VT 118 South.

23.4 Cross Missisquoi River.

27.1 Longley Covered Bridge is to the right. Continue straight on VT 118.

28.2 Village of Montgomery. Bear right, staying on VT 118.

30.6 Village of Montgomery Center. Bear right, staying on VT 118.

35.2 Avery's Gore Wildlife Management Area (picnic area) to the right.

38.7 Junction with VT 109. Turn right off VT 118 onto VT 109 South.

42.2 Village of Belvidere Center. Tallman's Store is on the right. Continue straight on VT 109.

49.1 Village of Waterville. Dan & Sheila's Country Store is on the right. Continue straight on VT 109.

49.6 Road forks. Hogback Road is to the left. Bear right, continuing on VT 109.

53.5 Junction with VT 108. Turn left onto VT 108 South.

53.7 Cross Lamoille River.

53.9 Intersection with VT 15. Cross VT 15, continuing straight on VT 108.

54.2 VT 108 South bears left. Bear right on Church Street in Jeffersonville.

54.3 Return to parking area behind post office.

Local Information

Smugglers Notch Chamber of Commerce Information Center, P.O. Box 364, Jeffersonville, VT 05464; (802) 644-8232; www.smugnotch.com.

Local Events/Attractions

Missisquoi Valley Rail Trail, 36 miles of flat pedaling and magnificent scenery along the Missisquoi River. Contact Northwest Vermont Rail Trail Council, 155 Lake Street, St. Albans, VT; (802) 524-5958; www.mvrailtrail.com.

Smugglers Notch State Park, 6443 Mountain Road (VT 108), Stowe, VT; (802) 253-4014; www.vtstateparks.com/htm/smugglers.cfm. Hiking, picnic area, and campground. The long history of clandestine travel through the notch started with the Embargo Act of 1807. Later, this was a corridor for fugitive slaves en route to Canada, and during Prohibition liquor was smuggled through here from the north.

Food

Smugglers Notch Inn and Village Tavern, 55 Church Street, Jeffersonville, VT; (802) 644-6607; www.smuggsinn.com. The tavern serves good pub food.

Jana's Cupboard Restaurant, 4807 VT 15, Jeffersonville, VT; (802) 644-5454.

Poppy's Market, 446 Main Street (VT 108), Bakersfield, VT; (802) 827-3025.

Sylvester's Market, 20 North Main Street, Mongomery Center, VT; (802) 326-4561.

Tallman's Store, Main Street (VT 109), Belvidere Center, VT; (802) 644-2751.

Dan & Sheila's Country Store, 21 Church Street (VT 109), Waterville, VT; (802) 644-6555.

Accommodations

Smugglers Notch Inn and Village Tavern, 55 Church Street, Jeffersonville, VT; (802) 644-6607; www.smuggsinn.com. They like bikers.

Black Lantern Inn, 2057 North Main Street (VT 118), Montgomery Village, VT; (802) 326-4507; www.blacklantern.com. This is a favorite overnight for some of the commercial bicycle touring organizations.

Phineas Swann B&B, 195 Main Street, Box 43, Montgomery Center, VT 05471; (802) 326-4306; www.phineaswann.com.

Bike Shop

Foot of the Notch Bicycles, 134 Church Street, Jeffersonville, VT; (802) 644-8182.

Map

DeLorme: Vermont Atlas & Gazetteer: Pages 46, 52.

15 Lake Willoughby Cruise

Willoughby is one of Vermont's most beautiful lakes, and it's largely undeveloped. This ride takes you along its shore and introduces you to Vermont's Northeast Kingdom. Bring a camera, water, and an extra layer, as weather can change quickly.

Start: Parking area at Crystal Lake State Park.
Length: 31.6 miles.
Terrain: Moderately steep uphill for the first 2.5 miles, descent, then relatively flat.

Traffic and hazards: Roads are narrow, and there will be more traffic during July and August, especially along Lake Willoughby.

Getting there: From St. Johnsbury, take Interstate 91 north to exit 25. Get on Vermont Highway 16 North, following signs for Barton. Continue on VT 16 through Barton. Turn right at the entrance to Crystal Lake State Park, just east of the downtown area. Leave your vehicle in state park's parking area (nominal day-use fee).

This is the center of Vermont's "Northeast Kingdom," an area whose geology and landscape have more in common with northern New Hampshire, Maine, and Quebec than with the rest of Vermont. It feels like a different "kingdom," characterized by conifer forests, deep, cold lakes, abundant wildlife, and people whose self-reliance is shaped by a rugged environment. Spring arrives late, fall comes early, and summer is particularly green.

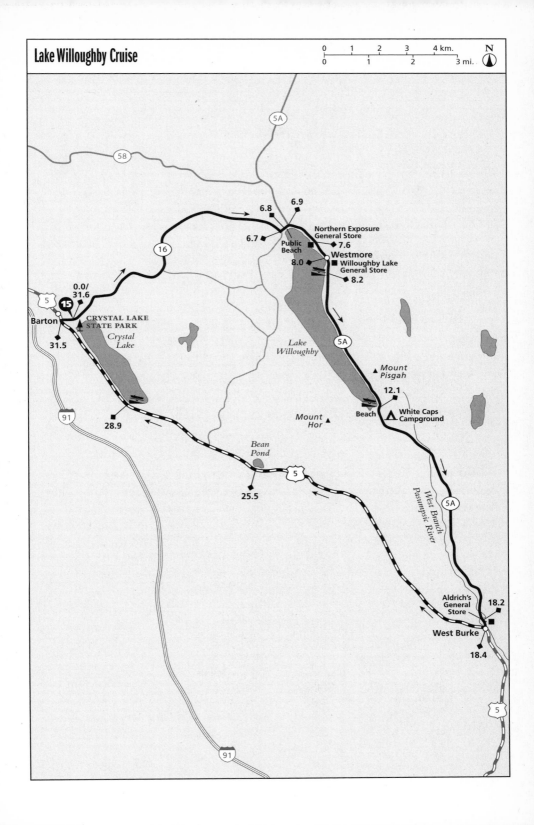

Lake Willoughby Cruise

0 1 2 3 4 km.
0 1 2 3 mi.

N

5A

58

6.9
6.8
6.7
Public
Beach

Northern Exposure
General Store
7.6
Westmore
8.0
Willoughby Lake
General Store
8.2

16

0.0/
31.6

5

15

Barton

31.5

CRYSTAL LAKE
STATE PARK

Crystal
Lake

Lake
Willoughby

5A

Mount
Pisgah

12.1

91

28.9

Beach

White Caps
Campground

Mount
Hor

Bean
Pond

5

25.5

West Branch
Pasumpsic River

5A

Aldrich's
General
Store

18.2

West Burke

18.4

91

5

The first 2.5 miles, on VT 16 East, are the most difficult part of the trip. VT 16 is a wonderful biking road (good surface, sparse traffic, great scenery), but it's uphill to the top of the watershed between Crystal Lake and Lake Willoughby. Notice the boggy area to your right at about 3 miles. It contains a beaver lodge and is, in general, a good wildlife spotting area.

More than any other part of Vermont, the Northeast Kingdom reminds us that, geologically speaking, the last ice age wasn't long ago. The bogs, sandpits, and deep, narrow lakes are all evidence of the retreat of the most recent continental glacier, a mere 11,000 years ago. At 6.3 miles, notice the sandpit to your right (a glacial deposit), and note the holes of bank swallows nesting in it.

At 6.7 miles you're at the north end of Lake Willoughby. The next 6 miles are going to be memorable. Lake Willoughby is typical of glacial lakes of the area (long and narrow, north to south). Most visitors agree that, although geologically typical, Willoughby is more spectacular than most. Folks who have traveled abroad often compare Willoughby with the lochs of Scotland. Geologists describing the lake talk about the retreat of the last glacier, a retreat interrupted by a temporary reversal. That was when "fingers" of glacial ice crept back down valleys, carving deep channels and leaving debris at the southern end as they retreated again (hence the uphill climb at the southern end of the lake). Not surprisingly, the cliffs on either side of the lake are mirrored by unusual depths: over 300 feet at the deepest spots. Vermont Highway 5A hugs the eastern shore of the lake on what feels like a narrow shelf between the lake and the steep cliffs to the east. The shoulder is adequate, and numerous pull-offs offer opportunities to admire the view. At the southern end of the lake, Mount Hor looms high on the west and Mount Pisgah rises straight up on the east.

VT 5A south from Lake Willoughby to West Burke is relatively flat. It follows the West Branch of the Pasumpsic River, whose boggy riverbanks are habitat for a variety of wildlife. Local papers print regular warnings, especially in spring and fall, about the dangers of hitting moose. They're big, and they're wild animals—keep a safe distance.

The general store in West Burke is a classic general store, where souvenirs for tourists are just a sideline, and life's necessities are the real stock. Directly across from the store is a public picnic area: buy lunch at the store and eat it across the street.

U.S. Highway 5 from West Burke back to Barton is also reasonably flat. It follows the Sutton River (upstream this time) and the Canadian Pacific Railway. The 12 miles between West Burke and Barton offer a snapshot of life in the Northeast Kingdom: logging, hillside farms, winter woodpiles, snowmobiles, camps and trailers, and, finally, Barton's beautiful Crystal Lake. Finish the trip with a swim at the state park, and begin plans for another ride in the Northeast Kingdom.

Miles and Directions

0.0   Turn right out of entrance to Crystal Lake State Park onto VT 16, heading east.

6.7   At the fork in the road, bear left to arrive immediately at north shore of Lake Willoughby.

6.8 Public beach at north end of Lake Willoughby.

6.9 At stop sign at junction with VT 5A, turn right onto VT 5A South, following signs for Westmore.

7.6 Northern Exposure General Store is on the right.

8.0 Village of Westmore. Willoughby Lake General Store is to your left.

8.2 Boat launch is on the right.

12.1 South end of Lake Willoughby. Boat launch and beach are on the right. White Caps Campground is on the left. Continue straight (south) on VT 5A.

18.2 Intersection at West Burke. Aldrich's General Store is on the left. Bear right, passing a playground/picnic area on the left.

18.4 Stop sign at a four-way intersection. Bear right onto US 5, heading north.

25.5 Bean Pond is on the right.

28.9 Crystal Lake boat launch is on the right.

31.5 Intersection with VT 16. Turn right onto VT 16 East.

31.6 Turn right at entrance to Crystal Lake State Park and return to parking area.

Local Information

Barton Area Chamber of Commerce, P.O. Box 343, Barton, VT 05822; (802) 525-1137; www.bartonareachamber.com.

Local Events/Attractions

Public beaches at northern and southern ends of Lake Willoughby.

Crystal Lake State Park, 96 Bellwater Avenue, Barton, VT; (802) 525-6205. Day use only. No camping.

Food

Northern Exposure General Store, 1266 VT 5A, Westmore, VT; (802) 525-3789. Sandwiches and the usual snacks and supplies.

Aldrich's General Store, 196 VT 5A, West Burke, VT. All the basics.

Willoughvale Inn, 793 VT 5A, Westmore, VT; (802) 525-4123 or (800) 594-9102; www.willoughvale.com. Fine dining, gracious atmosphere.

Step-Back Café, 16A Church Street, Barton, VT; (802) 525-4791. Sandwiches, soups, ice cream.

Accommodations

White Caps Campground, 5659 VT 5A, Westmore, VT; (802) 467-3345; www.whitecaps campground.com. At the southern end of Lake Willoughby. Access to lake and hiking trails.

Willoughvale Inn, 793 VT 5A, Westmore, VT; (802) 525-4123 or (800) 594-9102; www.willoughvale.com. Great views of Lake Willoughby.

LynBurke Motel, 791 Main Street, Lyndonville, VT; (802) 626-3346; www.lynburkemotel.com. Good basic lodging in a nearby college town.

Bike Shop

East Burke Sports, 439 Vermont Highway 114, P.O. Box 189, East Burke, VT 05832; (802) 626-3215.

Map

DeLorme: Vermont Atlas & Gazetteer: Page 54.

16 Northeast Kingdom Challenge

A glance at the map tells it all: This ride is a loop around a large tract of Vermont wilderness. There aren't any towns or paved roads inside the loop—just logging roads, hunting camps, lakes, snowmobile trails, and abundant wildlife. Be sure to take snacks, water, and tools for minor repairs, as there are stretches when you won't see anything but forest. Serious cyclists won't have trouble doing it in a day. Those anticipating a more leisurely pace should plan to stop overnight in Canaan.

Start: Parking area behind/next to Mike's Market in Island Pond. Overnight parking is okay. (It's wise to notify people at the market if leaving a vehicle overnight.)
Length: 67.2 miles.
Terrain: Varied. One significant climb, west of

Canaan. Vermont Highway 102 along the Connecticut River is very flat.
Traffic and hazards: Logging is an important industry in the Northeast Kingdom, so there will be logging trucks, especially on Vermont Highway 105 between Island Pond and Bloomfield.

Getting there: From the south, take exit 23 off Interstate 91. Get on U.S. Highway 5 North, following signs for Lyndonville. Proceed about 2.2 miles on US 5, through Lyndonville, to a four-way intersection. Bear right off US 5 onto Vermont Highway 114 North. Continue north on VT 114 for about 21 miles to a junction with VT 105. Turn right onto VT 105 East, following signs for Island Pond. Come to the village of Island Pond in about 2 miles. Mike's Market and parking area are at the end of the main street, where VT 105 makes a sharp turn to the right.

Cyclists have lively discussions about the best direction for riding this loop. As written here, it's done counterclockwise—the way my family likes to do it. Others prefer clockwise. The advantage of the clockwise direction has to do with the northern part of the circle, between Norton and Canaan. Done as written here, there's a steep climb as you head west out of Canaan, then a more gradual descent into Norton. I don't necessarily love the climb, but I like the long descent into Norton, and I also like being on the right, next to the Connecticut River, while heading north on VT 102. Take your pick: Either way, it's a great ride in a seldom visited part of the state.

Be on the lookout for moose on this trip. Anywhere is possible, but VT 105 between Island Pond and Bloomfield is a stretch of road where vehicle/moose collisions are especially common.

Island Pond, the starting point, is one of those Vermont communities that's gotten smaller in the past hundred years. This was once a bustling railroad hub. In fact, it was the site of the first international railroad junction in the United States. Today just a couple of tracks come through town, and the population is less than half of late-nineteenth-century levels. But trains still pass through, and you'll notice that much of this ride closely follows a track.

Route 102 along the Connecticut River

The general store in Bloomfield, at 16.2 miles, is a pleasant refueling stop. It will be the last—unless you make a detour into Colebrook, New Hampshire—before Canaan.

VT 102 between Bloomfield and Canaan is as nearly perfect as Vermont biking gets. A couple of years ago, *Vermont Life* did an article on best bike rides in the state. They called to ask me for my favorite. It was a tough choice. Local loyalty compelled me to settle on one of my favorite rides near home, in the west-central part of the state. But it was tempting to pick VT 102, along the Connecticut River between Bloomfield and Canaan. For almost 20 miles, traffic is sparse, views of the river are spectacular, and the terrain is gently rolling. Most riders will want to stop for a drink and a photo at the Columbia Covered Bridge, at 25.1 miles. And some may want to cross the next bridge, at 29.3 miles, to Colebrook, New Hampshire. Colebrook is a much larger town than any of the Vermont communities you'll see on this trip.

Cyclists who plan a two-day ride will want to stay in Canaan. There are a couple of possibilities. If you have enough energy left for a climb, the Pure Country Motel and Cabins on Wallace Pond, a little over 4 miles west of Canaan, is recommended (see information below). Note, though, that there isn't a restaurant or deli

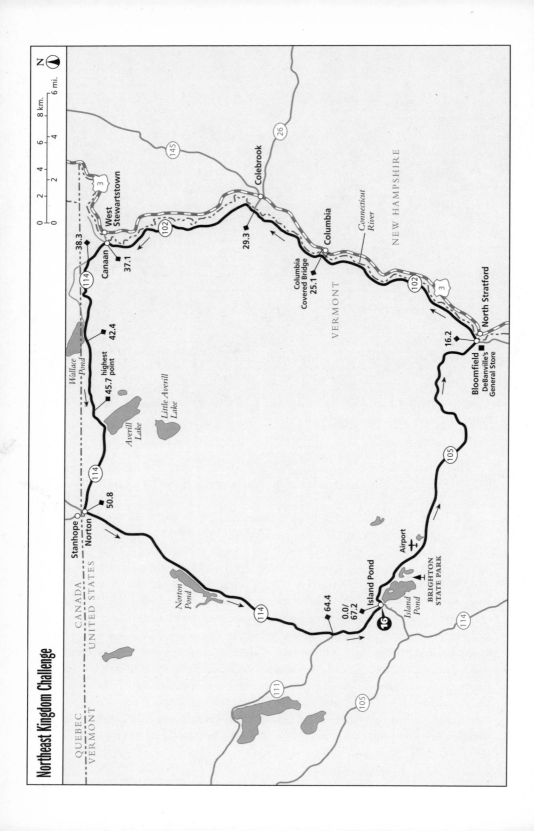

Northeast Kingdom Challenge

at Wallace Pond, so you might want to get a meal in the village of Canaan before heading west.

In the hamlet of Norton, VT 114 turns south, back toward Island Pond. You'll notice that all the road signs are bilingual. A turn to the right here would take you almost immediately into Quebec. As you head south on VT 114, you'll be paralleling the railroad again. Norton Pond, on the right about 6 miles south of Norton, is one of Vermont's hidden treasures. It's one of those long, deep, glacially formed lakes with almost no development. For a couple of miles, it's just the lake, the railroad track, and the road.

This ride will undoubtedly whet your appetite for more explorations of northeastern Vermont. Stop in and talk with the people at East Burke Sports for suggestions of both mountain and road bike rides.

Miles and Directions

0.0 Turn left out of parking area onto VT 105 East.

1.6 Road to Brighton State Park is on the right. Continue straight on VT 105.

3.6 Airport is to the left. Continue straight on VT 105.

16.2 Intersection with VT 102 in Bloomfield. DeBanville's General Store is on the corner. Turn left onto VT 102 North.

25.1 Columbia Covered Bridge is to the right. Continue straight on VT 102.

29.3 Bridge to Colebrook, New Hampshire, is to the right. Continue straight on VT 102.

37.1 Junction with VT 114 in Canaan. Turn left onto VT 114 West.

38.3 Road forks. Bear left, staying on VT 114. (Bearing right would take you north into Quebec.)

42.4 Road to right leads to boat access on Wallace Pond. Continue straight on VT 114.

45.7 Highest elevation.

50.8 Village of Norton. Bear left on VT 114, which heads south. (The road to the right crosses the border into Quebec.)

64.4 Junction with Vermont Highway 111 to the right. Bear left, continuing on VT 114.

67.2 Junction with VT 105. Parking area to the left.

Local Information

The Web site www.northcountry.org is an information source for several communities in northeastern Vermont and northern New Hampshire. Includes resources for Island Pond, Canaan, and Norton, Vermont.

Local Events/Attractions

Brighton State Park, 102 State Park Road, Island Pond, VT; (802) 723-4360; www.vtstateparks.com/htm/brighton.cfm. On Spectacle Pond. Swimming, picnic area, hiking, campground.

North Country Moose Festival. Organized by the North Country Chamber of Commerce, P.O. Box 1, Colebrook, NH 03576; (603) 237-8939 or (800) 698-8939; www.northcountry chamber.org/moosefestival.html. August events in Canaan, VT, Pittsburg, NH, and Colebrook, NH. Historical tours, exhibits, vendors, music, mooseburger BBQ, and more.

Food

Mike's Market, 12 Railroad Street (VT 114), Island Pond, VT; (802) 723-4747.

Jennifer's Restaurant, 18 Cross Street, Island Pond, VT; (802) 723-6135. A local favorite.

DeBanville's General Store, 47 VT 105, Bloomfield, VT; (802) 962-3311. The usual general store supplies, deli sandwiches, and pastries. Inside and outdoor seating, restroom.

Bessie's Diner, 166 Gale Street (VT 114), Canaan, VT; (802) 266-3310.

Norton Country Store, 564 VT 114 S, Norton, VT; (802) 822-5511.

Accommodations

Lakefront Inn and Motel, 127 Cross Street, Island Pond, VT; (802) 723-6507; www.the lakefrontinn.com. They advertise secure bike storage.

Brighton State Park, 102 State Park Road, Island Pond, VT; (802) 723-4360; www.vtstateparks.com/htm/brighton.cfm. Campsites, lean-tos, cabins.

Maurice's Motel, 125 Gale Street (VT 114), Canaan, VT; (802) 266-3453; www.mauricemotel.com. Handy to restaurants in Canaan, reasonable rates.

Pure Country Motel and Cabins, 4555 VT 114, Lake Wallace, Canaan, VT; (802) 266-3311; http://islandpond.com/purectry. About 4.5 miles west of Canaan.

Bike Shop

East Burke Sports, 439 VT 114, P.O. Box 189, East Burke, VT 05832; (802) 626-3215. The center for cycling in Vermont's Northeast Kingdom.

Map

DeLorme: Vermont Atlas & Gazetteer: Pages 55, 37.

New Hampshire

I t's possible that New Hampshire has the most varied terrain of any eastern state. Southern coastal areas are flat and quite densely populated. In central New Hampshire you'll find the stunning lakes regions (plural because there are several such clusters). And in the north there are the White Mountains, which have been called the most rugged terrain in the eastern two-thirds of the United States. Although its official headquarters is in Boston, the White Mountains are the spiritual headquarters of the Appalachian Mountain Club, one of the country's first and most active outdoor organizations. In the White Mountains, outdoor enthusiasts rule.

Nearing the top of the Dixville Notch

The rides in this collection are concentrated in central and northern New Hampshire. This is not to say there isn't lovely biking in the southern areas, but readers will probably agree that New England cycling doesn't get much better than the eleven rides included here.

A couple of cautionary notes: (1) Cyclists who have been pedaling in southern New England or in Vermont should note that New Hampshire soil, especially in the lakes regions, tends to be sandy. That means unpaved shoulders are sandy. While skinny tires can briefly manage an unpaved shoulder in Vermont, they're likely to sink in and precipitate a tumble in New Hampshire. Stay on the pavement. (2) New Hampshire is a mecca for motorcyclists. For the same reasons that cyclists like New Hampshire, motorcyclists are drawn to New Hampshire's roads in spring, summer, and fall. Motorcycles are particularly abundant during the weeklong rally in Laconia in June. Laconia is the center for the week, but motorcyclists range all over the state on day trips, and many arrive before the rally and stay after. They aren't a hazard to cyclists, just a bit of a surprise if you aren't expecting them. And it may take a few minutes to figure out why they look odd: Unlike most New England states, New Hampshire has no motorcycle helmet law.

Finally, kudos to the state of New Hampshire for its efforts to promote and support cycling. The Franconia Notch Bike Route (see description in Franconia/Kinsman Notch Challenge) is an example that all states should follow.

17 Charlestown Cruise

It's a fine ride in an historic part of New Hampshire: good exercise and classic New England scenery.

Start: Parking area at The Fort at No. 4, on New Hampshire Highway 11 north of Charlestown.
Length: 30.1 miles.
Terrain: Hilly, with a moderately difficult 2-mile climb to the village of Acworth.
Traffic and hazards: Traffic should be light to moderate on most roads. Expect more traffic on weekends. New Hampshire Highway 12 is the most heavily traveled road. Shoulders there vary from a few inches to about 8 feet. The 2.4 miles north of the turn onto New Hampshire Highway 12A have the narrowest shoulders. Watch for cars backing out of parking spaces on Main Street in Charlestown.

Getting there: From points south, take Interstate 91 north (on the Vermont side of the Connecticut River) to exit 7. Get on VT 11 East, following signs for Charlestown. Cross the Connecticut River and proceed about 0.3 mile to The Fort at No. 4, on the right. Park to the back of the large parking area at the fort.

It's hard to imagine this as a dangerous frontier, but in the mid-eighteenth century, Charlestown was the northernmost colonial settlement in the Connecticut River Valley. Before it became "Charlestown," the settlement was simply known as "Fort 4." What you see at the fort today is a reconstruction and living history museum, well worth a visit before or after the ride. The fort sets the stage for the ride: Like the pattern of colonial settlement, the route makes its way inland and upstream, following tributaries of the Connecticut.

NH 12 south of Charlestown is flanked by the railroad to the east and the Connecticut River to the west. There will be intermittent views of the river and the rich floodplain farmland that characterizes the Connecticut Valley.

Watch for the turn onto Cheshire Turnpike at 8.0 miles. Turn at the sign for the Fall Mountain Regional High School, but then make an immediate left onto Cheshire Turnpike. There's a road sign, but it's hard to spot.

If you checked a map and planned on crossing the Prentiss Covered Bridge at about 9 miles, you're going to be disappointed. The bridge is to the side of the road, on what used to be Cheshire Turnpike, and it isn't in very good shape. However, if you're willing to settle for an alternative piece of classic New England architecture, you're in luck. Immediately beyond the bridge, at the crest of the hill, is a farmhouse that's every bit as interesting. It's a fine example of the New England style commonly called "big house, little house, back house, barn." The buildings are all joined in a long line: You'll need a wide-angle lens to capture them all in one photo. It's a style that can be seen all over New England, but it becomes more prevalent the farther north you travel.

The Cold River at Vilas Pool PHOTO BY ENNIS DULING

As you make the left turn at the four-way intersection at 10.4 miles, the route begins following the Cold River. The road will parallel the river for most of the next 8 miles. You probably saw pictures and video footage of the Cold River in October 2005. This peaceful little stream is the one that caused massive flooding, property and road destruction, and loss of life. You can't miss the evidence of flooding and the rebuilding that's still taking place. In the Alstead Village Market, you can even buy a T-shirt that commemorates the recovery efforts.

A stop at the Alstead Village Market is recommended, as it's the last chance for refueling before the return to Charlestown. (There's no store in Acworth.) Buy snacks at the store and carry them to the town beach at Vilas Pool, about 0.8 mile farther along. Vilas Pool is a lovely little lake that was created by damming the Cold River. The town-owned facility has swimming and picnic areas and is staffed most afternoons during July and August. It's a good stop any time of year.

Until the turn onto Hill Road at 18.3 miles, the route has been moderately hilly. There's been a gradual increase in elevation, but climbs haven't been particularly steep or long. That's about to change. You'll soon discover that Hill Road is aptly named. The wise cyclist will take some water breaks during the next 2 miles.

The beautiful old cemetery on the left at 20.1 miles marks the outskirts of Acworth and the top of the climb. If you appreciate well-maintained colonial architecture—both brick and clapboard buildings—you'll enjoy Acworth. Residents are proud of their picturesque little community, high above the original settlement on the Connecticut River. As of this writing, the church steeple has been lifted to the ground for careful refurbishing.

From Acworth, it's downhill to Charlestown. Occasional short climbs punctuate the descent and give your brakes a rest.

Miles and Directions

0.0 Parking area at The Fort at No. 4.

0.1 End of road to the fort. Turn right onto NH 11 South.

0.7 Junction with NH 12. Turn right onto NH 12 South.

5.0 Turn right off NH 12 onto NH 12A, following signs for Alstead and Langdon. (NH 12A will loop over NH 12 and head east.)

8.0 Turn right off NH 12A, following sign for Fall Mountain Regional High School. Make an immediate left onto Cheshire Turnpike.

8.8 Stop sign. Lower Cemetery Road joins from the left. Turn right, continuing on Cheshire Turnpike, heading south.

9.0 Prentiss Covered Bridge is to the left.

10.4 At the four-way intersection, turn left onto New Hampshire Highway 123, heading northeast toward Alstead.

12.4 Intersection with NH 12A. Turn right (east) onto NH 12A/123, crossing bridge over Cold River.

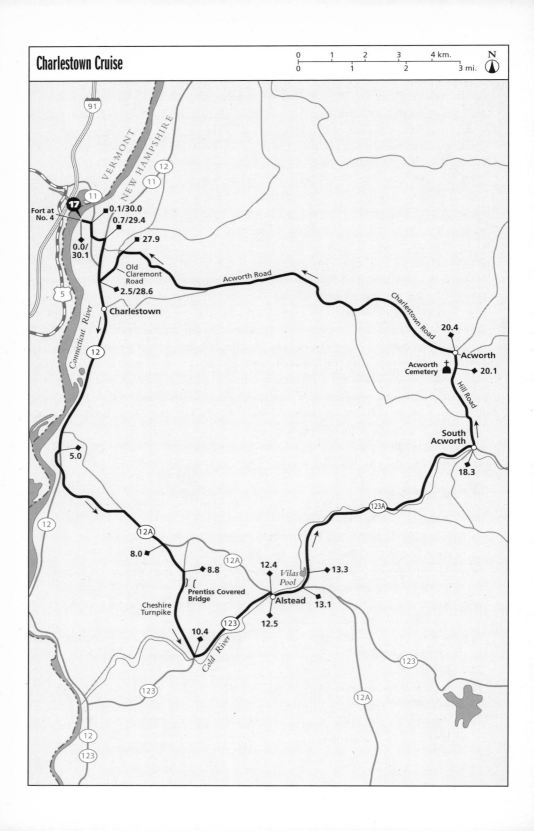

Charlestown Cruise

0 1 2 3 4 km.
0 1 2 3 mi.

N

91

VERMONT

NEW HAMPSHIRE

12

11

11

17

Fort at
No. 4

■ 0.1/30.0

■ 0.7/29.4

◆ 0.0/30.1

■ 27.9

Old
Claremont
Road

◆ 2.5/28.6

5

Connecticut River

○ Charlestown

12

Acworth Road

Charlestown Road

◆ 20.4

○ Acworth

Acworth
Cemetery

✝ ◆ 20.1

Hill Road

South
Acworth

◆ 18.3

◆ 5.0

12

12A

8.0 ◆

◆ 8.8

12A

123A

12.4
◆

Vilas
Pool

◆ 13.3

Prentiss Covered
Bridge

Cheshire
Turnpike

○ Alstead

◆ 13.1

12.5 ◆

123

◆ 10.4

Cold River

123

123

12A

123

12

123

12.5	NH 12A/123 makes a sharp left. Turn left, continuing on NH 12A/123 and heading north.
12.5	Alstead Village Market is on the right.
13.1	Turn left off NH 12A/123 onto New Hampshire Highway 123A East.
13.3	Vilas Pool (town beach) is on the left.
18.3	At the four-way intersection in South Acworth, turn left (north) onto Hill Road, following signs for Acworth.
20.1	Acworth Cemetery is on the left.
20.4	At the four-way intersection in Acworth, bear left (west) onto Charlestown Road (unmarked here), following signs for Charlestown.
27.9	Stop sign at junction with Old Claremont Road. Turn left onto Old Claremont Road, heading south toward Charlestown.
28.6	Junction with NH 12. Turn right onto NH 12 North.
29.4	Turn left off NH 12 onto NH 11 West, following signs for The Fort at No. 4.
30.0	Turn left off NH 11 at entrance to fort.
30.1	Return to parking area.

Local Information

The Greater Claremont Chamber of Commerce, 240 Opera House Square, Claremont, NH; (603) 543-1296; www.claremontnhchamber .org. Charlestown doesn't have a separate chamber of commerce, but it is one of the towns included in the Claremont area.
Springfield, Vermont, Chamber of Commerce, 14 Clinton Street, Suite 6, Springfield, VT 05156; (802) 885-2779; www.springfieldvt.com.

Local Events/Attractions

The Fort at No. 4, 267 Springfield Road, NH 11, P.O. Box 1336, Charlestown, NH 03603; (603) 826-3368; www.fortat4.com. A living history museum and reconstruction. Full schedule of demonstrations, conferences, reenactments.

Food

Heritage Diner, 122 Main Street, NH 12, Charlestown, NH; (603) 826-3110. Specializes in hearty breakfasts.

Alstead Village Market, 10 Mechanic Street (NH 12A/123), Alstead, NH; (603) 835-6758.

Accommodations

Go to the Greater Claremont Chamber of Commerce Web site for a list of lodging options. The Springfield, Vermont, Chamber of Commerce is likewise useful.
Holiday Inn Express, 818 Charlestown Road, Springfield, VT 05156; (802) 885-4516 or (800) 465-4329; www.hiexpress-springfield .com.

Bike Shops

Lane Road Cycle Shop, 603 Lovers Lane Road, Charlestown, NH; (603) 826-4435.
Claremont Cyclesport, 51 Pleasant Street, Claremont, NH; (603) 542-2453.

Map

DeLorme: New Hampshire Atlas & Gazetteer: Page 25.

18 New London Ramble

This short ramble takes riders through rural residential areas around New London. It's a quiet, easy ride with fine scenery: three lakes, an historic village, beautiful homes and gardens, and magnificent stone walls.

Start: New Hampshire Park & Ride parking lot at exit 12 off Interstate 89.
Length: 10.0 miles
Terrain: Gentle hills.
Traffic and hazards: Exercise caution on New Hampshire Highway 11 between the Park & Ride area and the turn onto Otterville Road:

The shoulder is wide, but traffic will be using the interstate on and off ramps. Zero to minimal shoulder width on most other roads, but traffic should also be minimal. If Main Street in New London is congested, walk bikes on the sidewalk.

Getting there: Take exit 12 off I-89 and head west on NH 11. Make the first left off NH 11, onto New Hampshire Highway 103A South. The New Hampshire Park & Ride lot is immediately on the left.

This is the western New Hampshire lakes region: not as well-known as the Winnipesaukee Lakes region but equally lovely and less crowded. Some consider this area one of New Hampshire's hidden treasures, bypassed by visitors on the interstate who head to Vermont or to the larger New Hampshire lakes to the northeast.

The ride begins with a leisurely swing around Little Sunapee Lake, where walkers and joggers are likely to outnumber cars on the road. Stop at the gravel pull-off immediately after the turn onto New Hampshire Highway 114 to watch kayakers, loons, and ducks happily sharing the water.

It's worth stopping to enjoy New London, too. Today New London is the cultural center for the western lakes region, with Colby-Sawyer College, a venerable summer theater, an active community of artists and artisans, and a well-rounded calendar of activities and attractions. History buffs will want to stop at the cemetery on Old Main Street (5.5 miles), where old headstones, surrounded by a classic white board fence, summarize the history of a New England community.

Bog Road descends to Messer Pond, whose clear water has a brownish tinge, a result of the peat in the adjacent bog. Then it's uphill again, under the interstate, and on to more rural roads and scenery. Tracy Road is a real treat. Most of the homes are relatively new, but they've all taken advantage of the magnificent old stone walls that extend the full length of the road on both sides. The historic marker at the turn onto Tracy Road explains that the walls were built a century ago by the Tracys, owners of the Willow Farm estate.

Old stone walls are one of New England's fascinating historic features—one that bikers get an opportunity to study more closely than auto-bound visitors. If you've

Stone wall along Tracy Road

been biking for a while in New England, you've surely noticed them, sometimes in unlikely places. Some are imposing shoulder-high fences, and others are mere mossy lines of rocks in the woods. If Robert Thorson, author of *Stone by Stone: The Magnificent History in New England's Stone Walls,* were along, he would tell us that the walls on Tracy Road are "double" walls: more carefully constructed than the more common "tossed" walls that served as places to pile unwanted field stones.

It would be hard to resist one more stop, to admire Herrick Cove on Lake Sunapee. It's obvious that Sunapee has been a resort community for a long time. The old summer homes—with their matching boathouses—are a far cry from the condos and boardwalks that characterize other lake regions. The historic marker at 9.3 miles tells about the steamboats that brought nineteenth-century visitors to this end of Lake Sunapee, where carriages took them to the inns of New London.

This short ramble is just a sample of biking in the New London area. Serious cyclists have probably heard of the annual race around Lake Sunapee, and they may want to try that loop. Another option is the loop around neighboring Pleasant Lake, an exhilarating descent from New London and a challenging climb on the return. The western lakes are an intriguing area, with many miles of back roads, clear lakes, historic sights, and plenty more stone walls.

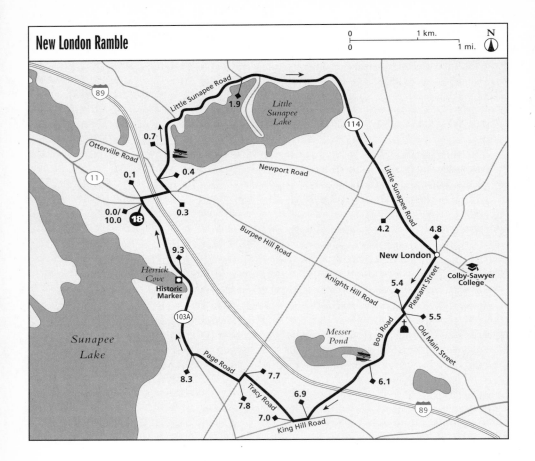

New London Ramble

0 — 1 km.
0 — 1 mi.

N

Miles and Directions

0.0 From Park & Ride area, turn right onto NH 103A, heading north.

0.1 Turn right onto NH 11, heading east and across I-89.

0.3 Turn left off NH 11 onto Otterville Road.

0.4 Turn right off Otterville Road onto Little Sunapee Road.

0.7 Public boat launch and picnic area on right.

1.9 Junction with NH 114. Turn right onto NH 114 South, following signs for New London.

4.2 Junction with Newport Road (also New London's Main Street). Turn left, heading into downtown New London.

4.8 At the four-way intersection, turn right off Main Street onto South Pleasant Street.

5.4 South Pleasant Street ends. Turn left (south) onto Old Main Street.

5.5 Turn right (west) off Old Main Street onto Bog Road.

6.1 Boat access on Messer Pond.

6.9 Junction with King Hill Road (unmarked here). Turn right (west) onto King Hill Road.

7.0 Turn right off King Hill onto Tracy Road. Note historic marker on corner.

7.7 Junction with County Road (unmarked here). Turn left onto County Road.

7.8 Turn right off County Road onto Page Road.

8.3 Junction with NH 103A. Turn right onto NH 103A North.

9.3 Herrick Cove and Lakeside Landing historic marker are on the left.

10.0 Return to parking area.

Local Information

Lake Sunapee Region Chamber of Commerce, P.O. Box 532, New London, NH 03257; (877) 526-6575 (toll free); www.sunapee vacations.com.

Local Events/Attractions

Lake Sunapee Bike Race. Since 1974, an annual May event, organized by S & W Sports Racing Team and Claremont Cycle Depot Club. For information on the race, contact Claremont Cycle Depot, 12 Plains Road, Claremont, NH; (603) 542-2453; www.claremontcycle.com.

New London Historical Society, 179 Little Sunapee Road, New London, NH; (603) 526-6564; www.newlondonhistoricalsociety.org. A collection of nineteenth-century buildings, carriages, etc. Call or check Web site for hours.

New London Barn Playhouse, 84 Main Street, New London, NH; (603) 526-4631; www.nl barn.com.

Food

Peter Christian's Tavern, 195 Main Street, New London, NH; (603) 526-4042; www.peter christianstavern.com. A local favorite, they advertise "victuals and strong waters."

Dunkin Donuts, 217 Main Street, New London, NH; (603) 526-4644. Look for the sign, as you wouldn't recognize the building. It's the classiest DD this cyclist has ever seen.

New London is a college town, with a wide assortment of interesting places to eat and to buy food.

Accommodations

Lamplighter Motor Inn, 34 Newport Road, New London, NH; (603) 526-6484; www.lamplightermotorinn.com. Check www.sunapeevacations.com for additional local lodging.

Days Inn, 135 State Street, New Hampshire Highway 120, Lebanon, NH; (603) 448-5070 or (800) DAYS INN. Located about 25 miles north, a quick trip on the interstate.

Bike Shop

Village Sports, 353 Main Street, New London, NH; (603) 526-4948. They have mountain bike rentals.

Map

DeLorme: New Hampshire Atlas & Gazetteer: Page 34.

19 Enfield Ramble

This is an easy pedal along the shores of two lakes, with an optional stop at the Enfield Shaker Village and Museum.

Start: Parking area for the Municipal Rail Trail, on Main Street in Enfield (next to the Laundromat and across from Twigs Bakery Café). If the parking area is full, or you anticipate the ride taking more than three hours, park in the lot behind the police station and municipal building, on the left just after the turn off U.S. Highway 4.

Length: 10.3 miles.

Terrain: First half of ride is quite flat, second half is hilly.

Traffic and hazards: Minimal shoulders on all roads. Light to moderate traffic on New Hampshire Highway 4A. Light traffic on other roads.

Getting there: Take exit 17 off Interstate 89 and get on US 4 East. In about 4 miles, turn right onto Main Street in Enfield. Proceed about 0.2 mile on Main Street to the parking area for the Municipal Rail Trail.

The Shaker "Great Stone Dwelling" on the shore of Mascoma Lake, at 2.0 miles, is a reminder that the Pilgrims were only the first in a long line of religious groups who built hopeful communities in New England. The Shakers are among the most interesting and most successful of nineteenth-century American communal societies. Shaker literature summarizes the Shaker religion as based upon a "commitment to common property, celibacy, confession of sins, equality of men and women, pacifism, and separation from the world." There are just a handful of Shakers left today, living in a Maine community. At their peak in the mid-nineteenth century, there were approximately 6,000 Shakers living in about twenty communities from Maine to Kentucky. The obvious question is how a celibate society managed to flourish for almost 200 years. The answer is their willingness to take in orphans, the homeless, and society's abandoned.

The Shakers' most prominent legacy is an elegantly simple style of furniture, a reflection of their love of simplicity combined with a commitment to labor-saving efficiency. They are also credited with inventing the screw propeller, a turbine water wheel, our everyday clothespin, a revolving oven, the first metal pens, flat brooms, and more. Their architecture is also famous. That enormous stone building in the Enfield Village is one of the Shaker buildings most often mentioned by historians. Constructed in 1837, it was the largest dwelling the Shakers built. At its peak, approximately 300 people lived and worked in the Enfield Shaker Community. Declining numbers forced closure of the community in 1923. In 1927 the Shakers sold the property to the LaSalettes, an order of Catholic priests—hence the present-day Catholic buildings on the grounds. Today the former Shaker village is owned by a nonprofit organization and is a museum and center for conferences, classes, and other events.

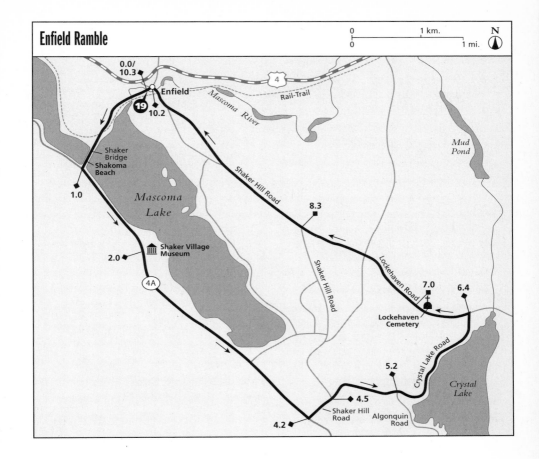

Enfield Ramble

The left turn off NH 4A marks the end of the flatter portion of the ride. Crystal Lake, the second lake of the trip, is at a higher elevation and is arguably even prettier than Mascoma Lake. On Crystal Lake Road there will be homes on your left and lakeshore on your right, with lovely views across the water. Unfortunately, the only public lake access is a boat launch at the end of Algonquin Road (to the right at 5.2 miles).

The Lockehaven Cemetery on the right at 7.0 miles marks the beginning of an exciting descent. Historians may want to stop here for the clues an old cemetery like this reveals about its inhabitants.

Miles and Directions

0.0 Turn left out of the Municipal Rail Trail parking area onto Main Street, heading west.

1.0 Junction with NH 4A. Turn left onto NH 4A South. Shakoma Beach (public swimming and boat launch) is on the left.

2.0 Shaker Village and Museum is on the left.

4.2 Turn left (east) off NH 4A onto Shaker Hill Road.

4.5 Bear right off Shaker Hill Road onto Crystal Lake Road.

5.2 Algonquin Road is to the right (boat launch). Continue straight on Crystal Lake Road.

6.4 Stop sign at junction of Crystal Lake Road with Lockehaven Road. Turn left onto Lockehaven Road, heading north.

7.0 Lockehaven Cemetery on right.

8.3 At junction of Lockehaven Road and Shaker Hill Road, turn right onto Shaker Hill Road, still heading northwest.

10.2 At four-way intersection in Enfield, turn left (west) onto Main Street.

10.3 Return to parking area.

Local Information

Greater Lebanon Chamber of Commerce, Village House, 1 School Street, P.O. Box 97, Lebanon, NH 03766; (603) 448-1203; www.lebanonchamber.com.

Local Events/Attractions

Enfield Shaker Museum, 447 NH 4A, Enfield, NH; (603) 632-4346; www.shakermuseum .org. Today the village is an "educational institution dedicated to interpreting and preserving the complex history of the Enfield Shaker Village and the Missionaries of La Salette."

Food

Twigs Bakery Café, 56 Main Street, Enfield, NH; (603) 632-3134. Hot and cold sandwiches, salads, paninis.

Accommodations

The Lebanon, West Lebanon, and Hanover areas will have the best variety of lodging possibilities. The Lebanon Chamber of Commerce Web site offers a comprehensive list of options.

Days Inn, 135 State Street, New Hampshire Highway 120, Lebanon, NH; (603) 448-5070 or (800) DAYS INN. Located about 7 miles from Enfield.

Bike Shop

Omer and Bob's Sport Shop, 7 Allen Street, Hanover, NH; (603) 643-3525; www.omerand bobs.com.

Map

DeLorme: New Hampshire Atlas & Gazetteer: Page 34.

20 Plymouth Ramble

The route takes secondary roads up the west side and down the east side of the Pemigewasset River, with nice river and mountain views. River/swim stops are possible at the two river crossings. The Blair Covered Bridge crossing is particularly scenic. Thanks to Michael Bombara at Rhino Bike Works for suggesting this one.

Start: Parking area at Rhino Bike Works, north of Plymouth.
Length: 24.8 miles.
Terrain: Gently rolling.
Traffic and hazards: Most of the heavy-duty north-south traffic will be using Interstate 93, which parallels the river, and U.S. Highway 3. Traffic on both sides of the river will be primarily local. Avoid morning and evening commuting times in order to encounter the least traffic. Shoulders range from minimal to spacious.

Getting there: Take exit 26 off I-93, following signs for US 3 and Plymouth. Get on US 3 North and proceed a very short distance (less than 0.1 mile) to a right turn with signs pointing to the Area Welcome Center and Plymouth Chamber of Commerce and Information Center. Rhino Bike Works is in the same building. Park at the far side of the parking lot.

Plymouth is an active little college town, with a healthy community of cyclists and outdoor enthusiasts. Its location, between the New Hampshire lakes region to the south and the White Mountains to the north, makes it a perfect starting point for a great variety of outdoor adventures. Its proximity to I-93 also makes for a quick trip to points north and south. What could be better than a week's vacation in Plymouth? A short drive each day gets you to a new ride, several of which are described in this book. And the bike shop (Rhino) is a friendly center for the local bike club. They're happy to offer many additional ride suggestions. Watch out: They'll surely suggest the ride they fondly call "The Grand Tour," a thigh-burning loop over the Kancamagus Highway and back through Crawford Notch. This route along the Pemigewasset is much easier and is one of the local club's regular weekly rides. It's a nice introduction to the area.

US 3 hugs the west bank of the Pemigewasset River for much of the first half of the ride. Pemigewasset is an Abenaki word meaning "swift current" or "rapids." It was also the name of a tribe that lived in the river valley. Locals refer to the river simply as the "Pemi." You'll start noticing views of the White Mountains a couple of miles before crossing the river at the northernmost point of the ride. The Pemi's source, Profile Lake in Franconia Notch, is up that way.

The only general store of the trip is at the intersection in Campton at 16.5 miles. The best picnic stop is a few miles farther, at the Blair Covered Bridge. New England towns are proud of their covered bridges and are generally happy to explain different styles, construction techniques, and the details of reconstruction efforts. The

Blair Covered Bridge PHOTO BY ENNIS DULING

Blair Bridge is the longest two-span covered bridge in New Hampshire. It's also one of the most picturesque of New Hampshire's bridges. The best photo spot is probably along the west bank of the river, south of the bridge. You can't miss the well-beaten path that swimmers and paddlers have made. The Country Cow Restaurant, on the west side of the bridge, is a good restaurant stop. The dining room overlooks the river and the bridge. There's also a friendly pub with good pub food.

The turn onto US 3 marks the completion of a loop. Head south for the return to the bike shop parking area, and begin planning the next trip.

Miles and Directions

0.0   Turn right out of Rhino Bike Works parking area onto US 3 North.

3.2   Blair Road to the right. Continue straight on US 3.

11.4   Turn right (east) off US 3 onto Cross Road and cross river on Thornton Memorial Bridge.

12.1   Stop sign at junction with New Hampshire Highway 175. Turn right onto NH 175.

16.5   At the intersection of NH 175 and New Hampshire Highway 49 in Campton, continue straight on NH 175.

20.8   Turn right (west) off NH 175 onto Blair Road, following signs for Covered Bridge #41.

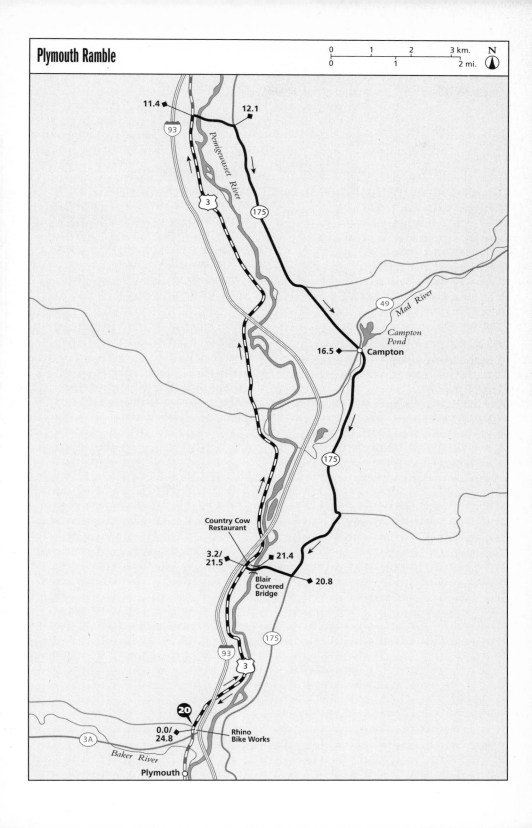

Plymouth Ramble

0   1   2   3 km.
0   1   2 mi.

N

93

11.4

12.1

Pemigewasset River

3

175

49   *Mad River*

*Campton
Pond*

16.5   Campton

175

Country Cow
Restaurant

3.2/
21.5   21.4

Blair
Covered
Bridge   20.8

175

93

3

20

0.0/
24.8

Rhino
Bike Works

3A

Baker River

Plymouth

21.4 Cross Blair Covered Bridge.

21.5 At the junction with US 3, turn left onto US 3 South.

24.8 Turn left off US 3 at entrance to Rhino Bike Works.

Local Information

Plymouth Chamber of Commerce, P.O. Box 65, Plymouth, NH 03264; (603) 536-1001 or (800) 386-3678; www.plymouthnh.org.

Local Events/Attractions

The White Mountains are New Hampshire's most famous attraction. The Plymouth region is widely considered a gateway to the White Mountain region, where hiking, camping, canoeing, and other outdoor activities rule. Contact the **White Mountain National Forest,** 719 North Main Street, Laconia, NH; (603) 528-8721; www.fs.fed.us/r9/forests/white_mountain.

Food

Country Cow Restaurant, 57 Blair Road, Campton, NH; (603) 536-1331; www.the-country-cow.com.

Plymouth is a college town, with a variety of restaurants such as:

Lucky Dog Tavern & Grill, 53 South Main Street, Plymouth, NH; (603) 536-2260; www.luckydogtavernandgrill.com. Good lunch and dinner options, reasonable prices.

Chase Street Market, 83 Main Street, Plymouth, NH; (603) 536-FOOD. Upstairs deli, downstairs pub.

Accommodations

There are numerous lodging options in the Plymouth area (see the Plymouth Chamber of Commerce Web site). Be sure to get advance reservations if planning a trip in mid-June. Lodging fills quickly during the annual Laconia Motorcycle Rally and Race Week.

Deep River Motor Inn, 166 Highland Street, Plymouth, NH; (603) 536-2155; http://deeprivermotorinn.com.

Days Inn, 1513 US 3, Campton, NH; (603) 536-3520; www.DaysInnCampton.com.

Bike Shop

Rhino Bike Works, 1 Foster Street, Plymouth, NH; (603) 536-3919. Stop in to chat about other bike routes. They sell snacks and they're glad to let you use their restroom.

Map

DeLorme: New Hampshire Atlas & Gazetteer: Page 39.

21 Squam Lake Cruise

This ride takes you around beautiful Squam Lake. It's no surprise that this is the actual "Golden Pond" of movie fame. Filming of the 1981 film took place at several locations in the area. Squam is a little to the northwest of Lake Winnipesaukee, at the southern edge of the White Mountain region. You'll catch occasional glimpses of the Whites as you circle the lake. Early fall is a particularly good time for this one: Traffic is reduced, and early autumn colors here are fine. Bring a camera, whatever time of year. Note that proximity to the lake might be misleading: Although not mountainous, the route isn't flat.

Start: Squam Lakes Natural Science Center in Holderness.
Length: 28.3 miles.
Terrain: Hilly.
Traffic and hazards: The New Hampshire Lakes region attracts many visitors in summer, and especially on summer weekends. Stay right and stay alert. The final section of the ride, on U.S. Highway 3/New Hampshire Highway 25, has the most traffic, and there are a few miles of NH 25 where shoulders are narrow. Be particularly careful between miles 21 and 26.

Getting there: Take exit 24 off Interstate 93. Follow US 3/NH 25 east to Holderness (about 4.5 miles). In Holderness, turn left off US 3/NH 25 onto New Hampshire 113. Proceed about 0.2 mile to the Squam Lakes Natural Science Center on the left. Park in the Science Center parking area.

This is a resort area, but residents favor an understated approach. Cottages and homes have typically been in the family for several generations. Buildings are discreetly camouflaged by trees, and loons are able to nest undisturbed by the fleets of motorcraft that swarm over neighboring Lake Winnipesaukee. Squam residents are proud of their loons, and their environmental policies are designed to keep the loons safely nesting on shores and calling from the waters.

Mileage begins at the exit from the Science Center, a worthwhile stop at the beginning or end of the ride. NH 113 is winding and fairly narrow. Shoulders are minimal, but traffic shouldn't be heavy here. For the first 11 miles, enjoy intermittent views of the lake, the White Mountains to the north, horse farms, a beaver pond, and magnificent stone walls. Although they can't top the lake for scenic appeal, those stone walls are a close second for "most impressive sight" on this trip.

A sign outside the Center Sandwich General Store, at 11.6 miles, announces that it's a ONE SHOP STOPPING CENTER. That's accurate, and the store is definitely biker friendly. They have a big deli, a large eating area (including an outdoor deck), a cozy woodstove, and a restroom. Snacks include muffins, soup, ice cream, and raspberry white chocolate cookies as well as the usual packaged biker fuels. The store was rescued from closure several years ago by a group of local citizens, who wisely figured

Squam Lake Cruise

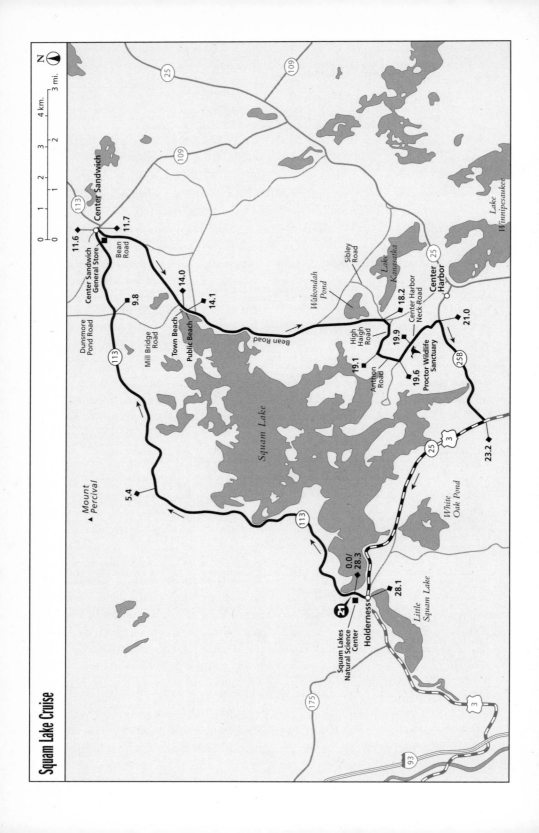

Mount Percival

Center Sandwich

11.6
Center Sandwich General Store
Bean Road
11.7

9.8
Dunsmore Pond Road
113
Mill Bridge Road
Town Beach
14.0
Public Beach
14.1

5.4

Bean Road

Squam Lake

Wakondah Pond
Sibley Road
Lake Kanasatka

Center Harbor Neck Road
18.2
High Haigh Road
19.9
Center Harbor
25
21.0
Amthon Road
19.1
19.6
Proctor Wildlife Sanctuary
25B
23.2

White Oak Pond

113
0.0/28.3

21
Squam Lakes Natural Science Center
Holderness
28.1
Little Squam Lake

175

25
3

93

109

109

25

113

Lake Winnipesaukee

N

0   1   2   3   4 km.
1   2   3 mi.

that having a general store was a way of maintaining their community. It was recently purchased by its current owners, who seem committed to long-term success.

The public beach at 14.1 miles even has a bike rack. If it's a warm day, this is the place for a swim. (Note that the small beach and boat launch about 100 yards before this one is for Squam residents only.)

The water to the left at 17.8 miles comes as a bit of a surprise, as you've been focusing on Squam to your right. That's Wakondah Pond, and it's the signal that a right turn onto High Haigh Road is coming soon, at 18.2 miles. Continuing straight instead on Bean Road is a possibility. But it would mean going through Center Harbor, a busy town at the north end of Lake Winnipesaukee. It would also mean a particularly nasty climb out of Center Harbor on New Hampshire Highway 25B. The route as mapped (with the right onto High Haigh Road) is the one favored by local bike clubs. Watch directions carefully here, being sure to take Anthon Road, then Center Harbor Neck Road. When you hit the uphill on Center Harbor Neck Road, you'll wonder how the alternative (climbing out of Center Harbor on NH 25B) could possibly be worse. Just trust the bike club—they've got it figured out. Take your time getting to the top of the hill (at about 20.8 miles). You'll pass the Proctor Wildlife Sanctuary, a New Hampshire Audubon Society work-in-progress, on your way up the hill. Stop, read the signs, do some wildlife viewing, have a drink, catch your breath.

The stop sign at 21.0 miles is the junction with NH 25B. Take a right here and right again onto US 3/NH25 in another couple of miles. Traffic on NH 25 is the heaviest of the trip, so exercise caution. Shoulders are modest until you enter the outskirts of Holderness at about 26 miles, where shoulders widen and views of the lake return.

Miles and Directions

0.0   From Natural Science Center exit, turn left onto NH 113.

5.4   Percival Trail to left. This is the trailhead for the climb up Mount Percival.

6.1   Town line Sandwich/Carroll.

9.8   Mill Bridge Road is to the right. Dunsmore Pond Road is to the left. Continue straight.

11.6   Center Sandwich. Center Sandwich General Store on right.

11.7   Immediately after the general store, turn right (south) off NH 113 onto Bean Road (unmarked as of this writing).

14.0   Town beach, boat access (Squam residents only).

14.1   Public beach, with bike rack.

17.8   Wakondah Pond is on the left.

18.2   Turn right (west) off Bean Road onto High Haigh Road.

19.1   Turn left (south) off High Haigh Road onto Anthon Road.

19.6   Stop sign at junction with Center Harbor Neck Road. Turn left onto Center Harbor Neck Road, heading southeast.

19.9 Proctor Wildlife Sanctuary (NH Audubon Society preserve).

20.7 Fine view of Squam Lake to the right. Good photo opportunity.

21.0 Stop sign. Turn right (west) onto NH 25B (unmarked here).

23.2 Junction with US 3/NH 25. Turn right (west) onto US 3/NH 25. Traffic increases, exercise caution.

23.9 Cross town line, into town of Holderness.

26.8 Shoulders widen, views of lake to right.

28.1 Turn right (north) off US 3/NH 25 onto NH 113, heading back toward the Science Center.

28.3 Turn left off NH 113 into the Science Center parking area.

Local Information

Squam Lakes Area Chamber of Commerce, (603) 968-4494; www.visitsquam.com. Use the "Vacationing" tab for lodging and restaurant directories, information on upcoming events, boating, shopping, etc.

Local Events/Attractions

Squam Lakes Natural Science Center, 23 Science Center Road, Holderness, NH; (603) 968-7194, www.nhnature.org. The starting point for this ride, it's open daily May 1 to November 1. They have ample parking and restrooms. Visitors to the center see plants and animals of the Squam area, walk on short hiking trails, and learn about the natural and geologic history of the region. The center also offers lake cruises.

Food

Holderness General Store, 863 US 3, Holderness, NH; (603) 968-3446.

Center Sandwich General Store, 6 Skinner Street (NH 113), Center Sandwich, NH; (603) 284-7200; www.sandwichgeneralstore.com.

Lucky Dog Tavern & Grill, 53 South Main Street, Plymouth, NH; (603) 536-2260; www.luckydogtavernandgrill.com. Good lunch and dinner options, reasonable prices.

Accommodations

See the Squam Lakes Chamber of Commerce Web site for a list of cabins, B&Bs, and campgrounds. Lodging in nearby Plymouth is likely to be less expensive, especially during summer months.

Deep River Motor Inn, 166 Highland Street, Plymouth, NH; (603) 536-2155; http://deeprivermotorinn.com, is convenient, clean, and reasonably priced.

Bike Shops

Rhino Bike Works, 1 Foster Street, Plymouth, NH; (603) 536-3919.

Riverside Cycles, 12 Riverside Drive, Ashland, NH; (603) 968-9676.

Map

DeLorme: New Hampshire Atlas & Gazetteer: Pages 39, 40.

22 Tamworth Ramble

Like the town of Tamworth, this ride is a real gem. Enjoy the ambience of a picturesque New England town, visit the Barnstormers Theatre, and stop at the Remick Country Doctor Museum and Farm. Traffic noise won't be the dominant sound on this ride. Instead, you'll pedal to the sounds of the Swift River and birdsongs.

Start: Public parking area next to town office building in Tamworth. The parking lot is on the north side of Main Street, across from the Village Store and the public library.
Length: 22.8 miles.

Terrain: Intermittent uphill for the first 6 miles, then a long descent.
Traffic and hazards: The only significant traffic will be on New Hampshire Highway 25, where shoulders are large.

Getting there: Tamworth is north of Lake Winnipesaukee. Take exit 24 off Interstate 93 and proceed east on U.S. Highway 3/NH 25, following signs for Holderness. Come to Holderness in about 4.5 miles. Continue straight on US 3/NH 25 to the junction with New Hampshire Highway 25B, about 4.6 miles east of Holderness. Turn left onto NH 25B. Proceed about 3 miles to the junction with NH 25. Turn left onto NH 25 and proceed about 14.6 miles, through South Tamworth, to the intersection with New Hampshire Highway 113 North and signs for Tamworth. Turn left onto NH 113 North and proceed 2 miles. Turn left off NH 113 onto Main Street in Tamworth. The public parking area is 0.2 mile farther on the right.

Although the Sandwich range of mountains provides the backdrop to the north, this route is not particularly difficult: one long, gradual climb at the beginning, then small hills and miles and miles of long, gradual descent.

Be sure to stop and read the historical marker at the corner of Main Street and New Hampshire Highway 113A. It gives a quick history of the Barnstormers Theatre, one of Tamworth's several claims to fame. Although the summer playhouse now has a permanent home here, it started as a traveling troupe, with an 80-mile circuit of local barns in which productions were staged.

Approximately the first 13 miles of the ride are on NH 113A—also called the Chinook Trail—a paved road that skirts the edge of the White Mountains. There are no stores and only one notable business (a garden center) on the road: just lovely old homes and the occasional local driver. It's uphill for about the first 6 miles, much of it following the Swift River. Uphill, but not relentlessly steep. It's hard to imagine a more beautiful mountain stream, and there are ample opportunities to stop and visit the river.

Just before the top of the climb, there's an historical marker on the left at 5.6 miles. It marks the site of the Chinook Kennels, where Milton and Eva Seeley bred and raised sled dogs that were used on Antarctic expeditions. The old buildings look

Wonalancet Union Chapel

abandoned but with a little imagination you can picture what this area looks like in the winter, with malamutes and huskies running through the snowy woods.

After the Chinook Kennels, most of the trip will be downhill. It's worth a quick stop at the Wonalancet Union Chapel, at 6.7 miles. It only has services in summer, but cyclists can stop anytime to admire the building and to visit the adjacent picnic area by the river. Immediately after the chapel, be sure to bear left with NH 113A as it makes a sharp turn toward the south. Several more miles of a rolling downhill bring you to the intersection with NH 113, where you'll make a left and start heading east.

If you're ready for a snack or a water bottle refill, make a very short detour at the junction of NH 113A and NH 113. Instead of bearing left, go straight (on NH 113 West) for less than 0.1 mile to the North Sandwich Store. They go out of their way to be bicycle friendly and are likely to offer water bottle refills even before you can ask. They also have a deli and eating area, hardware supplies, an art gallery, and the local post office. And there's a pleasant little park across the street.

Two wildlife refuge areas along NH 113 (the Alice Bemis Thompson Wildlife Refuge and the Jackman Pond Wildlife Area) may be good moose spotting opportunities. Even if the moose aren't around, you'll probably see tracks along the side of the road and in the mud by Jackman Pond. Bird-watchers will be pleased with the variety of species to be seen from the bridge at Jackman Pond.

The junction with NH 25, at 17.3 miles, signals a significant increase in traffic. Fortunately, there's also a significant increase in the size of the paved shoulder. This section of the trip is also beautiful, with the Bearcamp River to the left. Watch for the turn off NH 25, then head back to Tamworth on NH 113 East.

Miles and Directions

0.0   Exit public parking area on Main Street in Tamworth. Turn left onto Main Street, heading east.

0.2   At the four-way intersection, turn left onto NH 113A North.

5.6   Chinook Kennels is on the left.

6.7   Wonalancet Union Chapel is on the right. Picnic area is by the river.

6.9   NH 113A makes a sharp left, heading south. Continue on NH 113A.

13.5   Junction with NH 113 in North Sandwich. Turn left onto NH 113 East. Go right here for a stop at the North Sandwich Store, then return to this intersection.

17.3   Intersection with NH 25. Turn left onto NH 25/113 East.

20.6   Turn left off NH 25/113 onto NH 113 North, following signs for Tamworth.

22.6   Turn left off NH 113 onto Main Street in Tamworth.

22.8   Return to parking area.

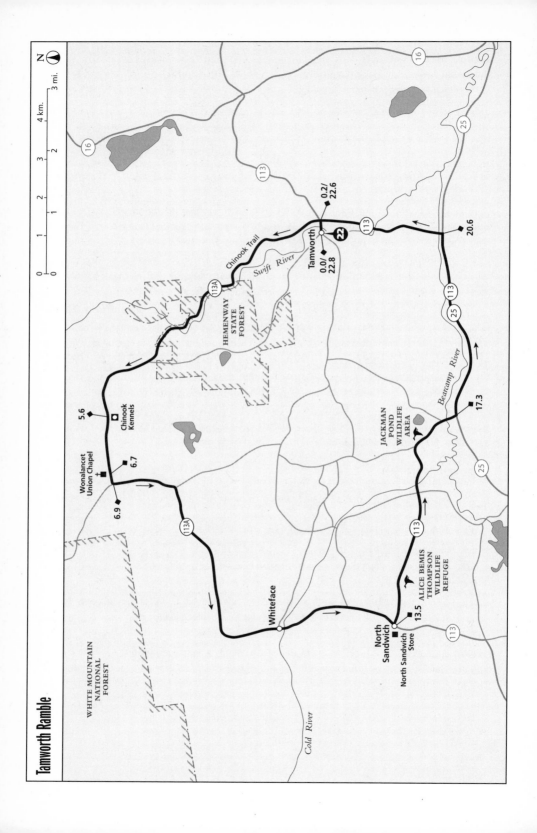

Tamworth Ramble

N

3 mi.

4 km.

16

16

25

113

0.2/
22.6

113

22

20.6

113

25

Chinook Trail

Swift River

Tamworth

0.0/
22.8

113A

HEMENWAY
STATE
FOREST

Bearcamp River

5.6

Chinook Kennels

JACKMAN
POND
WILDLIFE
AREA

17.3

25

6.7

Wonalancet
Union Chapel

6.9

113A

Whiteface

113

WHITE MOUNTAIN
NATIONAL
FOREST

North
Sandwich

ALICE BEMIS
THOMPSON
WILDLIFE
REFUGE

13.5

North Sandwich Store

113

Cold River

Local Information

The Mount Washington Valley Chamber of Commerce and Visitor's Bureau covers the Tamworth area. P.O. Box 2300, North Conway, NH 03860; (603) 356-5701 or (800) 367-3364; www.mtwashingtonvalley.org/chocorua tamworth.

Local Events/Attractions

Barnstormers Theatre, P.O. Box 434, 100 Main Street, Tamworth, NH 03886; (603) 323-8500; www.BarnstormersTheatre.org.

Remick Country Doctor Museum & Farm, 58 Cleveland Hill Road, Tamworth, NH; (603) 323-7591 or (800) 686-6117; www.remick museum.org. Just west of town, it celebrates 200 years of rural New England life. Free admission.

Food

Olde Village Store, 85 Main Street, Tamworth, NH; (603) 323-9222.

The Other Store, 77 Main Street, Tamworth, NH; (603) 323-8872; www.otherstore.qpg.com.

Tamworth Inn, 15 Cleveland Hill Road, Tamworth, NH; (603) 323-7721 or (800) 642-7352; www.tamworth.com. Upscale dining and pub fare.

North Sandwich Store, 2 Maple Ridge Road, North Sandwich, NH; (603) 284-7147.

Accommodations

Tamworth Inn, 15 Cleveland Hill Road, Tamworth, NH; (603) 323-7721 or (800) 642-7352; www.tamworth.com. A beautiful country inn with all the amenities. One of the inns on the "Bike the Whites" tour. Bike rentals available.

Bike Shops

The Bike Shop, 90 North South Road, North Conway, NH; (603) 356-6089.

Rhino Bike Works, 1 Foster Street, Plymouth, NH; (603) 536-3919.

Map

DeLorme: New Hampshire Atlas & Gazetteer: Page 40.

23 Conway Cruise

Situated at the eastern end of the Kancamagus Highway, Conway serves as a gateway to the White Mountains. But, as this lovely ride demonstrates, it's also a side door to New Hampshire's extensive lakes region. The route goes by at least ten named lakes and ponds, so there are plenty of opportunities to picnic on a beach. Like all summer resort areas, traffic is heaviest in July and August.

Start: Parking lot next to the post office and Laundromat and across the street from the middle/senior high school, on Main Street in Conway.

Length: 31.8 miles.

Terrain: Gentle to moderate hills.

Traffic and hazards: Traffic in the town of Conway can be terrible, approaching an unfortunate gridlock at its worst. If you happen to be there at rush hour, walk the bike on the sidewalk for the short distance from the start to the turnoff onto New Hampshire Highway 153. Traffic should be fairly light for the next 20 miles. The most hazardous pedaling will be from Madison north to the junction with New Hampshire Highway 16. After the junction with NH 16, traffic increases but shoulders are ample. Be particularly careful of soft shoulders on the Ossipee Lake Road, where soil is sandy.

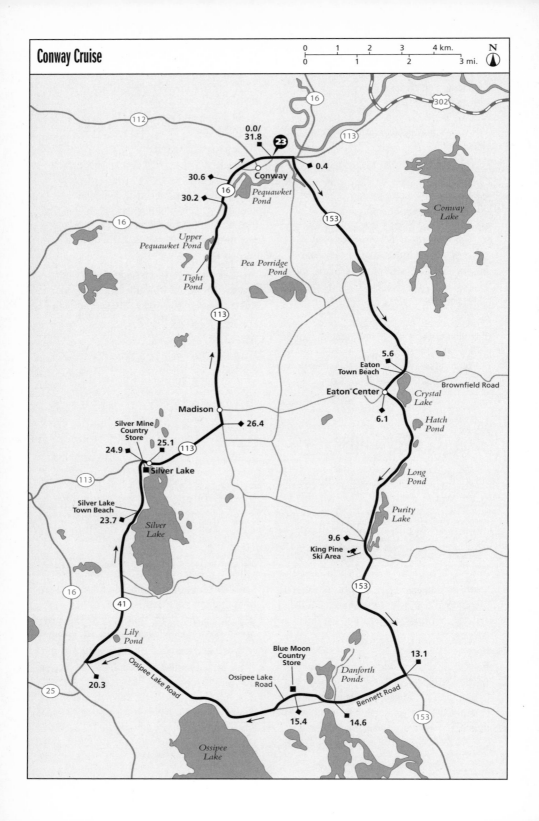

Conway Cruise

0   1   2   3   4 km.
0   1   2   3 mi.

N

302

112

16

0.0/
31.8   **23**

113

0.4

30.6

Conway

30.2

16

Pequawket Pond

153

Conway Lake

16

Upper Pequawket Pond

Pea Porridge Pond

Tight Pond

113

5.6

Eaton Town Beach

Brownfield Road

Eaton Center

Crystal Lake

6.1

Hatch Pond

Madison

26.4

Silver Mine Country Store

25.1

Long Pond

24.9

113

Silver Lake

Purity Lake

Silver Lake Town Beach

23.7

Silver Lake

9.6

King Pine Ski Area

113

153

16

41

Lily Pond

13.1

20.3

25

Ossipee Lake Road

Blue Moon Country Store

Danforth Ponds

Ossipee Lake Road

Bennett Road

153

15.4

14.6

Ossipee Lake

Getting there: Conway is in eastern New Hampshire, close to Maine, about midway between the state's northern and southern borders. From southern New Hampshire, take Interstate 93 to exit 32, following signs for Lincoln and the Kancamagus Highway (New Hampshire Highway 112). Take the Kancamagus Highway (NH 112) east for about 35 miles, to the junction with NH 16/113. Turn left onto NH 16 North/NH 113 East. Proceed about 0.6 mile to the parking area next to the post office in the center of Conway.

Lakes are the theme of this ride. Your first lake stop is likely to be soon, at 5.6 miles. This is Crystal Lake, and that's the Eaton Town Beach on your left. Immediately beyond the beach there's a small picnic area that beckons. Immediately after Crystal Lake, you'll pass Hatch Pond, Long Pond, Purity Lake, and a couple of ponds that are too small for names. Although not all have public access, there will be plenty of opportunities to stop and admire the views. One of the advantages of biking is the ability to stop for a drink and a photo almost anywhere along the road.

Watch carefully for the turn off NH 153 onto Bennett Road (there's no stop sign or light at the intersection). Bennett Road and Ossipee Lake Road appear to be a geologic boundary: Although you've been by plenty of lakes already, to the south is the beginning of the official New Hampshire Lakes Region. Notice all that sand, and imagine the washout from the retreating glaciers of the last ice age. This section of the trip is quite flat, traffic is very sparse, and there will be occasional glimpses of Ossipee Lake to the south and Danforth Lakes to the north. You'll pass summer camps, a Lutheran Conference Center, and lots of pine trees and blueberry bushes. Notice that distinctive smell of pine and sand: It triggers memories of summer camp in New Hampshire for many visiting cyclists. The Bennett Road/Ossipee Lake Road section of the ride doesn't have paved shoulders, except for a very short section—between approximately miles 16 and 18—where there is an official bike lane. Be especially careful if you're on skinny tires: Leaving the pavement and sinking into the sand would mean a fall. The Blue Moon Country Store on the right at about 15.4 miles is a good refueling spot.

The right turn onto New Hampshire Highway 41 at 20.3 miles signals the start of more traffic. Between here and the return to Conway, you'll pass "Pine Tree Power," a biomass electrical generating plant (they burn wood chips—and more—to make electricity), a lumber mill, and at least one large sand and gravel operation. Pines and sand are important elements of the local economy as well as of the picturesque landscape. From a cyclist's point of view, sand and gravel pits and lumber mills mean big trucks. Stay right and stay alert.

It would be hard to pedal past the town beach on Silver Lake without stopping. They have a welcoming picnic area and sandy beach. There isn't much parking space but, fortunately, you don't have to worry about parking a car. After the beach it's just a couple of miles to the Silver Mine Country Store in the town of Silver Lake. Their "Maine Black Bear" ice cream is guaranteed to fuel the climb out of Madison (coming soon). There's a comfortable picnic area, too, right next to the store and on the lakeshore. Notice the carefully restored railroad station, now the post office, across the street.

The climb out of Madison seems long but not as long as the glorious downhill on the other side. A couple more little lakes on the left, and you're almost back to Conway. Traffic looks terrible when you get to the junction with NH 16, but the center turning lane gives motorists some extra room, and then, in less than 0.5 mile, the shoulder widens to 6 to 8 feet and brings you safely back into town.

Miles and Directions

0.0   Entrance to parking lot at post office and Acorn Wash & Dry Laundromat. Turn right onto NH 16/113, heading east.

0.4   Turn right off NH 16/113 onto NH 153.

0.7   Tasker Hill Road bears right. Continue south on NH 153.

5.6   Brownfield Road and Eaton Town Beach to left. Continue straight (south) on NH 153.

6.1   At the four-way intersection, bear left, continuing south on NH 153.

8.4   Nice pull-off on left, next to lake.

9.6   King Pine Ski area is on the right.

13.1   At the four-way intersection, turn right (west) off NH 153 onto Bennett Road.

14.6   Stop sign at four-way intersection. Bennett Road ends. Continue straight onto Ossipee Lake Road. Danforth Bay will be on your right at the bottom of the hill.

15.4   Blue Moon Country Store on right.

20.3   At the junction with NH 41, turn right onto NH 41 North.

23.7   Town beach and picnic area on Silver Lake, on right.

24.9   At junction with NH 113, turn right onto NH 113 East, following signs for Madison.

25.1   Village of Silver Lake. Silver Mine Country Store on right.

26.4   Stop sign. Bear left, continuing on NH 113 East, following signs for Conway.

30.2   Junction with NH 16. Turn right onto NH 16/113 East. Traffic increases.

30.6   Shoulder widens to 6 to 8 feet.

31.8   Return to parking area.

Local Information
Conway Village Area Chamber of Commerce, 230 West Street, Conway, NH; (603) 447-2639; www.conwaychamber.com.
Mount Washington Valley Chamber of Commerce and Visitor's Bureau, P.O. Box 2300, North Conway, NH; (603) 356-5701 or (800) 367-3364; www.mtwashingtonvalley.org.

Local Events/Attractions
Outdoor adventures in the White Mountains are the main attractions. See the above Web sites for details.

Food
Blue Moon Country Store, 612 Ossipee Lake Road, Freedom, NH; (603) 539-1001.
Silver Mine Country Store, 1374 Village Road, Silver Lake, NH; (603) 367-8171.

Accommodations
North Conway has the best motel options. The Mount Washington Valley Chamber of Commerce has a good list of lodging possibilities.
HI (Hostelling International) Hostel, 36 Washington Street, Conway, NH; (603) 447-1001. For reservations call (800) 886-4284.

Reasonable dorm rates and private rooms. Open all year.

Bike Shop

The Bike Shop, 90 North South Road, North Conway, NH; (603) 356-6089.

Map

DeLorme: New Hampshire Atlas & Gazetteer: Page 41.

24 Franconia/Kinsman Notch Challenge

Thanks to Bob Lesmerises at Littleton Bike & Fitness for sharing this, one of his favorite rides. It's the very best of White Mountain cycling: stunning scenery, sparse traffic, breathtaking descents, and opportunities for sightseeing and recreational stops. The route takes you through two of the Whites' famous "notches." For serious riders it's a solid workout in a heavenly place. Weekend vacationers could even stretch it out over a couple of days, with sightseeing/hiking stops along the way and an overnight in Franconia.

Start: The Flume Gorge Visitor Center, at exit 34A off Interstate 93.
Length: 38.3 miles.
Terrain: Mountainous.
Traffic and hazards: The first 6.5 miles are on the Franconia Notch Bike Route. Obey bike route speed limits and regulations. Traffic will be heaviest on U.S. Highway 3 in North Woodstock. During busy periods, it's safest to walk the bike on the sidewalk for the short distance through town. After North Woodstock, the US 3 portion of the trip is on a designated bike lane.

Getting there: Take exit 34A off I-93, following signs for US 3 North and the Flume Gorge Visitor Center. The parking area for the visitor center is the first right. The bike route begins at the north end of the parking area.

A kiosk at the visitor center explains that a "notch" is a V-shaped passage between mountains. Early settlers thought those passages looked like the notches they cut when felling trees. In other states these passages are called "gaps" or "passes." But in the White Mountains, they're almost always "notches." This ride takes you through two of them: Franconia Notch and Kinsman Notch.

The parking area where the ride starts is at the southern end of Franconia Notch. Franconia is a very narrow notch. In fact, it's so narrow that there simply wasn't room for both the old US 3 and the new I-93. So, just north of the Flume Gorge Visitor Center, engineers merged the two roads. A little farther north, as the notch narrows even more, the merged I-93/US 3 is reduced to two lanes—one northbound and one southbound—with heavy traffic. At this point in the tale, one wants to invoke a blessing on the state of New Hampshire. Some wise group realized that since bicycles aren't permitted on interstate highways, this new road arrangement meant cyclists would simply be unable to get through Franconia

Misty mountains near Franconia Notch

Notch. So they built the completely separate 8.8-mile paved bike route. It's the kind of bike lane that Europeans have been building and using for a long time, but that's rarely found in the United States.

The Franconia Notch Bike Route parallels I-93/US 3, with an occasional underpass to switch sides. It also parallels the Pemigewasset River, which flows southward through the notch. The bike route is essentially uphill heading north. There are numerous pull-offs, parking areas, trailheads, a couple of campgrounds, historical markers, etc. You could do the first 6.5 miles of the ride—the section on the bike route—quite quickly. Or you could stop for the sights and hikes. At the very least, plan to stop near Profile Lake (the headwaters of the Pemigewasset River) for a nostalgic look at the site of the Old Man of the Mountain. Of course you won't see the Old Man anymore: The rock formation collapsed on May 3, 2003. However, you may spot the formation that resembles the barrel of a cannon—hence "Cannon Mountain"—straight ahead.

When you get to the northern end of Echo Lake, there will be an underpass where the bike route goes under New Hampshire Highway 18. Immediately before the underpass, there is an unmarked left spur that connects the bike route to the road. This is where our route leaves the bike route. It's easy to miss this turn (the

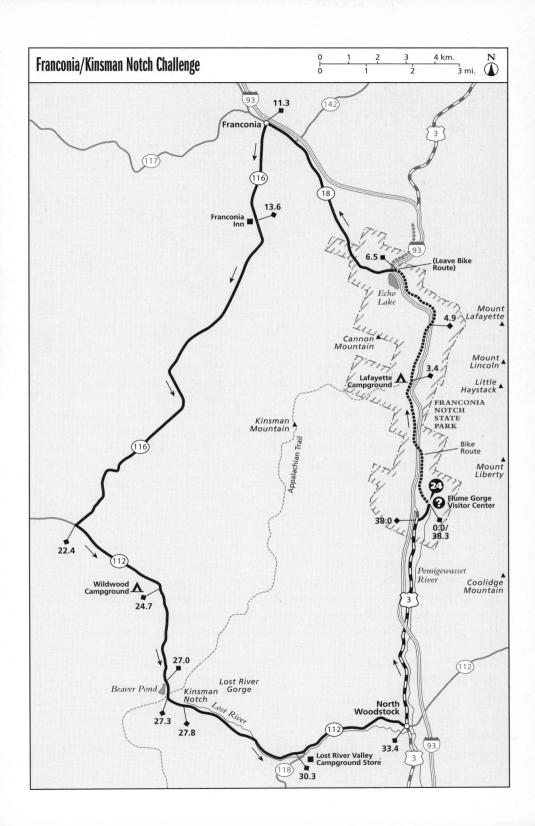

Franconia/Kinsman Notch Challenge

0 1 2 3 4 km.
0 1 2 3 mi.

N

93
11.3
142
Franconia
3

117

116
13.6
18
Franconia Inn

93
6.5
(Leave Bike Route)

Echo Lake

4.9
Mount Lafayette

Cannon Mountain

3.4
Mount Lincoln

Lafayette Campground
Little Haystack

116
FRANCONIA NOTCH STATE PARK

Kinsman Mountain

Appalachian Trail

Bike Route

Mount Liberty

24
?
Flume Gorge Visitor Center

38.0
0.0/ 38.3

22.4

112
Pemigewasset River
Coolidge Mountain

Wildwood Campground
24.7

3

27.0

Beaver Pond
Kinsman Notch
Lost River Gorge

Lost River

112

27.3

27.8
North Woodstock

112

33.4
93

Lost River Valley Campground Store
118
30.3
3

voice of experience here), as the scenery is great and you're starting a gentle descent. An error here isn't catastrophic, but it adds a few miles to the trip.

The parking area for Echo Lake access is on the left, just after the turn onto NH 18. Stop here for a swim at elevation 1,931 feet. A little after the lake is the entrance to Cannon Ski Area, your signal that it's time to test the brakes, as a long downhill is just ahead. The distance between the ski area and the village of Franconia is more than 4 miles, with a thousand-foot drop in elevation. NH 18 has at least a minimal shoulder and very light traffic: It's a glorious descent.

Franconia is a delightful little village with all the biker amenities (restaurant, grocery store, even a bicycle shop). If you happen to arrive in mid to late June, you'll catch the annual Fields of Lupine Festival, a celebration of those tall, feisty purple (and blue and white and pink) flowers you've been spotting along the roadside.

New Hampshire Highway 116 south from Franconia is 11 miles of pleasant pedaling with magnificent views. This is a popular cycling road, and with good reason. It's hilly but not difficult, rural landscape is beautiful, and traffic is almost nonexistent.

The junction with New Hampshire Highway 112 means the beginning of an ascent through Kinsman Notch. NH 112 has the appearance of being a major road. It's wide and fairly straight here, with big shoulders. Some of the "notches" in the While Mountains are heavily traveled. The road through a notch is often the only way to get across, and everybody seems in a hurry to get to the other side. Not so with this one. It's a great road, but evidently not a major east-west route. Traffic is light.

Wildwood Campground and picnic area, on the right at 24.7 miles, has a handy water faucet, in case you want to refill a water bottle before the climb. It's a significant climb, but never horribly steep. Beaver Brook Scenic Area is at the top of Kinsman Notch. There are several attractive hiking options from here if you have a little energy left. The Appalachian Trail crosses just a little beyond the crest of the notch, and there are hikes from Lost River Gorge and Boulder Caves, at 27.8 miles.

It's a quick trip from the top of Kinsman Notch down to North Woodstock. North Woodstock, a bustling little town, represents the only real traffic problem of the ride. If it's a busy time of day, just get off and walk the bike on the sidewalk for the short distance through town. North of North Woodstock, US 3 has an enormous shoulder that's marked as an official bike lane. Traffic is significant on US 3, and the tourist "attractions" along here (dancing bears and water slides) are a little dismaying after all the magnificent wilderness you just pedaled through. But the bike lane is wide, and it's not far to the outskirts of the Franconia Notch State Park and the visitor center parking area.

Miles and Directions

0.0 Beginning of the Franconia Notch Bike Route, at the northwestern corner of the Flume Gorge Visitor Center parking area.

3.4 Lafayette Campground is on the left.

4.9 Observation point for views of Profile Lake and former Old Man of the Mountain.

6.5 Exit bike route and get on NH 18 West.

6.8 Echo Lake State Park is to the left. Continue straight on NH 18.

11.3 At the four-way intersection in village of Franconia, turn left off NH 18 onto NH 116 South, following signs for Easton and the Robert Frost Museum.

13.6 Franconia Inn is on the right, and gliderport is on the left. Continue straight on NH 116 South.

22.4 Junction with NH 112. Turn left onto NH 112 East.

24.7 Wildwood Campground and picnic area. Fill water bottles and continue straight on NH 112 East.

27.0 Beaver Brook Scenic Area is at the top of the notch.

27.3 Appalachian Trail crosses road.

27.8 Lost River Gorge and Boulder Caves. Continue straight on NH 112 East.

30.3 Lost River Valley Family Campground and Camp Store is on the right. Continue straight on NH 112 East.

33.4 Junction with US 3 in North Woodstock. Turn left onto US 3 North.

38.0 Turn right off US 3 at entrance to Flume Gorge Visitor Center.

38.3 Return to parking area at Flume Gorge Visitor Center.

Local Information

Franconia Notch Chamber of Commerce, P.O. Box 780, Franconia, NH 03580; (603) 823-5661; www.franconianotch.org.

Flume Gorge Visitor Center, Franconia Notch State Park, 852 US 3, Lincoln, NH; (603) 745-8391; www.flumegorge.com. Open early May through late October.

Local Events/Attractions

Franconia Notch State Park includes Flume Gorge, Old Man of the Mountain Historic Site, Cannon Mountain Aerial Tram, the recreation/bike trail, many miles of hiking trails, and other attractions. From May to October, contact the Flume Gorge Visitor Center, 852 US 3, Lincoln, NH; (603) 745-8391; www.flumegorge.com. In winter, contact the Cannon Mountain Aerial Tramway, 9 Franconia Notch, Franconia, NH; (603) 823-8800; www.franconianotchstatepark.com.

Lost River Gorge & Boulder Caves, 1712 Lost River Road (NH 112), North Woodstock, NH; (603) 745-8031; www.findlostriver.com.

Fields of Lupine Festival, P.O. Box 780, Franconia, NH 03580; (603) 823-5661; www.franconianotch.org/lupine.festival.html. In June, a two-week series of exhibits, tours, special events, and sales.

Food

Quality Bakery, 467 Main Street, Franconia, NH; (603) 823-5228.

Store at Lost River Valley Campground, 951 Lost River Road (NH 112), North Woodstock, NH; (603) 745-8321. North Woodstock is a tourist town, with lots of restaurants, delis, ice cream shops, etc.

Accommodations

Stonybrook Motel & Lodge, 1098 Profile Road, Franconia, NH; (603) 823-5800 or (800) 722-3552; www.stonybrookmotel.com.

Gale River Motel & Cottages, 1 Main Street, Franconia, NH; (603) 823-5655 or (800) 255-7989; www.galerivermotel.com.

Franconia Inn, 1300 Easton Road, Franconia, NH; (603) 823-5542 or (800) 473-5299; www.franconiainn.com.

Lost River Valley Campground, 951 Lost River Road (NH 112), North Woodstock, NH; (603) 745-8321 or (800) 370-5678.

Wildwood Campground, administered by Pro Sport, Inc., concessionaire for the White Mountain National Forest. (603) 726-7737 or

(888)-CAMPS NH; www.campsnh.com /wildwood.htm.

Bike Shops

Rhino Bike Works, 1 Foster Street, Plymouth, NH; (603) 536-3919.
Littleton Bike Shop, 87 Main Street, Littleton, NH; (603) 444-3437; www.littletonbike.com.

Franconia Sports Shop, 334 Main Street, Franconia, NH; (603) 823-5241; www.franconia sports.com.

Map

DeLorme: New Hampshire Atlas & Gazetteer: Page 43.

25 Lancaster/Connecticut River Cruise

The Connecticut River is the centerpiece of this two-state ride. There will be almost constant views of the river and the hills beyond. This is an unusually flat route—an easy pedal with magnificent scenery. It could be shortened to a 23-mile ramble (a particularly nice ride for beginning cyclists) by turning right at 16.7 miles, crossing the covered bridge, and returning north to Lancaster on New Hampshire Highway 135. To capture the best light, photographers will want to plan this trip for early morning or late afternoon and evening, shooting from the New Hampshire side in the morning and from Vermont in the afternoon.

Start: Public parking lot next to the Great North Woods Welcome Center on the south side of Main Street (U.S. Highway 2) in the center of Lancaster. The Welcome Center is across the street from the high school and next to the Lancaster Motor Inn.
Length: 35.4 miles.
Terrain: Flat, with a few minor hills.

Traffic and hazards: Significant traffic in Lancaster: Walk bikes on the sidewalk during busy times of day. U.S. Highways 2 and 3 are major roads, with a lot of truck traffic, including logging trucks. There is an adequate shoulder and good visibility on the short stretch of US 2 in Vermont. US 3 in New Hampshire has very wide shoulders for most of the distance between the Guildhall bridge and Lancaster.

Getting there: From Littleton (exit 41 off Interstate 93), take New Hampshire Highway 116 north to Whitefield and the intersection with US 3. Proceed on US 3 north to Lancaster. US 3 joins US 2 on the outskirts of Lancaster. The Welcome Center parking area is on the south side of US 2/3 in the center of town.

The turn onto scenic NH 135 South is just 0.1 mile from the parking area, so don't be discouraged by traffic in bustling downtown Lancaster. There is a short climb as you start south on NH 135, then it's clear sailing next to the river on a delightfully flat and surprisingly quiet road—for many miles. Watch for waterfowl (herons, ducks, geese). If you're lucky, you might spot an osprey fishing.

An early photo stop will probably be the Mount Orne Covered Bridge, at 5.2 miles. At 11.3 miles there's another interesting photo angle as the route crosses the Connecticut, from Dalton, New Hampshire, to Gilman, Vermont.

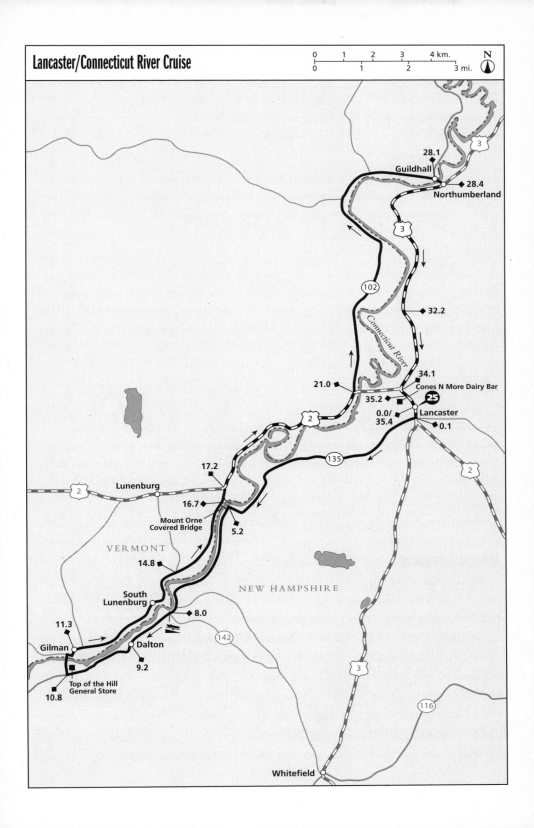

Lancaster/Connecticut River Cruise

0   1   2   3   4 km.
0   1   2   3 mi.

N

28.1
Guildhall
28.4
Northumberland
3
102
32.2
34.1
21.0
Cones N More Dairy Bar
35.2
25
0.0/
35.4
Lancaster
0.1
2
135
17.2
Lunenburg
2
16.7
Mount Orne
Covered Bridge
5.2
VERMONT
14.8
South
Lunenburg
NEW HAMPSHIRE
8.0
11.3
142
Gilman
Dalton
Top of the Hill
General Store
9.2
10.8
3
116
Whitefield

Connecticut River

As you begin heading north along the Vermont side, you'll pass the Dirigo Paper Company, one of the area's largest employers. Logging is an important business in the Great North Woods, and many of those logs are turned into paper. Before the days of modern logging rigs and interstate highways, logs were floated down the Connecticut River. Old photos show enormous log jams, with lumberjacks jumping from one floating log to another.

Just north of Gilman, cross the track of the Maine Central railroad. The track will remain between the road and the river for about 3 miles. The west side of the Connecticut River is just as lovely as the east, with gentle hills, scarce traffic, and river views that are a photographer's delight. The approach to the Mount Orne Covered Bridge is an opportunity for some real calendar shots. If a shorter ride (the 23-mile ramble) is planned, turn right and cross the covered bridge here.

The junction with US 2 means heavier traffic for the next 3.8 miles. Views are still great, but stay focused on the road. Leave US 2 at 21.0 miles—noticing the marker that explains US 2's significance in northern New England history—and return to serene pedaling on Vermont Highway 102. VT 102 is a popular biking destination. Locals from both Vermont and New Hampshire have fond memories of family cycling trips here. It's a perfect place to introduce kids to the joys of road biking.

In Guildhall the road forks. VT 102 swings left, and this route bears right over the bridge and back into New Hampshire. Guildhall is worth at least a short stop: no general store, but some interesting architecture. The Essex County Court House is on the left, and be sure to notice the stained-glass windows in the library, on the left just before the bridge.

US 3 is a scenic but busy road, with an unfortunate number of trucks. However, the shoulder is at least adequate (3 to 4 feet) for the first couple of miles, then more than adequate (5 to 7 feet) for the rest of the distance back to the junction with US 2 in Lancaster. Get off the bike at the junction of US 3 and US 2, and cross carefully. US 2 has wide shoulders here, but they're occasionally used for parking. A stop at the Cones N More Dairy Bar on the right makes a satisfying end for the ride.

Miles and Directions

0.0 Turn right (southeast) out of the Welcome Center parking area onto Main Street (US 2/3).

0.1 Turn right off Main Street onto NH 135 South.

5.2 Mount Orne Covered Bridge straight ahead. Bear left, continuing south on NH 135.

8.0 New Hampshire Highway 142 to left. Continue straight on NH 135 South. Public boat launch, small beach are on the right.

9.2 Town of Dalton. No general store here.

10.8 Top of the Hill General Store on right. Turn right (northwest) off NH 135 onto Gilman Road, following signs for Gilman, Vermont.

11.2 Cross Connecticut River and enter Gilman, Vermont.

11.3 Turn right onto River Road (unmarked here as of this writing), heading northeast.

14.8   South Lunenburg Road is to the left. Continue straight (north) on River Road.

16.7   Mount Orne Covered Bridge is to the right. Continue straight (north) on River Road. (This is where you'll turn right and cross the bridge if the shorter, 23-mile ramble is planned.)

17.2   Junction with US 2. Turn right onto US 2 East.

21.0   US 2 bears right, toward a bridge over the Connecticut River. Turn left off US 2 onto VT 102 North.

28.1   Guildhall, Vermont. Turn right (east) off VT 102, following signs for US 3 and Northumberland, New Hampshire.

28.3   Cross bridge over Connecticut River.

28.4   Turn right onto US 3 South.

32.2   Railroad tracks cross road at oblique angle. Use extreme caution.

34.1   Intersection with US 2. Turn left onto US 2 East, heading toward Lancaster.

35.2   Cones N More Dairy Bar is on the right.

35.4   Return to Welcome Center parking area.

Local Information

Northern Gateway Chamber of Commerce, 25 Main Street, Lancaster, NH; (603) 788-2530 or (877) 788-2530; www.northerngateway chamber.org. This chamber of commerce covers a number of towns north of Lancaster.

Great North Woods Welcome Center, 25 Park Street, Lancaster, NH; (603) 788-3212. Lancaster prides itself on being a gateway to the "Great North Woods." Friendly staff provides maps, brochures, and answers to your questions. And there's a public restroom.

Local Events/Attractions

Lancaster Fair, US 3, Lancaster, NH; (603) 788-4531; www.lancasterfair.com. Labor Day weekend. Agricultural exhibits and competitions, music, a large midway, and more. Fairgrounds are located on US 3, 1 mile north of the junction of US 2 and US 3.

Weeks State Park, US 3, Lancaster, NH; (603) 788-4004; www.nhstateparks.com/wingate .html. On the grounds of the John Wingate Weeks Estate. Includes buildings, fieldstone fire tower, picnic grounds, hiking.

Food

Top of the Hill General Store, 395 Dalton Road, Dalton, NH; (603) 837-9153.

Cones N More Dairy Bar, 176 Main Street, Lancaster, NH; (603) 788-2154. Just west of the Welcome Center. Lancaster is a busy commercial center, with a good assortment of restaurants, convenience stores, and fast food.

Accommodations

Lancaster Motor Inn, 112 Main Street, Lancaster, NH; (603) 788-4921 or (800) 834-3244; www.lancastermotorinn.com.

Bike Shops

Tobin's Bicycle, 129 Main Street, Lancaster, NH; (603) 788-3144.

Littleton Bike Shop, 87 Main Street, Littleton, NH; (603) 444-3437; www.littletonbike.com.

East Burke Sports, 439 Vermont Highway 114, P.O. Box 189, East Burke, VT 05832; (802) 626-3215.

Map

DeLorme: New Hampshire Atlas & Gazetteer: Page 47.

26 Dixville Notch Classic

It's an ambitious ride, but not as difficult as it may appear. You'll cross the White Mountains twice, but the crossings are much gentler than crossings to the south. And there are long stretches of relatively flat pedaling along the Androscoggin and Connecticut Rivers. Scenery is magnificent, with moose sightings likely. The ride is recommended as a two-day trip, with an overnight in Errol. Serious riders could do it in a day but would have to forego the many stops for wildlife and scenery.

Start: The large parking area next to Emerson Outdoor Outfitters, on U.S. Highway 3 in Groveton. They're happy to have cars left overnight but would like to be notified so as to avoid worry over missing adventurers at the end of the day.
Length: 91.1 miles.
Terrain: Generally moderate, with one short, steep climb over Dixville Notch.

Traffic and hazards: Logging is probably the most important industry in the North Woods, so there are logging trucks. Sections of New Hampshire Highway 26 have minimal shoulder and significant numbers of these trucks. Exercise extra caution here, especially between the top of Dixville Notch and Colebrook.

Getting there: From the south, take Interstate 93 in New Hampshire north to Littleton, then New Hampshire Highway 116 and US 3 north to Lancaster, then US 3 north to Groveton. Alternatively, take Interstate 91 in Vermont north to St. Johnsbury, then U.S. Highway 2 east to Lancaster, and US 3 north to Groveton. Proceed through Groveton and continue north on US 3. Emerson Outdoor Oufitters is on the left, about 0.8 mile north of the intersection of US 3 and New Hampshire Highway 110.

NH 110 east of Groveton (also called Stark Highway) is a designated "Scenic and Cultural Byway." It has good shoulders, very moderate grade, and stunning scenery. The railroad tracks on the map are a clue that this is a relatively painless way to cross the Whites. Trains aren't good climbers, so builders of the railroad that parallels NH 110 had to find the easiest way to cross the mountains. Sights to enjoy along the way include the Ammonoosuc River north of the road, rocky peaks in the distance, and the little village of Stark at about 7.5 miles. A couple of miles east of Stark, on the right, notice the historical marker. There's nothing but forest here now, but in the 1940s this was the site of a World War II prisoner of war camp. A few years ago, local newspapers featured a story about the reunion that was held in the area, where friendships between former German prisoners and their American guards were remembered and renewed.

Don't miss the left turn off NH 110 onto New Hampshire Highway 110A at 14.5 miles. There is a general store on NH 110, just beyond (and within sight of) the turn onto NH 110A—the last chance for refueling for the next 21 miles. NH 110A doesn't have a shoulder, but traffic will be reduced. Cedar Pond, at 16.3 miles,

Dixville Notch Classic

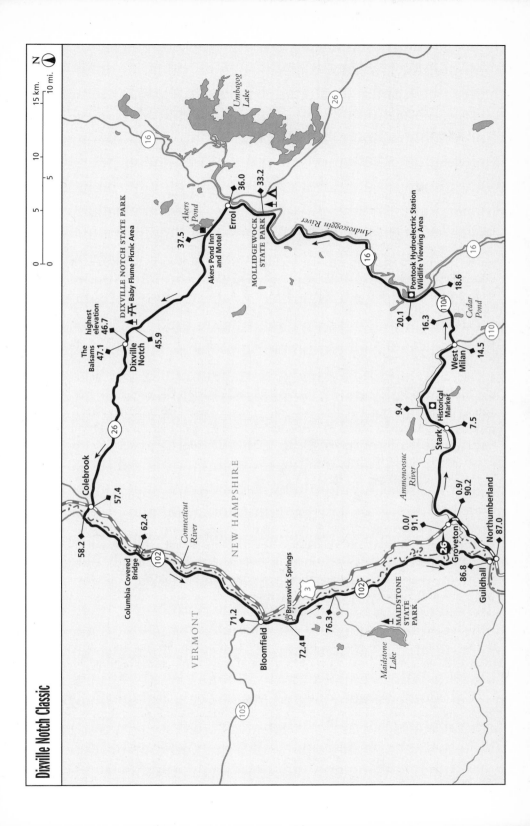

has a nice little campground and a public boat launch. Then it's a short distance to the end of NH 110A and the turn onto New Hampshire Highway 16.

NH 16 hugs the bank of the Androscoggin River, a fast-moving stream that's a favorite of canoe and kayak paddlers. It's also the destination for moose watching tours from points south. You'll see churned-up muddy areas on both sides of the road, where moose have been browsing. Moose sightings are most likely in the morning and evening, but possible any time of day. I've pedaled this section of NH 16 twice and spotted moose both times. There are many pull-offs and wildlife viewing areas. The Pontook Hydroelectric Station, at 20.1 miles (picnic area, restrooms, boat launch), is a good place to watch ospreys fishing. If you stop and see the sights along NH 16, this 17.4 miles—even though it's smooth sailing—can take quite awhile.

The town of Errol has a real North Woods frontier feel. Tourism here means moose hunting, kayaking, and snowmobiling. An outdoors mentality prevails, and bikers fit in nicely. If a two-day trip is planned, Errol is the likely overnight stop. There are several campgrounds and motels. The Akers Pond Inn and Motel, just west of Errol on NH 26, is recommended (see below).

Pedaling over Dixville Notch is not as difficult as it sounds or might appear on the map. (Hint: One full water bottle will be enough, as there's a refill location just over the top.) NH 26 actually has a very moderate uphill grade for all but the last 1.5 miles of ascent. The last mile is steep, but it could be worse. The Baby Flume picnic area on the right at about 45 miles is a good rest stop before that final mile. As you reach the crest and start downhill on the western side, The Balsams Hotel incongruously appears, a lavish resort nestled in the north woods wilderness. During the nineteenth and early twentieth centuries, the White Mountains were dotted with grand hotels. The Balsams is one of only a few that remain. To make this trip an upscale event, consider staying at The Balsams instead of in Errol. But be prepared for upscale rates.

To fill water bottles, make a right at the entrance to The Balsams and proceed less than 0.1 mile to the "Cold Spring" on the right.

If you've been trying to remember why Dixville Notch sounds familiar, think presidential elections. The tiny hamlet of Dixville is that place in New Hampshire where the whole handful of registered voters stay up past midnight on Monday in order to cast their ballots during the first minutes of election day on Tuesday. This all takes place in the "ballot room" at The Balsams.

From The Balsams, NH 26 descends to Colebrook. The wide shoulder continues just a short distance past The Balsams, then vanishes. In terms of traffic, this is the most difficult section of the trip. Stay focused, stay right, and give those logging trucks all the respect they deserve.

In Colebrook the route crosses the Connecticut River into Vermont. It would be possible to finish the loop by heading south on the New Hampshire side of the Connecticut River—on US 3—to Groveton. US 3 generally has a wide shoulder, but it's heavily traveled. Vermont Highway 102, on the Vermont side, carries much less traffic and is unanimously preferred by local cyclists. In fact, it's hard to imagine almost 30 miles of road that's better biking than this.

DeBanville's General Store in Bloomfield, Vermont, at 71.2 miles, is a good rest stop. Then, just a little over a mile south of Bloomfield, on the left and across the road from the Brunswick Town Offices, is a dirt path that leads to Brunswick Springs. If time permits, it's worth the short hike. (Bikes must be left at the road.) The springs are mineral rich and leave colorful deposits where they flow from the riverbank into the Connecticut River. But their main claim to fame is the curse that is said to have been placed on them by an Abenaki shaman. You'll notice the remains of at least one early-twentieth-century spa that burned—the fate decreed for any for-profit use of the springs. You'll also notice the tokens left by contemporary Abenakis, who still consider this a holy spot. See Joe Citro's *Green Mountain Ghosts, Ghouls & Unsolved Mysteries* for further details.

South of Brunswick, VT 102 is slightly inland from the river, but it offers splendid views of Connecticut River Valley farmlands and the New Hampshire mountains beyond. Traffic continues to be sparse until you cross the river again and join US 3. US 3 has a wide shoulder here, and it's a quick and easy return to the parking area in Groveton.

Miles and Directions

0.0   Parking area at Emerson Outdoor Outfitters. Turn right out of parking area onto US 3 South.

0.8   Turn left off US 3 to cross the pedestrian/cyclist covered bridge, just before the intersection with NH 110.

0.9   End covered bridge crossing and junction with NH 110. Turn left onto NH 110 East.

7.5   Village of Stark.

9.4   Historical marker at site of former prisoner of war camp.

14.5   Turn left off NH 110 onto NH 110A, heading east.

16.3   Cedar Pond. Campground and boat launch.

18.6   Junction with NH 16. Turn left onto NH 16 North.

20.1   Pontook Hydroelectric Station wildlife viewing, picnic, and boat launch area.

33.2   Mollidgewock State Park and Campground on right.

36.0   At the intersection of NH 16 and NH 26 in Errol, turn left onto NH 26 West.

37.5   Akers Pond Inn and Motel on right.

45.9   Dixville Notch State Park. Baby Flume picnic area to right.

46.7   Highest elevation.

47.1   Entrance to The Balsams on right. **Option:** Stop here for "Cold Spring" water refill.

57.4   At the intersection with US 3 in Colebrook, turn right onto US 3 North.

57.5   Turn left off US 3 onto Bridge Street.

58.2   After crossing the Connecticut River, turn left onto VT 102 South.

62.4   Columbia Covered Bridge on left.

71.2 Four-way intersection in Bloomfield. DeBanville's General Store is on southwest corner of intersection. Continue straight on VT 102 South.

72.4 Brunswick Town Offices on right. Dirt path to Brunswick Springs on left (unmarked). Continue straight on VT 102 South.

76.3 Road to Maidstone State Park on right. Continue straight on VT 102 South.

86.8 Town of Guildhall. Turn left (east) off VT 102, following signs to US 3 and to Northumberland, New Hampshire.

87.0 Immediately after crossing the Connecticut River, turn left onto Old Village Road, heading north.

87.8 At junction with US 3, turn left onto US 3 North.

90.2 At junction with NH 110, bear left, staying on US 3 North.

90.5 Stay on Truck Route US 3 North through Groveton.

91.1 Return to parking area at Emerson Outdoor Outfitters.

Local Information

Northern Gateway Chamber of Commerce, 25 Main Street, Lancaster, NH; (603) 788-2530 or (877) 788-2530; www.northerngateway chamber.org. This chamber of commerce covers a number of towns north of Lancaster.

North Country Chamber of Commerce, P.O. Box 1, Colebrook, NH 03576; (603) 237-8939 or (800) 689-8939; www.northcountrychamber.org.

Local Events/Attractions

Annual Moose Festival, sponsored by the North Country Chamber of Commerce. Held in late August with events in Colebrook. Includes street fair, moose stew cook-off, moose calling contest, entertainment, sidewalk sales, etc.

Umbagog Wildlife Festival, sponsored by the Lake Umbagog National Wildlife Refuge, the town of Errol, and the Umbagog Chamber of Commerce. Kids' games, canoe tours, edible plant walk, loon calling contest, and more. Held in early August. Visit www.fws.gov /northeast/lakeumbagog/events.htm.

Food

Northern Exposure Restaurant and Black Bear Pub, 12 Main Street, Errol, NH; (603) 482-3468. Elk burgers, homemade donuts.

Errol 'Cream Barrel and Chuck Wagon, 39 Colebrook Road (NH 26), Errol, NH; (603) 482-3258. Just west of the junction of NH 16 and NH 26 in Errol. A *Yankee Magazine Travel Guide* editor's pick. Seafood, barbecue chicken dinners, Joe's famous spaghetti sauce, homemade ice cream.

Wilderness Restaurant, 181 Main Street, Colebrook, NH; (603) 237-8779. Just south of the junction of NH 26 and US 3.

DeBanville's General Store, 47 VT 105, Bloomfield, VT 05905; (802) 962-3311. The usual general store supplies, deli sandwiches, and pastries. Inside and outdoor seating, restroom.

Accommodations

Akers Pond Inn & Motel, 820 Colebrook Road (NH 26), Errol, NH; (603) 482-3471; www.akerspondinn.com. Located 1.5 miles west of Errol, on the right (just after the "Errol International Airport" on the left). They welcome bikers and invite use of their clothesline for hanging out jerseys and shorts. They also have lake access and a canoe, and they provide a continental breakfast with enough calories to get you over the notch.

The Balsams Grand Resort Hotel, 100 Cold Spring Road, Dixville Notch, NH; (800) 255-0600 (in New Hampshire, 800-255-0800); www.thebalsams.com.

Clear Stream Natural Campground, off NH 26, 0.5 mile west of Errol, P.O. Box 131 Errol, NH 03579; (603) 482-3737.

Mollidgewock State Park and Campground, on the Androscoggin, off NH 16 about 2.8 miles south of Errol, (603) 482-3373; www.nhstateparks.org.

The North Country Chamber of Commerce
(www.northcountrychamber.org) provides a
lengthy list of lodging possibilities.

East Burke Sports, 439 Vermont Highway 114,
P.O. Box 189, East Burke, VT 05832; (802)
626-3215.

Bike Shops

Tobin's Bicycle, 129 Main Street, Lancaster,
NH; (603) 788-3144.
Littleton Bike Shop, 87 Main Street, Littleton,
NH; (603) 444-3437; www.littletonbike.com.

Map

DeLorme: New Hampshire Atlas & Gazetteer:
Pages 46, 47, 48, 50, 51.

27 Connecticut Lakes Challenge

This is the Great North Woods: A moose sighting isn't guaranteed, but it's likely. The
route takes you upstream along five lakes to the headwaters of the Connecticut River
and the Canadian border, then back. Ordinarily, out-and-back routes aren't as much
fun as loops, but this is an exception. Beyond the first few miles, there won't be any
traffic (or services), and scenery is incredible. Most cyclists will do it in a day, but the
campground about 4 miles south of the border could serve as a midpoint for a
leisurely two-day excursion.

Start: The boat launch off U.S. Highway 3, on
Lake Francis, about 1.1 miles north of Pitts-
burg. Plenty of parking.
Length: 44.6 miles.
Terrain: Hilly, with a net increase in elevation
of about 1,000 feet between Pittsburg and the
Canadian border.

Traffic and hazards: Light traffic in the vicinity
of Pittsburg. Minimal traffic farther north.
Watch for moose in the road, and don't be
fooled by their docile appearance. Take pictures from a distance.

Getting there: Take US 3 north from Lancaster about 50 miles to Pittsburg. Continue north on
US 3 from Pittsburg 1.1 miles to the boat launch on Lake Francis.

This is New Hampshire's last frontier, and it still has the feel of northern wilderness.
Hunting, fishing, and snowmobiling are the main tourist attractions. (Room amenities at the local motel probably include a gun rack.) But cyclists fit in the mix quite
nicely. A bike affords the perfect pace for admiring the river, the lakes, and the natural beauty of the Great North Woods. After pedaling around lakes in southern New
Hampshire, where cottages and homes seem to occupy every available piece of lakeside real estate, it's refreshing to find large bodies of water surrounded by nothing
but mountains and trees and wildlife.

It isn't surprising to learn that much of this remote corner of New England was
once an independent republic: the Republic of Indian Stream. An historical marker
in Pittsburg explains that a territorial dispute between the United States and Canada

Moose sighting on the Connecticut Lakes Challenge

prompted settlers to declare autonomy. The area became part of Pittsburg in 1836 and was officially declared U.S. territory in 1842.

At about 4.2 miles (and again at 38 miles), you'll pass through a hamlet with the delightful name of Happy Corner. One explanation credits the name to an elderly gentleman who lived on the corner and enjoyed entertaining friends with his Victrola. Evidently, his taste in music was upbeat. Turn right here for a very short side-trip to the Happy Corner Covered Bridge, over Perry Stream.

The dam at the southern end of First Connecticut Lake is at 5.4 miles, with a boat launch and road to a picnic area just beyond. The boat launch and beach on Second Connecticut Lake, farther ahead, may be the best spot for a swim. To get to the beach, turn right off US 3 at 12.8 miles onto a dirt road, following signs for the boat launch. The beach is about a half mile off US 3. During midweek, even in July and August, you're likely to be alone on the lake.

Deer Mountain Campground is to the left at 16.3 miles. This would be a good overnight stop for those who want to combine some hiking with biking, and turn the trip into a two-day adventure.

The boat launch and beach on Third Connecticut Lake is on the left at 20.0 miles. In practical terms, this is the headwater of the Connecticut River. Technically, the headwater is the Fourth Connecticut Lake (really a very tiny pond) about a mile to the northwest. But no road—not even a dirt one—goes there. If you wanted to paddle a canoe the entire length of the Connecticut River, from its beginning to its end in Long Island Sound, the Third Connecticut Lake is where you'd start.

The Canadian border, and the highest elevation of the trip, is about a mile farther. The route turns around at the border, but some cyclists may want to cross into Canada and explore a bit of rural Quebec. This is a rather sleepy border crossing. They're very professional, but they don't get a lot of business. As of spring 2008, a government issued photo I.D. (driver's license) and proof of citizenship (birth certificate), or a green card, is sufficient for a North American land or sea border crossing. However, beginning in June 2009 a passport, "passport card," or green card will be required (unless the law is changed).

The return trip will be easier. There are those same hills, but with a net loss of 1,000 feet in elevation. Instead of returning the whole way on US 3, the route makes a short loop onto Back Lake Road and returns to the parking area through the village of Pittsburg.

Miles and Directions

0.0   Turn right out of boat launch parking area onto US 3 North.

4.2   Hamlet of Happy Corner. Continue straight on US 3 North. **Option:** Take 0.1-mile side trip to the right (South) to the Happy Corner Covered Bridge.

5.4   Dam at southern end of First Connecticut Lake.

9.1   Moose Alley Cones is on the right.

12.8   Road to boat launch and beach on Second Connecticut Lake, to right.

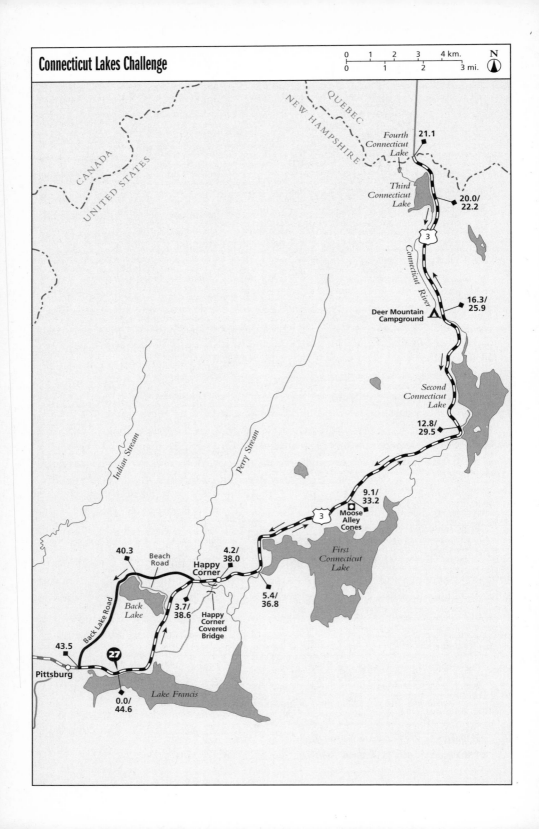

Connecticut Lakes Challenge

0   1   2   3   4 km.
0   1   2   3 mi.

N

QUEBEC
NEW HAMPSHIRE
CANADA
UNITED STATES

Fourth
Connecticut
Lake   **21.1**

Third
Connecticut
Lake   **20.0/
                      22.2**

3

Connecticut River

Deer Mountain
Campground   **16.3/
                      25.9**

Second
Connecticut
Lake

**12.8/
29.5**

Indian Stream

Perry Stream

**9.1/
33.2**

3   Moose
    Alley
    Cones

First
Connecticut
Lake

40.3   Beach
           Road   **4.2/
                       38.0**
Happy
Corner   **5.4/
                       36.8**

Back Lake Road

Back
Lake   **3.7/
            38.6**
            Happy
            Corner
            Covered
            Bridge

43.5

27

Pittsburg

**0.0/
44.6**   Lake Francis

16.3	Deer Mountain Campground is to the left.
20.0	Boat launch and beach on Third Connecticut Lake, to left. Continue straight on US 3.
21.1	U.S./Canadian border. Turn around.
22.2	Third Connecticut Lake is to the right.
25.9	Deer Mountain Campground is to the right.
29.5	Road to beach on Second Connecticut Lake, to left.
33.2	Moose Alley Cones is on the left.
36.8	Dam at southern end of First Connecticut Lake.
38.0	Hamlet of Happy Corner.
38.6	Turn right (west) off US 3 onto Back Lake Road.
40.3	Beach Road to left. Continue straight on Back Lake Road.
43.5	Junction with US 3. Pittsburg Trading Post (general store) is across the road. Turn left onto US 3 North.
44.6	Parking area at Lake Francis.

Local Information

Northern Gateway Chamber of Commerce, 25 Main Street, Lancaster, NH; (603) 788-2530 or (877) 788-2530; www.northerngateway chamber.org. This chamber of commerce covers a number of towns north of Lancaster.

North Country Chamber of Commerce, P.O. Box 1, Colebrook, NH 03576; (603) 237-8939 or (800) 689-8939; www.northcountry chamber.org.

Information booth on the green next to the Methodist Church in Pittsburg.

Local Events/Attractions

North Country Moose Festival. Organized by the North Country Chamber of Commerce, P.O. Box 1, Colebrook, NH 03576; (603) 237-8939 or (800) 698-8939; www.northcountry chamber.org/moosefestival.html. August events in Canaan, VT, Pittsburg, NH, and Colebrook, NH. Historical tours, exhibits, vendors, music, mooseburger BBQ, and more.

Food

Pittsburg Trading Post, 1624 Main Street (US 3), Pittsburg, NH; (603) 538-6533.
Good place to stock up, as there may not be other opportunities.

Moose Alley Cones, US 3, First Connecticut Lake, Pittsburg, NH; (603) 538-6380. Next to Partridge Cabins, about 10 miles north of Pittsburg, on US 3. They serve Northland Ice Cream, made in Berlin, New Hampshire. Open May through September.

Accommodations

Spruce Cone Cabins, 2067 North Main Street (US 3), Pittsburg, NH; (603) 538-6572 or (800) 538-6361. Rustic cabins, good views of Lake Francis.

Deer Mountain Campground, 5309 North Main Street (US 3), Pittsburg, NH; (603) 538-6965. Reservations: (603) 271-3628.

Lake Francis State Park Campground, off US 3, Pittsburg, NH; (603) 538-6965. Reservations: (603) 271-3628.

Go to www.northcountrychamber.org for additional lodging options.

Bike Shops

Tobin's Bicycle, 129 Main Street, Lancaster, NH; (603) 788-3144.

Littleton Bike Shop, 87 Main Street, Littleton, NH; (603) 444-3437; www.littletonbike.com.

East Burke Sports, 439 Vermont Highway 114, P.O. Box 189, East Burke, VT 05832; (802) 626-3215.

Map

DeLorme: New Hampshire Atlas & Gazetteer: Pages 52, 53.

Maine

Maine is a big state, with vast areas of wilderness and superb opportunities for long-distance biking. The rides included in this section just scratch the surface of the possibilities. Most rides included here are in coastal areas that will be relatively easy destinations for visitors. Once bikers get a taste of Maine, however, it's almost certain they'll want more. Be sure to get hold of the Maine Department of Transportation's *Explore Maine by Bike: 25 Loop Bicycle Tours*,

The Park Loop Road on Mount Desert Island

available from the Maine Department of Transportation or online at www.explore maine.org/bike/bike_tours.html. They've done a fine job of mapping out twenty-five long routes, generally with two or three shorter alternatives. A couple of the following rides are variations on their routes.

It's estimated that, as the crow flies, Maine has only about 228 miles of coastline. If you measured the shoreline along all those peninsulas, bays, and coves, however, you'd get about 3,500 miles. That's a lot of coast—about the same as California. It's no surprise that the ocean is at the heart of much that's unique about Maine and her people. Maine seems to have a larger than average share of talented authors (many of them women) who have described their lives and passion for the sea in ways that capture imaginations far beyond Maine's borders. Think of Sarah Orne Jewett, Rachel Carson, and recently, Linda Greenlaw. They've let us all—even the most dedicated city dwellers— know what it means to be from "downeast."

Special notes about biking in Maine: (1) Traffic in coastal areas will be heavy in summer. Although U.S. Highway 1 is particularly congested, many sections of it have very wide shoulders, often making it feasible for use as a connector on a loop. (2) Fog rolls in quickly in coastal areas. In a matter of minutes, you can become invisible to drivers. Very bright reflective clothing is essential in foggy conditions. Even if you add a light for better safety, assume that drivers cannot see you. Be ready to escape onto a shoulder or into a ditch if necessary. (3) Much of the land in northern Maine is owned or leased by paper companies. For bikers that means lots of big logging trucks. Don't argue with them. (4) Biking, especially long-distance biking, consumes incredible numbers of calories. This is your opportunity to enjoy—in quantities no auto-bound visitor can possibly imagine—the foods for which Maine is famous: chowders, lobster, beans, blueberry pies. You're going to love them all.

28 Southwest Coastal Challenge

This is one of the rides recommended by the Maine Department of Transportation, with a few modifications. Scenery is fantastic, and it's easy, flat pedaling. I last pedaled the route on a Saturday in mid-October. Many summer residences, and some shops, were closed for the season. It was a sparkling warm day when fall colors were at their peak, and traffic was quite tolerable. That won't be the case in July or August. Plan this one for spring or fall.

Start: Wells National Estuarine Research Reserve at Laudholm Farm. They have a large parking area. A gatehouse at the entrance requests registration and a donation of $2 per adult. That's a bargain for parking, and the buildings and trails are interesting places to visit before or after the ride. The entrance to the parking area is gated at sunset, so plan accordingly.

Length: 44.0 miles.

Terrain: Flat to gently rolling.

Traffic and hazards: The route uses side roads and sections of main roads with mostly adequate shoulders. Nevertheless, traffic will be heavy in summer. Be visible and pedal defensively. Bring a lock, as you'll almost certainly want to make beach stops.

Getting there: Take exit 19 off Interstate 95, getting on Maine Highway 9/109 South. Proceed about 1.4 miles to a junction with U.S. Highway 1 in Wells. Turn left onto US 1 East and continue east about 1.5 miles. Turn right off US 1 onto Laudholm Farm Road. Continue on Laudholm Farm Road for about 0.4 mile, then bear left off Laudholm Farm Road onto Skinner Mill Road. The entrance to the Wells National Estuarine Research Reserve is almost immediately on the right.

A bike is the best (some would say the only) way to see the Maine coast. It's an especially good way to visit this area—the southwest coast—where sandy beaches extend for miles and the coastal plain reaches far inland. The southwest coast was the earliest settled and is the most densely populated section of Maine coastline. Except for public beaches and areas of public land designated as the Rachel Carson National Wildlife Refuge, the area is heavily developed. Parking a car to get to a beach can be almost impossible in the summer, and may be tricky other times of year. But on a bike, it's easy.

Official beach stops may include Kennebunk Beach (starts at about 4 miles), Goose Rocks Beach (starts at about 16 miles), and Fortunes Rocks (starts at about 20 miles). And on a bike, spontaneous ocean stops can happen at many locations in between.

The town of Kennebunkport is the best bet for shops, restaurants, and assorted tourist attractions. It's also the most congested section of the ride. The town provides public restrooms at the "hospitality center" on the left, shortly after the turn onto Ocean Avenue. Kennebunkport's biggest claim to fame appears a bit outside of town, at about 8.1 miles, where you'll probably notice cars stopped along the road, cameras aimed at Walker Point. That's the occasional residence of former president

Watching the boats at Cape Porpoise

George Bush Sr. This is as close as you (or any other tourists) are going to get, but it's a clear view of the house and grounds.

The short trip to the end of the peninsula at Cape Porpoise shouldn't be missed. Tourism is the theme and livelihood for most of the southwest Maine coast, but Cape Porpoise is an exception. This is a working fishing harbor. Local fishermen's trucks occupy a big section of the parking lot, and their boats are moored in the harbor. You can walk out on the pier for a close-up look at stacks of lobster traps and assorted fishing gear. There's a restaurant next to the pier (Pier 77), or you may want to pedal the half mile back to the town of Cape Porpoise, where both restaurants boast homemade chowders, pies, and other downeast favorites.

Fortunes Rocks Beach at 20.2 miles is especially beautiful. The road is separated from the beach by huge blocks of granite and a hedge of beach roses. Smell the salt air and the beach roses: It's the essence of the Maine coast.

Just after Fortunes Rocks Beach, at 21.1 miles, come to the intersection with Maine Highway 208. But don't turn north onto ME 208 yet. Head straight east on Milestretch Road toward the village of Biddeford Pool (not to be confused with the town of Biddeford). The "Pool" is the body of water to your left, an unusually well-protected harbor whose only ocean access is a very narrow inlet at the eastern end.

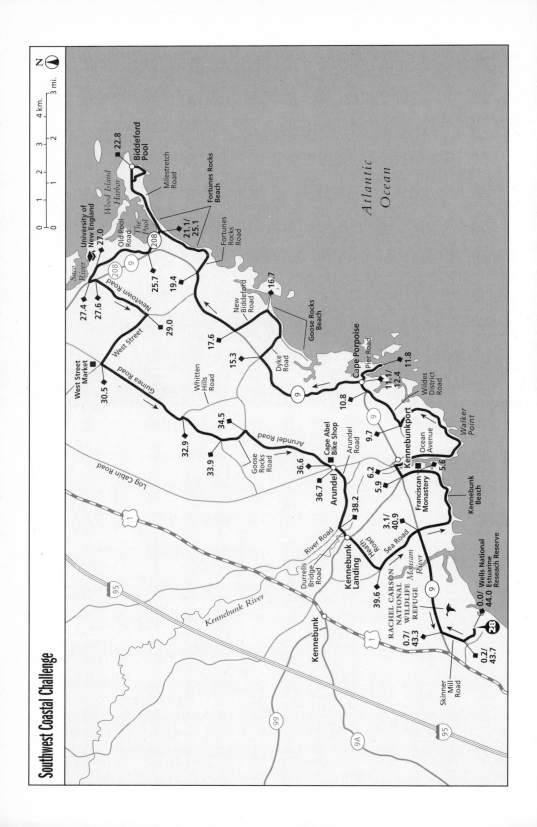

Southwest Coastal Challenge

Don't worry about getting lost in the village of Biddeford Pool; just head east, follow the road close to the water, admire the summer cottages and their amazing vistas, then head back west.

Old Pool Road (the right turn at 25.7 miles) is a quiet, shady, winding road. No ocean views—just homes and forest. The University of New England campus is straight ahead at the turn at 27.0 miles. Nice location! Not surprisingly, they offer programs in marine science and marine biology.

Starting at the University of New England, watch directions carefully, as it's easy to miss a couple of turns. (In particular, watch for the turn at 32.9 miles, where Guinea Road bears right.) This section of the route takes you inland. Farther up the coast, pedaling inland means hills, and even mountains. Not so here. It's lovely flat coastal plain. You're likely to see an assortment of fellow cyclists taking advantage of the opportunity to crank in a high gear.

The Cape Able Bike Shop, at 36.6 miles, signals your arrival in the village of Arundel. If you've read *Arundel,* the novel by Kenneth Roberts, you may need to make a few extra stops to check historical markers, headstones in the cemetery, or pay a visit to the Historical Society (a short distance south on Log Cabin Road). In early spring or late fall, or if you can't resist the challenge of summer coastal traffic, you could elect to continue south from Arundel into Kennebunkport, then return west on ME 9. Sticking to the route on Arundel Road (becomes River Road) then crossing the river on Durrells Bridge Road is a lot more peaceful. Sea Road, an official bike route, brings you back to ME 9. Turn west onto ME 9 and head back to the research center parking area.

Miles and Directions

0.0 Exit parking area at Wells National Estuarine Research Reserve, returning north on the reserve entrance road.

0.2 Junction with Skinner Mill Road. Turn right onto Skinner Mill Road, heading east.

0.7 Junction with ME 9. Turn right onto ME 9 East.

0.8 Rachel Carson National Wildlife Refuge is on the right.

3.1 Traffic light at a four-way intersection. Turn right (south) off ME 9 onto Sea Road, following signs for Kennebunk Beach.

5.6 Entrance to Franciscan Monastery Guest House is on the right.

5.9 Traffic light at four-way intersection. Turn right onto ME 9 East.

6.1 Cross Kennebunk River.

6.2 Turn right (south) off ME 9 onto Ocean Avenue.

8.1 Views of Walker Point are on the right.

9.7 Turn right onto Wildes District Road, heading east.

10.8 Junction with ME 9. Turn right onto ME 9 East.

11.1 At the four-way intersection in the village of Cape Porpoise, continue straight onto Pier Road.

11.8   Pier on end of Cape Porpoise Peninsula. Turn around and return north on Pier Road.

12.4   At the four-way intersection in the village of Cape Porpoise, turn right onto ME 9 East.

15.3   At the four-way intersection, turn right (south) off ME 9 onto Dyke Road.

16.0   Bear left onto Kings Highway.

16.7   Stop sign at a four-way intersection. Turn left (north) onto New Biddeford Road.

17.6   Junction with ME 9. Turn right onto ME 9 East.

19.4   Turn right (south) off ME 9 onto Fortunes Rocks Road.

21.1   Intersection with ME 208. Continue straight (east) onto Milestretch Road.

22.8   End of the peninsula, in village of Biddeford Pool. Road bears right.

23.4   Stop sign. Turn left onto Seventh Street (unmarked here).

23.6   Junction with First Street. Bear left onto First Street, heading west.

23.7   Junction with Milestretch Road (unmarked here). Turn left onto Milestretch Road, heading west.

25.1   Intersection with ME 208. Turn right onto ME 208 North.

25.7   Turn right off ME 208 onto Old Pool Road, heading north. The turn is just before the junction with ME 9.

27.0   Junction at the University of New England campus. Bear left, remaining on Old Pool Road (unmarked here).

27.4   Junction with ME 9/ME 208. Turn left onto ME 9 West/ME 208 South. Sea Star Market is directly opposite.

27.6   Turn right (southwest) off ME 9/ME 208 onto Newtown Road.

29.0   Stop sign. Turn right off Newtown Road onto West Street (unmarked here).

30.5   Stop sign at a four-way intersection. Turn left onto Guinea Road, heading west. The West Street Market is on the corner.

32.9   Bear right, staying on Guinea Road. (Whitten Hills Road continues straight.)

33.9   Junction with Goose Rocks Road (unmarked here). Turn left onto Goose Rocks Road, heading south.

34.5   Turn right (west) off Goose Rocks Road onto Arundel Road.

36.6   Cape Able Bike Shop is on the left.

36.7   Junction with Log Cabin Road (unmarked here). Turn left (south) onto Log Cabin Road and make an immediate right (west) onto Arundel Road, which becomes River Road.

38.2   Stop sign. Turn left (west) off River Road onto Durrells Bridge Road.

38.3   Cross Kennebunk River.

38.5   Junction with Maine Highway 9A. Turn left onto ME 9A South.

38.6   Turn right (west) off ME 9A onto Heath Road.

39.6   Junction with Sea Road (unmarked here). Turn left (south) onto Sea Road.

40.9   At the traffic light at the four-way intersection, turn right onto ME 9 West.

43.3   Turn left (south) off ME 9 onto Skinner Mill Road.

43.7   Turn left off Skinner Mill Road at entrance to Wells National Estuarine Research Reserve.

44.0   Return to parking area.

Local Information

Wells Chamber of Commerce, P.O. Box 356, Wells, ME 04090; (207) 646-2451; www .wellschamber.org.

Kennebunk-Kennebunkport Chamber of Commerce, P.O. Box 740, Kennebunk, ME 04043; (207) 967-0857; www.kennebunk kennebunkportchamber.com.

Local Events/Attractions

Wells National Estuarine Research Reserve at Laudholm Farm, 342 Laudholm Farm Road, Wells, ME; (207) 646-1555; www.wells reserve.org. Features 1,600 acres of preserved forest, beach, and salt marsh. Restored farm buildings house a visitor center and museum. Miles of hiking trails. This place is one of Maine's coastal treasures.

Food

The Maine Diner, 2265 Post Road (US 1), Wells, ME; (207) 646-4441; www.mainediner .com. Great diner food: prize-winning chowders, homemade pies, and more.

Wayfarer Restaurant, 2 Pier Road, Kennebunkport, ME; (207) 967-8961.

Pier 77, 79 Pier Road, Kennebunkport, ME; (207) 967-0123.

The Clam Shack, ME 9, at the Kennebunkport Bridge, Kennebunkport, ME; (207) 967-2560. A local institution.

Accommodations

The Wells and the Kennebunk-Kennebunkport Chambers of Commerce Web sites contain comprehensive listings of lodgings. Motels along US 1 are likely to offer most reasonable rates. Oceanfront accommodations are pricey during summer months, but rates are much lower in spring and fall.

USA Inn, 1017 Post Road (US 1), Wells, ME; (207) 646-9313; www.usainn.com.

Atlantic Motor Inn is directly on the beach and is a good choice for the off-season. P.O. Box 386, Wells Beach, ME 04090; (207) 646-7061; www.atlanticmotorinn.com. Consider an alternative to the usual motel or inn and try the **Guest House** at St. Anthony's Franciscan Monastery, 28 Beach Avenue, Kennebunk, ME; (207) 967-4865; www.francis canguesthouse.com. Open mid-May through late October. Rates are comparatively reasonable, and breakfast is included.

Bike Shop

Cape Able Bike Shop, 83 Arundel Road, Kennebunkport, ME; (207) 967-4382; www.cape ablebikes.com.

Breton's Bike Shop, 879 Post Road (US 1), Wells, ME; (207) 646-4255.

Map

DeLorme: Maine Atlas & Gazetteer: Page 3.

29 Popham Ramble

Although the vast majority of the rides in this book are loops of one sort or another, there were a couple of "out-and-back" rides that begged to be included. The Popham ride is one. This one will be a favorite with beach lovers and historians. Those who just want a short rolling pedal through coastal countryside will be delighted as well.

Start: Parking area at the Center Pond Preserve, on Parker Head Road in Phippsburg.
Length: 15.4 miles.
Terrain: Moderately hilly.
Traffic and hazards: Parker Head Road is nar-row and winding, with no shoulder. Compared with major roads, traffic is light. But local drivers may be moving fast, so pedal defensively. There will be beach traffic on Maine Highway 209 during summer months.

Getting there: From U.S. Highway 1 in Bath, take ME 209 south about 6.7 miles. Turn left off ME 209 onto Parker Head Road, in the town of Phippsburg. Proceed about 0.5 mile on Parker Head Road to the parking area for the Center Pond Preserve. The preserve is on the right, just after a short causeway.

The peninsula south of Bath is home to fascinating historic sites, beautiful beaches, and terrific scenery. Unfortunately, ME 209—the main north-south road—carries heavy traffic during summer months, and its shoulders are spotty. The length of ME 209 can only be recommended for biking during the off-season. It's possible to make a loop around much of the Bath peninsula using secondary roads (several very rough dirt and gravel) on a fat-tire bike, but it's not recommended for road bikes. Fortunately, this short out-and-back ride takes cyclists past some of the peninsula's most impressive sights.

You can't help but notice the cemeteries along Parker Head Road. Within a stretch of just 3 or 4 miles, you'll pass at least six tiny cemeteries. (The first two are at about 0.3 mile—one on each side of the road.) This area was more heavily populated a century or two ago. In fact, an English settlement at Popham predated the Plymouth colony by thirteen years. The settlement was ultimately unsuccessful, but its colonists managed to construct the first large ship built in North America before they abandoned the site.

After the turn onto ME 209, at 4.5 miles, the terrain becomes quite flat and pedaling gets easy. The beach at Popham Beach State Park is a must stop, either on the way out or back. If possible, try to be at the beach at low tide, or a couple of hours on either side, when you can walk out and explore North Fox Island. At low tide, water is about waist deep at the deepest part of the walk. Lifeguards announce when it's safe to head for the island and when it's time to return.

Fort Popham, at the end of the peninsula, is another must stop. There is no visitor center, information booth, or entrance fee: just ruins that visitors are welcome

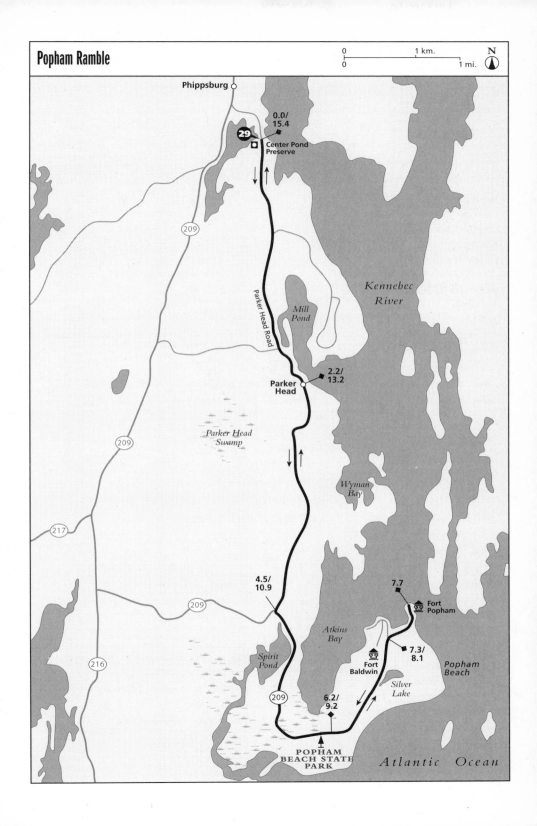

Popham Ramble

0   1 km.
0   1 mi.

N

Phippsburg

29

0.0/
15.4

Center Pond
Preserve

209

Mill
Pond

*Kennebec
River*

Parker Head Road

2.2/
13.2

Parker
Head

*Parker Head
Swamp*

209

*Wyman
Bay*

217

4.5/
10.9

7.7

Fort
Popham

209

*Atkins
Bay*

7.3/
8.1

Fort
Baldwin

*Popham
Beach*

216

*Spirit
Pond*

*Silver
Lake*

209

6.2/
9.2

**POPHAM
BEACH STATE
PARK**

Atlantic Ocean

to explore. Many people are surprised to learn that the fort was built during the Civil War. A Civil War fort in Maine? Yes, indeed. This is the mouth of the Kennebec River. Not too far upstream is the town of Bath, home of Bath Ironworks, where military shipbuilding is still an important industry. Fort Popham was built to protect the Ironworks from Confederate attack. Fort Baldwin—the optional side-trip at 7.3 or 8.1 miles—was also built to protect the Ironworks, but during World War I. Fort Baldwin is a fascinating site, too, and makes an interesting comparison with the Civil War–era fort. Cyclists on road bikes may need to walk the last short stretch of the entrance to Fort Baldwin when the road turns to dirt and becomes quite steep. It's a great view, and you can imagine how improved artillery could do a good job of protecting the river from here.

Return the way you came, perhaps stopping to admire the quaint little village of Parker Head: no stores or tourist attractions, just beautiful views of the river.

Miles and Directions

0.0   Turn right out of parking area at Center Pond Preserve onto Parker Head Road, heading south.

2.2   Village of Parker Head. Very narrow, twisting road. Go slow and stay right.

4.5   Junction with ME 209. Turn left onto ME 209 East.

6.2   Entrance to Popham Beach State Park is on the right. Continue straight on ME 209.

7.3   Fort Baldwin Road is to the left. **Option:** Turn here for the side-trip to Fort Baldwin. Otherwise, continue straight on ME 209.

7.6   Entrance to Fort Popham State Historic Site. Continue straight.

7.7   Ruins of Fort Popham at end of the peninsula. Turn around for return trip.

8.1   Fort Baldwin Road is to the right. **Option:** Turn here for the side-trip to Fort Baldwin. Otherwise, continue straight on ME 209.

9.2   Entrance to Popham Beach State Park on left. Continue straight on ME 209.

10.9   Turn right off ME 209 onto Parker Head Road, heading north.

13.2   Village of Parker Head.

15.4   Return to Center Pond Preserve.

Local Information

Southern Midcoast Maine Chamber of Commerce, 59 Pleasant Street, Brunswick, ME; (207) 725-8797 or (877) 725-8797; www.midcoastmaine.com.

Local Events/Attractions

Fort Popham State Historic Site, 10 Perkins Farm Road, Phippsburg, ME; park season: (207) 389-1335; off-season: (207) 624-6080.

Fort Baldwin, Sabino Hill, Phippsburg, ME. The fort is now part of Fort Popham State Historic Site, 10 Perkins Farm Road, Phippsburg, ME; park season: (207) 389-1335; off-season: (207) 624-6080.

Popham Beach State Park, ME 209, Phippsburg, ME; (207) 389-1335.

Maine Maritime Museum, 243 Washington Street, Bath, ME; (207) 443-1316; www.mainemaritimemuseum.org.

Food

Both of the following are at the end of the peninsula, near the entrance to Fort Popham.
Spinney's Oceanfront Restaurant, 987 Popham Road, Phippsburg, ME; (207) 389-1122.
Percy's Store, 6 Sea Street, Phippsburg, ME; (207) 389-2010.

Accommodations

The Southern Midcoast Maine Chamber of Commerce site has lodging information. Most motels are in the Bath or Brunswick area.
Holiday Inn of Bath, 139 Richardson Street, Bath, ME; (207) 443-9741 or (866) 258-7245.

Hermit Island Campground. Summer address: 6 Hermit Island Road, Phippsburg, ME. Winter address: 42 Front Street, Bath, ME; (207) 443-2101 (same phone year-round); www.hermitisland.com. Open mid-May to mid-October. Tents only, reservations necessary during summer months.

Bike Shop

Bath Cycle and Ski, 115 Main Street (US 1), Woolwich, ME; (207) 442-7002; www.bike man.com.

Map

DeLorme: Maine Atlas & Gazetteer: Page 6.

30 Pemaquid Challenge

One of the beauties of the Pemaquid Peninsula is its width. Unlike many of Maine's coastal peninsulas, it's wide enough to have more than one north–south road. That's good news for cyclists who like to do loops and who prefer not competing with all the traffic in one place. Actually, there are lots of roads on the Pemaquid Peninsula, all leading to fascinating explorations. This would be a good area in which to plan several days of cycling. Thanks to Debbie Robinson, biking companion extraordinaire, for planning and being tour guide on this one.

Start: Boat launch at the north end of Biscay Pond, about 4 miles east of Damariscotta.
Length: 41.3 miles.
Terrain: Flat to rolling hills, with one notable descent and return climb.
Traffic and hazards: This is the Maine coast, and traffic is heavier during summer months.

Shoulders range from adequate to nonexistent. The route is planned to avoid major roads and to take advantage of less-traveled scenic routes. There are two short sections of unpaved road that shouldn't be a problem for road bikes.

Getting there: From U.S. Highway 1 in Newcastle, take Business US 1 through Damariscotta. About 1.3 miles after crossing the Damariscotta River, turn right off Business US 1 onto Biscay Road, heading east. Proceed about 2.8 miles on Biscay Road to the public boat launch and fishing access on the right, at the north end of Biscay Pond.

The ride begins east of Damariscotta at the northern end of Biscay Pond, one of several freshwater ponds on the Pemaquid Peninsula. Biscay and Folger Roads, both quiet, shady back roads, take you south along the eastern shore of the pond toward

Pemaquid Point Lighthouse

Bristol. The first short section of dirt road (about 0.7 mile long) comes shortly after the turn onto Split Rock Road. Road bikes will have to slow down a bit, but traffic will be nearly nonexistent on Split Rock Road. After the turn onto Maine Highway 129 South, watch for an almost immediate right onto Clarks Cove Road and prepare for a plunge to sea level. Enjoy the views of the Damariscotta River at sea level, then downshift for the inevitable return climb.

Be sure to make the right off Maine Highway 130, at 16.0 miles, to Fort William Henry and Pemaquid Beach, the first must-see stops of the trip. The Colonial Pemaquid State Historic Site includes the fort, a visitor center and museum, and a self-guided tour of the remains of a colonial village. This has been a strategic site—and a bone of contention—since the first English fishermen and settlers landed. Several forts were constructed here by the English and destroyed in attacks by the locals: native Wabanaki and Etchemen. The buildings you see today are a partial reconstruction of Fort William Henry, built in 1692 and destroyed in 1696. On a hot day, you'll definitely want to plan a stop at Pemaquid Beach, to the right just south of the fort.

The next must-see stop is the Pemaquid Point Lighthouse, at the southern tip of the peninsula. If you think it looks familiar, you're probably right. It's the lighthouse on the quarter and on countless calendars and posters as well. It's still in use, and they give tours. The small fishermen's museum attached is quintessential Maine and would be a worthwhile destination even without the lighthouse.

Head back north from the lighthouse and make a refueling stop at the C. E. Reilly & Son grocery store in New Harbor. You may want to carry purchases the short distance to the Rachel Carson Salt Pond Preserve, the next must-see stop. Watch for the turn onto Maine Highway 32 North at 24.5 miles. (The only indication is a little street sign with the route number.) ME 32 is particularly lovely, with surprisingly little traffic, even during summer months. The Rachel Carson Salt Pond Preserve is the tidal pool used by Rachel Carson in some of her studies for *The Edge of the Sea*. It's rather an honor to share a picnic spot with the memory of Maine's most famous naturalist and author.

As you're cruising north on ME 32, notice the old stone walls on either side of the road. It's all forest today, with amazingly few signs of human habitation. But the stone walls, and the old cemetery on the right at about 29.1 miles, are reminders that there were fields and farms and even villages here during the eighteenth and nineteenth centuries.

Don't miss the penny candy at the Granite Hall Store, to the right in the village of Round Pond, near the harbor. Well-protected Round Pond Harbor is thought to have been a safe haven for pirates, including Captain Kidd.

At 33.5 miles the route makes a right off ME 32 onto Shore Road, which rejoins ME 32 again in a couple of miles. Shore Road has almost no traffic, more forest, and a fine view of Greenland Cove. For 0.7 mile it is unpaved: good hard-packed dirt that shouldn't be a problem for road bikes. During spring mud season, however, or

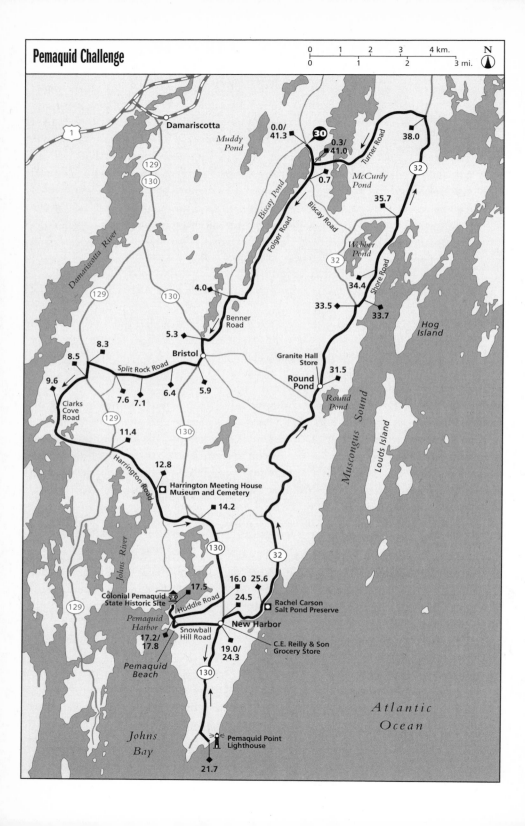

Pemaquid Challenge

0   1   2   3   4 km.
0   1   2   3 mi.

N

Damariscotta

Muddy Pond

0.0/ 41.3

30

0.3/ 41.0

38.0

Turner Road

0.7

McCurdy Pond

35.7

32

Biscay Pond

Folger Road

Biscay Road

Webber Pond

34.4

Shore Road

4.0

Benner Road

33.5

33.7

Hog Island

5.3

Bristol

Granite Hall Store

Split Rock Road

31.5

8.3

8.5

Round Pond

Round Pond

9.6

7.6 7.1

6.4

5.9

Clarks Cove Road

Muscongus Sound

Louds Island

129

11.4

Harrington Road

12.8

Harrington Meeting House
Museum and Cemetery

14.2

130

32

Johns River

16.0 25.6

24.5

Colonial Pemaquid
State Historic Site

17.5

Rachel Carson
Salt Pond Preserve

Huddle Road

Pemaquid Harbor

Snowball Hill Road

New Harbor

C.E. Reilly & Son
Grocery Store

17.2/
17.8

19.0/
24.3

Pemaquid Beach

130

Johns Bay

Atlantic Ocean

Pemaquid Point
Lighthouse

21.7

if you're in a hurry, you could simply continue north on ME 32 instead of taking Shore Road. (Shore Road is actually shorter, but the unpaved part will mean a slower pace.)

If you're lucky, there will be time for a swim in Biscay Pond at the end of the ride.

Miles and Directions

0.0   Boat launch at north end of Biscay Pond. Turn right onto Biscay Road, heading east.

0.3   Turner Road is to the left. Bear right, continuing on Biscay Road.

0.7   Turn right off Biscay Road onto Folger Road, heading south.

4.0   Stop sign at junction with Benner Road. Turn left (south) onto Benner Road, heading toward Bristol.

5.3   At the junction of Benner Road and ME 130 (Bristol Road), turn left onto ME 130 South.

5.9   Turn right (west) off ME 130 onto Split Rock Road.

6.4   Road surface turns to dirt.

7.1   Road surface returns to asphalt but remains very narrow.

7.6   Road forks. Bear right, remaining on Split Rock Road.

8.3   Junction with ME 129. Turn left onto ME 129 South.

8.5   Turn right (west) off ME 129 onto Clarks Cove Road.

9.6   Darling Marine Center is to the right. Continue straight on Clarks Cove Road.

11.4   Cross ME 129. Get on Harrington Road, heading east.

12.8   Harrington Meeting House Museum and Cemetery on left.

14.2   Junction with ME 130. Turn right onto ME 130 South.

16.0   Turn right (west) off ME 130 onto Huddle Road, following signs for Pemaquid Beach and Fort William Henry State Historic Site.

17.2   At the four-way intersection, turn right (north) onto Old Fort Road, following signs for the state historic site. Bear right, following signs for the visitor center.

17.5   Parking area at the state historic site. Turn around.

17.8   Return to four-way intersection. Continue straight (south) onto Snowball Hill Road.

18.0   Pemaquid Beach is to the right. Continue straight on Snowball Hill Road.

19.0   Junction with ME 130 in town of New Harbor. Turn right onto ME 130 South.

21.7   Pemaquid Point Lighthouse. Turn around and return north on ME 130.

24.3   Intersection in New Harbor. Continue straight on ME 130 North.

24.5   Turn right (east) off ME 130 onto ME 32 North.

25.6   Rachel Carson Salt Pond Preserve on right.

31.5   Village of Round Pond. Granite Hall Store is to the right.

33.5   Turn right off ME 32 onto Shore Road, still heading north.

33.7   Road surface turns to dirt.

34.4   Road surface returns to asphalt.

35.7   At the junction of Shore Road and ME 32. turn right onto ME 32 North.

38.0 Turn left off ME 32 onto Turner Road, heading west.

41.0 Junction with Biscay Road. Turn right onto Biscay Road, heading west.

41.3 Return to parking area.

Local Information

Damariscotta Region Chamber of Commerce, P.O. Box 13, Damariscotta, ME 04543; (207) 563-8340; www.damariscottaregion.com.

Local Events/Attractions

Colonial Pemaquid State Historic Site, P.O. Box 117, New Harbor, ME 04554; (207) 677-2423; www.maine.gov/doc/parks or www.friendsofcolonialpemaquid.org. Open Memorial Day through Labor Day.

Pemaquid Point Lighthouse and Fishermen's Museum, 3007 Bristol Road (ME 130), New Harbor, ME; (207) 677-2494; www.pemaquid lighthouse.com. Open daily Memorial Day through Columbus Day.

Food

Bristol Diner, 1267 Bristol Road (ME 130), Bristol, ME; (207) 563-8000. A hometown diner.

Cupboard Café, 137 Huddle Road, New Harbor, ME; (207) 677-3911. A good stop on the road to the fort and the beach.

C. E. Reilly & Son Grocery Store, 2576 Bristol Road, New Harbor, ME; (207) 677-2321.

The Sea Gull Restaurant and Gift Shop, 3119 Bristol Road, New Harbor, ME; (207) 677-2374. Next to the Pemaquid Lighthouse.

Shaw's Fish & Lobster Wharf, 129 ME 32, New Harbor, ME; (207) 677-2200. Classic Maine seafood and atmosphere.

Granite Hall Store, 9 Back Shore Road, Round Pond, ME; (207) 529-5864.

Accommodations

Hotel Pemaquid, ME 130, 3098 Bristol Road, New Harbor, ME; (207) 677-2312; www.hotelpemaquid.com. Classic old hotel with adjoining bungalows. Practically next door to the lighthouse. Open mid-May to mid-October.

Gosnold Arms, 146 ME 32, New Harbor, ME; (207) 677-3727; www.gosnold.com. Open mid-May to mid-October.

Pemaquid Point Campground, 2850 Bristol Road (ME 130), New Harbor, ME; (207) 677-CAMP; www.midcoast.com~ed.

Bike Shop

Bath Cycle and Ski, 115 Main Street (US 1), Woolwich, ME; (207) 442-7002; www.bike man.com.

Map

DeLorme: Maine Atlas & Gazetteer: Page 7.

31 Belgrade Lakes Cruise

The beautiful Belgrade Lakes area is home to many people who work in Augusta, the state capital. In fact, this ride is popular with Augusta area cyclists, who love the enormous shoulders on Maine Highways 8/11/27. Proximity to an urban area means this one isn't as bucolic as some lake rides, but the scenery is fine, and the rolling hills make for a good, fast workout.

Start: Boat launch and public access parking area at the south end of Messalonskee Lake.
Length: 26.9 miles.
Terrain: Flat to hilly.
Traffic and hazards: Shoulders on the major roads of the route are generally wide. No shoulder on Maine Highway 225, but less traffic. As of this writing, there is an inadequate shoulder and considerable traffic for approximately 3 miles between the junction of ME 8 and ME 11 and the major intersection where ME 8/11 joins ME 27. Exercise extra caution here. As always in lakes regions, use a rearview mirror to watch for vehicles pulling boat trailers: Drivers may forget how wide the trailer is, so be ready to get out of the way.

Getting there: Take exit 112B off Interstate 95 and get on ME 8/11/27 North. Proceed about 7.4 miles to the public boat launch on the right, on Messalonskee Lake.

Maine is rich in lakes. The four lakes on this route are Messalonskee Lake, Great Pond, Long Pond, and Salmon Lake. Don't assume the traditional distinction that defines a "pond" as smaller than a "lake." Great Pond is by far the largest, and Salmon Lake is quite small. Salmon Lake, the farthest east, is at the highest elevation, followed by Great Pond, then Long Pond, the westernmost lake. Those three lakes are connected: Salmon Lake flows into Great Pond, which flows into Long Pond. The falls and dams between lakes are among the most interesting sights on the route.

"Messalonskee" is Abenaki for "white clay here," which may explain why atlases list "Snow Pond" as an alternative name for Messalonskee Lake. Although views of the four lakes on this trip will be infrequent, you'll never be far from water. Geologists explain that the lakes here in the Augusta area were largely formed from glacial outwash. They tend to be long and thin, in a north–south line, and are blessed with some lovely sandy beaches.

The first stop of the ride will probably be in the village of Belgrade Lakes, which is situated at the falls where Great Pond flows into Long Pond. Day's Store, on the left at 6.9 miles, is one of those wonderful New England full-service general stores. Stop there to buy a snack, then carry it 0.2 mile farther to Peninsula Park, where there's a picnic area with a fine view of the falls and Long Pond.

ME 8/11/27 is a heavily traveled road, especially during summer months. However, it has such wide shoulders that traffic is not an issue. The state of Maine should be congratulated on its "share the road" efforts. New road construction and repaving

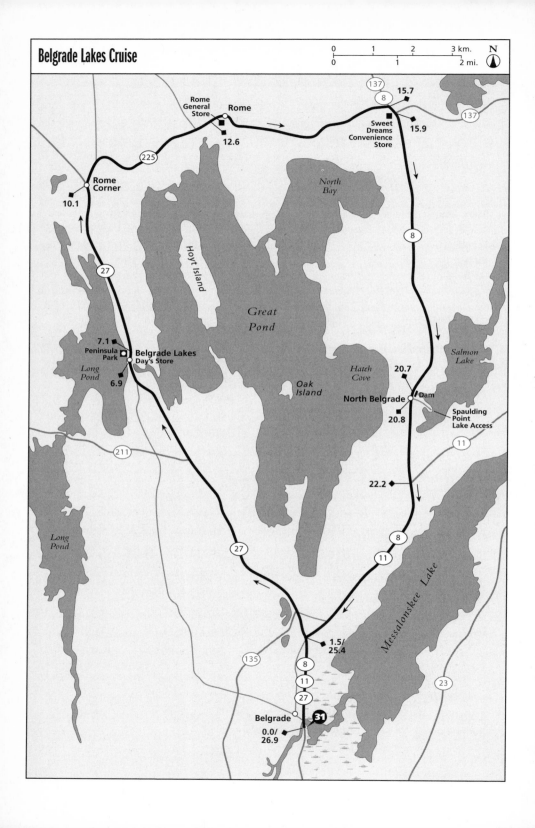

Belgrade Lakes Cruise

0   1   2   3 km.   N
0   1   2 mi.

Rome General Store
Rome
12.6

225

(137)
8   15.7

Sweet Dreams Convenience Store   15.9

Rome Corner
10.1

27

8

North Bay

Hoyt Island

Great Pond

Salmon Lake

7.1
Peninsula Park
Belgrade Lakes
Day's Store
6.9

Long Pond

Oak Island

Hatch Cove
20.7
North Belgrade   Dam
20.8

Spaulding Point Lake Access

11

211

22.2

Long Pond

27

11

8

Messalonskee Lake

135

1.5/ 25.4

8
11
27

23

Belgrade
0.0/ 26.9

31

projects generally include very wide shoulders—sometimes the width of an additional lane. The trick is to find scenic loops that take advantage of these recently widened roads. This loop does pretty well, but you'll be disappointed at the turn off ME 8/11/27 onto ME 225, which has no shoulder at all. Traffic is light, but cyclists should stay right and be on the lookout for vehicles pulling boat trailers. Better to bail out into a ditch than get sideswiped by a driver who has forgotten how wide their trailer is.

There's a general store on the right in Rome. Pay attention if you're planning to refuel there. Rome, Maine, has nothing in common with its namesake. Perhaps its early settlers had grand expectations, but today it's a "blink and you'll miss it" kind of place—even on a bicycle.

If you happened to be talking, or swatting a blackfly, or some other brief distraction made you miss the store in Rome, not to worry. There's another general store (Sweet Dreams Convenience Store) on ME 8, coming up soon.

The second lake connection, between Salmon Lake and Great Pond, is at 20.7 miles. Again, the road crosses the stream that connects the two lakes. There's a small dam to the left. Just after the dam there's a dirt road to the left that goes to a boat launch and public access on Salmon Lake.

Miles and Directions

0.0 Turn right out of boat launch parking area onto ME 8/11/27 North.

1.5 Four-way intersection. ME 8/11 bears right. Continue straight (north) on ME 27.

6.9 Village of Belgrade Lakes. Day's Store is on the left.

7.1 Peninsula Park is on the left.

10.1 Turn right off ME 27 onto ME 225 East, following signs for Rome.

12.6 Rome General Store is on the right.

15.7 At junction with ME 8/Maine Highway 137, turn right onto ME 8/137, heading south.

15.9 ME 137 goes to the left. Continue straight on ME 8 South. Sweet Dreams Convenience Store is on the right.

20.7 Dam and spillway between Salmon Lake and Great Pond.

20.8 Dirt road to the left leads to Spaulding Point lake access.

22.2 ME 11 joins Route 8 from the left. Continue straight (south) on ME 8/11.

25.4 At the junction with ME 27, turn left (south) onto ME 8/11/27.

26.9 Turn left off ME 8/11/27 into parking area at the boat launch.

Local Information

Find comprehensive Belgrade Lakes Region information at www.belgradelakesmaine.com.

Local Events/Attractions

Old Fort Western, 16 Cony Street, Augusta, ME; (207) 626-2385; www.oldfortwestern.org.

In downtown Augusta, on the banks of the Kennebec River. Eighteenth-century stockaded fort and museum.

Great Pond Mailboat, 171 Main Street, Belgrade Lakes, ME (207) 215-7520.

Two to four hours of touring and delivering mail, Monday through Saturday in June through September. Call ahead for reservations. The boat departs from the dock next to the post office in the village of Belgrade Lakes.

Food

Day's Store, P.O. Box 277, Belgrade Lakes, ME 04918; (207) 495-2205 or (800) 993-9500; www.go2days.com.

Rome General Store, 517 Rome Road, Rome, ME; (207) 397-2758.

Sweet Dreams Convenience Store, 164 Village Road, Smithfield, ME; (207) 362-2010.

Accommodations

The Belgrade Lakes Web site lists inns and B&Bs. The best options for budget accommodations are in Augusta, about 10 miles to the south.

Super 8 Motel, 395 Western Avenue, Augusta, ME; (207) 626-2888; www.the.super8.com/augusta03486. Offers reasonably priced rooms.

Bike Shops

Auclaire Cycle & Ski, 64–66 Bangor Street, Augusta, ME; (207) 623-4351 or (800) 734-7171; www.auclaircycle.com.

Kennebec Bike & Ski, 276 Whitten Road, Hallowell, ME; (207) 621-4900; www.Kennebec BikeSki.com.

Map

DeLorme: Maine Atlas & Gazetteer: Pages 12, 20.

32 China Lake Cruise

This ride is just plain good pedaling on quiet back roads in an area of rural Maine that's easily accessible from the interstate and from coastal regions.

Start: Memorial Park in South China. Memorial Park is a tiny green space and monument at the four-way intersection in South China. It has a small parking area that should generally have space. If parking isn't possible here, use the post office parking lot, on the north side of Maine Highway 3, about 0.2 mile west of South China.

Length: 34.3 miles.

Terrain: Hilly.

Traffic and hazards: Exercise extreme caution crossing ME 3/Maine Highway 9/U.S. Highway 202 (at 0.1 and 10.2 miles). The crossing at 10.2 miles is particularly hazardous: It's at the crest of a hill, and you won't be able to see traffic in either direction. Get off the bike and listen before crossing. The final stretch of the ride (about 6.6 miles) is on ME 9/US 202, a major road that carries a substantial volume of traffic. The good news is that this section of ME 9/US 202 has a large shoulder (4 to 8 feet). Traffic is a nuisance but shouldn't be dangerous as long as cyclists stay right and pedal defensively. Most of the ride is on quiet back roads. Note that road signs are not always present at intersections, so pay attention to mileages and directions.

Getting there: Take exit 109 off Interstate 95 and proceed east on US 202. Drive through Augusta and across the Kennebec River, staying on US 202. It's about 14.5 miles from exit 109 to the left turn off US 202 in South China. Then it's just 0.1 mile to the four-way intersection and Memorial Park in South China.

Road sign in South China

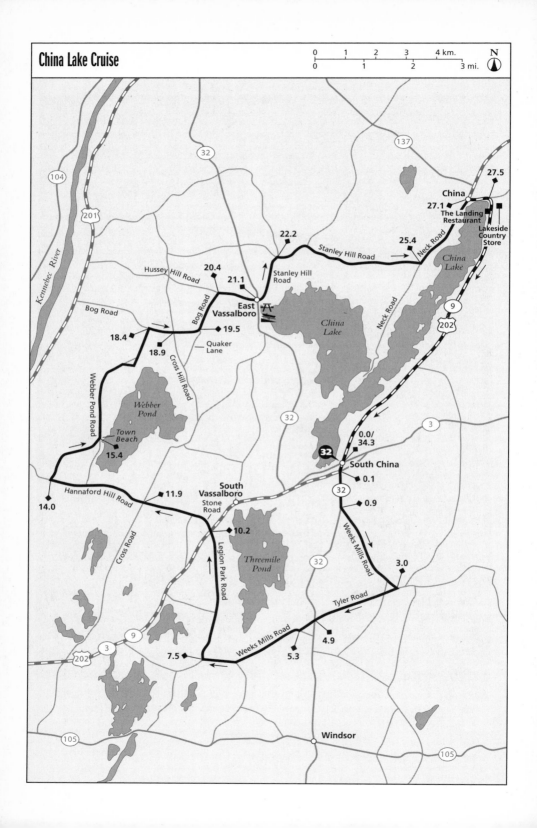

China Lake Cruise

0 1 2 3 4 km.
0 1 2 3 mi.

N

104
201

Kennebec River

32

137

China
27.1 **27.5**
The Landing
Restaurant
Lakeside
Country
Store

China
Lake

22.2
Stanley Hill Road **25.4** Neck Road
20.4
Hussey Hill Road
21.1
Stanley Hill
Road
Bog Road
East
Vassalboro
9
202

18.4
19.5
Bog Road
Quaker
Lane
18.9
Cross Hill Road

China
Lake

Neck Road

Webber Pond Road

Webber
Pond

32

3

Town
Beach
15.4

**0.0/
34.3**

32

11.9
South China **0.1**

14.0
Hannaford Hill Road
South
Vassalboro
Stone
Road
32
0.9

Cross Road
10.2
Legion Park Road
Threemile
Pond
Weeks Mills Road
32
3.0

Tyler Road
4.9

202
3
9
7.5
Weeks Mills Road
5.3

105

Windsor
105

A study of Maine's place names is intriguing. Many of the most melodic names are derived from Native American words. Names like "Mooselookmeguntic" roll off the tongues of local eight-year-olds but are sure to give pause to visitors. Likewise the "exotic" names, common in a broad swath settled in the early nineteenth century, seem perfectly ordinary to local folks. Imagine a bike trip through China, Norway, Peru, Madrid, Mexico, Rome, and Egypt. It's quite possible—in just a few days—in central Maine. Conventional wisdom holds that the Chinas of this trip (China, South China, and China Lake) are named not for the country but for a hymn that was popular with early settlers.

The first 10 miles of the ride are gently rolling. You'll be looping around Three-mile Pond (guess how long it is) but won't catch even a glimpse of this particular body of water. If a picnic by the water is part of your plan, just keep pedaling. Webber Pond and China Lake are coming up soon.

The steepest climb of the ride is on Stone Road, after crossing ME 3/ME 9/US 202 at 10.2 miles. Then it's pretty much downhill to Webber Pond. Early settlers were not terribly consistent, but generally modest, in naming bodies of water. Webber, like many Maine "ponds," would almost certainly be a "lake" elsewhere.

After the turn onto Bog Road, directions become especially important. There are several turns and frequent intersections without road signs. Keep a map handy. If you do make a wrong turn, relax; it just means an opportunity to see a little more of rural Maine. If you need to ask for directions, say you're heading for East Vassalboro. (Some readers may remember the old "Bert and I" recording where the frustrated tourist, who's been back and forth in front of the narrator's house several times, asks for directions to East Vassalboro. "Don't ya move a gol darn inch," is the reply.)

East Vassalboro is a good spot for a break. The general store is friendly, and there's a great picnic spot on China Lake, just a short distance from the store. (See directions below at 21.1.) If your timing is right, you may be able to visit the Vassalboro Historical Society as well. You may notice signs in the general store about the local Friends Meeting. Most of us picture Pennsylvania when we think of Quakers, but there were pockets of Quaker settlers all over the northeast. Many Quaker communities, such as those in this area, are still active. As you leave East Vassalboro on Stanley Hill Road, you'll pass a Quaker Meeting House and cemetery on your left.

From East Vassalboro, you'll be heading toward China. The beach along Causeway Road, at the north end of the lake, and in the town of China, is another good spot for a break. Ice cream at The Landing Restaurant on the corner of Causeway Road and ME 9/US 202 should fuel the final miles back to South China.

Miles and Directions

0.0 Turn right (south) out of the Veterans' Memorial Park parking area onto Old Windsor Road, heading toward ME 3/ME 9/US 202.

0.1 Cross ME 3/ME 9/US 202 and proceed south on Maine Highway 32.

0.9 Turn left (southeast) onto Weeks Mills Road.

3.0 Turn right off Weeks Mills Road onto Tyler Road.

4.9 Cross ME 32 (here called Ridge Road) and continue straight (west) on Weeks Mills Road. (Yes, that's correct. This is another Weeks Mills Road.)

5.3 Reach a T intersection. Bear right, continuing on Weeks Mills Road (unmarked here), and continuing west.

7.5 Turn right off Weeks Mills Road onto Legion Park Road, heading north.

10.2 Cross ME 3/ME 9/US 202 and continue straight (north) on Stone Road.

11.9 Four-way intersection. Cross Road goes to the right and left. Continue straight on what is now called Hannaford Hill Road. This is just about the highest elevation of the ride.

14.0 At junction with Webber Pond Road, turn right onto Webber Pond Road, heading north.

15.4 Dam Road on right leads to boat launch and town beach. Continue straight (north) on Webber Pond Road.

18.4 At junction with Bog Road, turn right onto Bog Road, heading east.

18.9 Four-way intersection. Taber Hill Road is to the left, Cross Hill Road is to the right. Continue straight on Bog Road.

19.5 Quaker Lane to the right. Continue straight on Bog Road.

20.4 Hussey Hill Road to the left. Continue straight on Bog Road.

21.1 Four-way intersection in East Vassalboro. Continue straight (east) across ME 32 onto Stanley Hill Road. **Option:** Turn right onto ME 32 and proceed about 0.1 mile south for a stop at Vassalboro Historical Society, picnic area, and boat launch on China Lake.

22.2 Four-way intersection. Bear right (east), continuing on Stanley Hill Road.

25.4 Junction with Neck Road. Turn left onto Neck Road, heading north toward China.

27.1 Turn right (east) off Neck Road onto Causeway Road.

27.5 Turn right off Causeway Road onto ME 9/US 202 South. Lakeside Country Store is across the road on ME 9/US 202.

34.1 Turn right off ME 9/US 202 onto Jones Road (unmarked here).

34.3 Back to parking area.

Local Information

China Area Chamber of Commerce, P.O. Box 189, South China, ME 04358; (207) 445-2890.

Mid-Maine Chamber of Commerce, 1 Post Office Square, Waterville, ME; (207) 873-3315; www.midmainechamber.com.

Local Events/Attractions

Trek Across Maine: Sunday River to the Sea. A 3-day, 180-mile bicycle tour from Bethel in northwestern Maine to the coast at Belfast. Sponsored by the American Lung Association of Maine, 122 State Street, Augusta, ME; (207) 622-6394; www.mainelung.org/Events /Trek/index.asp.

China Community Days, 571 Lakeview Drive, China, ME; (207) 445-2014; www.china.gov office.com. Annual August event includes food, music, demonstrations, competitions, fireworks, and more. Sponsored by various local organizations.

Vassalboro Historical Society Museum, 327 Main Street, East Vassalboro, ME; (207) 923-3533.

Food

Dog Days Gourmet Bakery & Café, 241 ME 3, South China, ME; (207) 445-4798. Deli, soups, pastries.

The Country Store, 342 Main Street (ME 32), East Vassalboro, ME; (207) 923-3300. All the usual necessities, plus a deli and pizza.

Lakeside Country Store, 1390 Lakeview Drive, China, ME; (207) 968-3663.

Accommodations

The best motel options are in Augusta or Waterville.

Super 8 Motel, 395 Western Avenue, Augusta, ME; (207) 626-2888; www.the.super8.com /augusta03486.

Best Western Waterville, 356 Main Street, Waterville, ME; (207) 873-3335.

Waterville Econo Lodge, 455 Kennedy Memorial Drive, Waterville, ME; (207) 872-5577.

Bike Shops

Auclair Cycle & Ski, 64–66 Bangor Street, Augusta, ME; (207) 623-4351 or (800) 734-7171; www.auclaircycle.com.

Kennebec Bike & Ski, 276 Whitten Road, Hallowell, ME; (207) 621-4900; www.Kennebec BikeSki.com.

Map

DeLorme: Maine Atlas & Gazetteer: Page 13.

33 Norridgewock Ramble

The route is primarily on quiet secondary roads, where traffic is scarce. Rural scenery includes farms and two rivers. With two short sections of unpaved road, this is a perfect ride for a group that includes beginners on hybrid bikes.

Start: Public parking lot in Norridgewock on the south side of U.S. Highway 2, just west of the railroad track crossing. If this lot is full, there's another public lot just east of the railroad crossing, on the north side of US 2.
Length: 16.2 miles.
Terrain: Flat to hilly.
Traffic and hazards: The two short sections of unpaved road total about 4 miles. In spite of

proximity to the Kennebec and Sandy Rivers, where soils are likely to be sandy, the unpaved sections of road are good hard-packed dirt and gravel, suitable for road bikes as well as bikes with fatter tires. The final 3 miles are on US 2, a major east-west route with significant traffic. Shoulders here are enormous, however, and visibility is good.

Getting there: Take exit 130 off Interstate 95 and get on Maine Highway 104 North, following signs for Skowhegan. At about 4.7 miles, bear left off ME 104 onto Maine Highway 139 North. Proceed north on ME 139 another 8 miles to a junction with US 2 in Norridgewock. Bear left onto US 2 West. Proceed about 0.1 mile west on US 2 to the public parking area on the left.

"Ramble" is a good word to describe this one: a pleasant, leisurely jaunt on quiet roads with fine views of the rural countryside and two rivers.

The first river is the Kennebec, which flows from Moosehead Lake in the north, through the state capital, Augusta, past Bath Ironworks, then into the Atlantic at Popham. This is the river that Benedict Arnold and companions traveled on the grueling autumn 1775 expedition to Quebec. Chances are good they camped along the shore near Winding Hill Road after portaging around Norridgewock Falls. Arnold's men paddled, poled, and dragged their bateaux upstream to Bingham, a little north

Norridgewock Ramble

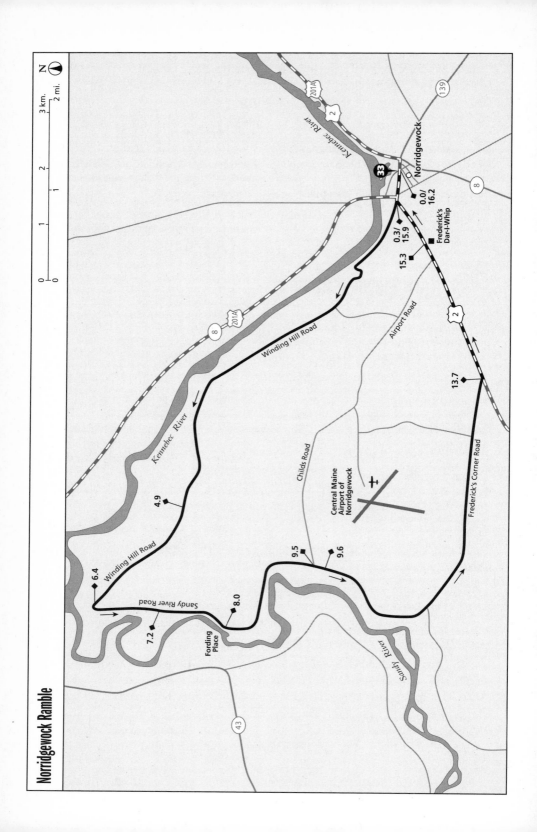

N

3 km.
2 mi.

Kennebec River

201A
2

Norridgewock
139

8

0.0/
16.2

0.3/
15.9
Frederick's
Dari-I-Whip

15.3

201A
8

Winding Hill Road

Airport Road

2

13.7

Childs Road

Central Maine
Airport of
Norridgewock

Frederick's Corner Road

Kennebec River

4.9

6.4
Winding Hill Road

9.5

9.6

Sandy River Road

7.2

8.0
Fording
Place

Sandy River

43

of here, where they carried the boats and gear to Dead Creek, then north into Quebec. It's a much happier experience on a bike, on a quiet back road, on a fine summer day.

At about 6.4 miles you'll reach the northern end of the ride, at a prosperous-looking farm on the floodplain where the Sandy River joins the Kennebec. During the next few miles, farms, farm equipment, and farm animals will be more likely than cars. Chickens wander in yards, and you may even spot an occasional cat napping in the road.

The fording place, at 8.0 miles, is an interesting stop. During summer months it's still a quicker way to the other side than driving all the way to the bridge in Norridgewock. Notice that the fording place is even on the DeLorme map. Bridges have replaced most official fording places like this in New England today. But this is a sparsely populated area, and the Sandy River extends over 17 miles from New Sharon to the Kennebec without a bridge. Our route doesn't cross the ford but continues straight on Sandy River Road.

Don't be surprised if a low-flying plane seems to be heading at you. The Central Maine Regional Airport is in the center of this loop.

Frederick's Dar-I-Whip, on the right on US 2, just before the village of Norridgewock, is a perfect way to end the ride. I recommend the homemade blueberry pie topped with homemade ice cream. This is the kind of restaurant cyclists dream of finding.

Miles and Directions

0.0 Turn left out of the public parking area in Norridgewock onto US 2 West.

0.3 Traffic light at a five-way intersection. Cross the intersection, then bear right off US 2 onto Upper Main Street (later called Winding Hill Road), heading north along the west side of the Kennebec River.

1.2 Road swings away from the river and begins steep climb.

4.9 Road surface turns to dirt.

6.4 Road surface returns to pavement. This is now called Sandy River Road.

7.2 Road surface turns to dirt again.

8.0 Fording place is to the right. Continue straight on Sandy River Road.

9.5 Childs Road (paved) to left. Continue straight on Sandy River Road.

9.6 Road surface returns to pavement. Name has changed to Frederick's Corner Road.

13.7 Junction with US 2. Turn left onto US 2 East.

15.3 Frederick's Dar-I-Whip on the right. Continue straight on US 2.

15.9 Traffic light at five-way intersection. Continue straight on US 2 East.

16.2 Turn right off US 2 into public parking area in Norridgewock.

Norridgewock Chamber of Commerce, P.O. Box 32, Norridgewock, ME 04957; (207) 634-4962; www.norridgewock.com.

Local Events/Attractions

Norridgewock Historical Society & Museum, 11 Mercer Road (US 2), Norridgewock, ME; (207) 634-5032.

Food

Frederick's Dar-I-Whip & Homespun Family Dining, 120 Mercer Road (US 2), Norridgewock, ME; (207) 634-4962. Homemade pies and ice cream, chowders, sandwiches, daily specials.

Accommodations

Norridgewock Colonial Inn, 15 Upper Main Street, P.O. Box 932, Norridgewock, ME 04957; (207) 634-3470.

Best Western Waterville, 356 Main Street, Waterville, ME; (207) 873-3335; www.best western.com.

Waterville Econo Lodge, 455 Kennedy Memorial Drive, Waterville, ME; (207) 872-5577; www.choicehotels.com.

Bike Shops

Northern Lights Bike Shop, 639 Wilton Road, Farmington, ME; (207) 778-6566.

Auclair Cycle & Ski, 64–66 Bangor Street, Augusta, ME; (207) 623-4351 or (800) 734-7171; www.auclaircycle.com.

Kennebec Bike & Ski, 276 Whitten Road, Hallowell, ME; (207) 621-4900; www.Kennebec BikeSki.com.

Map

DeLorme: Maine Atlas & Gazetteer: Page 20.

34 Islesboro Ramble

Flat terrain, magnificent scenery, and light traffic combine to make this ride a popular one. Throw in the ferry ride, a swim or two, photo stops, and ice cream and you've got a whole day's worth of fun. If time is limited, or the group includes beginners, the ride could be shortened to just the northern or the southern end of the island.

Start: Parking area at the ferry terminal in Lincolnville, on the mainland. Ride mileages begin at the ferry landing in Islesboro.
Length: 27.2 miles.
Terrain: Relatively flat, with occasional gentle hills.

Traffic and hazards: No shoulders on island roads. Some delivery and construction trucks, especially on Main Road. The last ferry leaves Islesboro at 4:30 p.m., so plan accordingly.

Getting there: Follow U.S. Highway 1 south from Belfast about 13 miles to Lincolnville. The ferry terminal is well marked, on the left. During summer months, a ferry departs from Lincolnville every hour on the hour, from 8:00 a.m. to 5:00 p.m. It departs from Islesboro every hour on the half hour, with the last ferry leaving Islesboro at 4:30 p.m.

A recent issue of *Down East*—the glossy monthly with articles on Maine communities, people, and attractions—featured Islesboro. *Down East* favors attractive spreads of travel destinations, but occasionally it gently tackles controversial subjects. The

On the Islesboro Ferry

feature on Islesboro begins with celebrity spotting in Dark Harbor, an easy pastime on an island populated with the rich and famous. But the article goes on to analyze the frictions created in a small isolated community with an enormous gulf between the haves and have-nots.

Historically, the wealthy have settled on the southern part of Islesboro. The working folks who take care of the wealthy (the landscapers, construction workers, caterers, etc.) live to the north. Although that dichotomy seems to be fading, with northern island property values on a steep upward curve, it's still evident. On the northern part of the island, you'll see some fine homes, but most are still rural middle class.

You won't see stacks of lobster traps and backyard chickens in the southern part of the island. You will see estates with service entrances and gated drives. In fact, the estates you see are the less lavish: The grandest aren't visible from the road.

The Islesboro Historical Society, at the junction of West Bay and Main Roads, is an interesting stop if your timing is right. It's open from 12:30 to 4:30 p.m., Saturday to Wednesday. Islesboro's recorded history dates back to the mid-eighteenth century, when farming, fishing, and boatbuilding dominated. The late nineteenth century marked the beginning of the era of great estates and summer people.

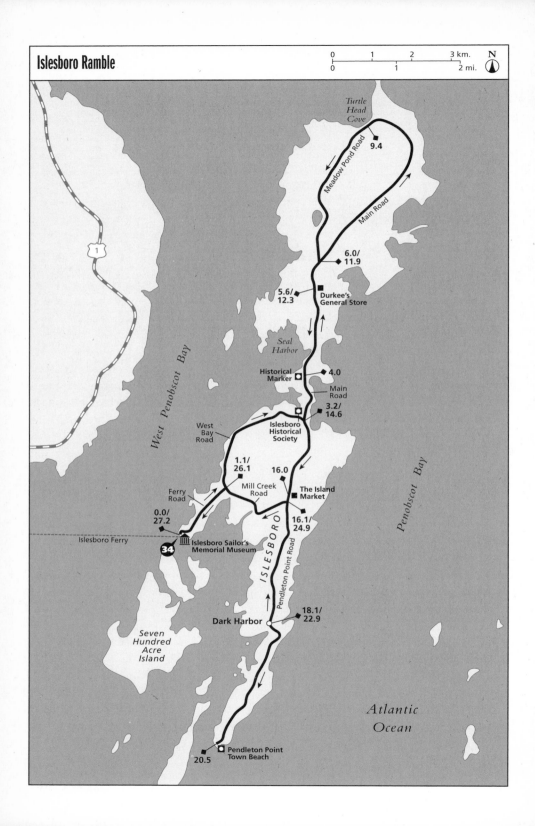

Islesboro Ramble

0   1   2   3 km.

0   1   2 mi.

N

Turtle Head Cove

Meadow Pond Road

9.4

Main Road

6.0/ 11.9

5.6/ 12.3

Durkee's General Store

Seal Harbor

West Penobscot Bay

Historical Marker

4.0

Main Road

3.2/ 14.6

Islesboro Historical Society

West Bay Road

1.1/ 26.1

Mill Creek Road

16.0

The Island Market

Penobscot Bay

Ferry Road

0.0/ 27.2

16.1/ 24.9

Islesboro Ferry

34

Islesboro Sailor's Memorial Museum

ISLESBORO

Pendleton Point Road

18.1/ 22.9

Dark Harbor

Seven Hundred Acre Island

20.5

Pendleton Point Town Beach

Atlantic Ocean

1

Notice the historical marker on the left at 4.0 miles. It marks the site of the first recorded observation of a total solar eclipse in North America, in 1780. Be glad you're on a bike. Visitors in cars generally miss that tidbit of scientific history.

At about 4.3 miles the road swings close to the shore along Seal Harbor. There's a tiny parking area and a path to a small beach at the north end of the harbor. You'll pass this spot again on the return.

Durkee's Store is on the right shortly before the road forks to make the northern loop. There are no supermarkets on the island, so this (and the Island Market to the south) are more than "convenience" stores. For locals, unless you plan a ferry ride, this is where you shop.

The loop at the northern end of the island could be done in either direction. Either way you'll want to make a photo stop at Turtle Head Cove, the only section of the northern loop with postcard views of beach and ocean.

After completing the northern loop, head back south on Main Road. If 4:30 p.m. is approaching, the intersection of Main Road and West Bay Road is where you'll shorten the trip by making a right and heading toward the ferry. If it's early yet, continue straight on Main Road to finish the ride with a tour of the southern section of the island.

At some point Main Road gets a name change and becomes Pendleton Point Road. Pendleton Point is the southern tip of the island, where there is a secluded public beach and picnic area. It's a gravel beach, with several small coves. Even on a hot day in July, you might find yourself alone.

As you headed south to Pendleton Point, you passed through the village of Dark Harbor. In a Harry Potter era, the name sounds a little sinister. In reality it simply means that nineteenth-century sailors had trouble seeing it. The highlight of the village today—from a cyclist's point of view—is probably the Dark Harbor Shop. Their specialty is ice cream, served at an old-fashioned soda fountain.

A short tour through the Islesboro Sailor's Memorial Museum, adjacent to the ferry terminal, is a fine ending for the ride.

Miles and Directions

0.0   Ferry terminal on Islesboro. Proceed straight (east) on Ferry Road.

1.1   At junction of Ferry Road and West Bay Road, turn left onto West Bay Road, heading north.

3.2   At junction of West Bay Road and Main Road, turn left onto Main Road, heading north. Islesboro Historical Society is on the left.

4.0   Historical marker on left.

4.3   Seal Harbor on left.

5.6   Durkee's General Store on right.

6.0   Road forks. Bear right, staying on Main Road and heading north.

9.4   Road is now called Meadow Pond Road. Turtle Head Cove is to the right.

11.9 Junction with Main Road. Bear right onto Main Road, heading south.

12.3 Durkee's General Store on left.

13.5 Seal Harbor to the right.

14.6 West Bay Road is to the right. Continue straight (south) on Main Road.

16.0 The Island Market is on the left. This is now called Pendleton Point Road.

16.1 Mill Creek Road to the right. Continue straight (south) on Pendleton Point Road.

18.1 Dark Harbor Shop on right.

20.3 Road surface turns to dirt.

20.5 Pendleton Point Public Beach. Turn around and return north on Pendleton Point Road.

20.7 Road surface returns to asphalt.

24.9 Turn left off Pendleton Point Road onto Mill Creek Road, heading west.

26.1 Turn left (west) off Mill Creek Road onto Ferry Road.

27.2 Return to ferry terminal.

Local Information

Islesboro Historical Society, 388 Main Road, Islesboro, ME; (207) 734-6733. Open Saturday through Wednesday, 12:30 to 4:30 p.m., July 1 through August 31. Full schedule of summer events and displays.

Local Events/Attractions

Pendleton Point Public Beach, at the southern tip of Islesboro. Picnic areas, restroom.

Islesboro Sailor's Memorial Museum, P.O. Box 137, Islesboro, ME 04848; (207) 734-2253. Adjacent to the ferry slip on Islesboro. The museum is located in the former Grindle Point Lighthouse keeper's home.

Food

Durkee's General Store, 863 Main Road, Islesboro, ME; (207) 734-2201. Full stock of groceries plus deli sandwiches, lunch specials.

The Island Market, across from the post office, 113 Maine Road, Islesboro, ME; (207) 734-6672. Groceries and more.

Dark Harbor Shop, Pendleton Point Road, Dark Harbor, ME; (207) 734-8878. Ice cream.

Accommodations

There are no motels on Islesboro, and just a couple of B&Bs.

Aunt Laura's Bed and Breakfast, 812 Main Road, Islesboro, ME; (207) 734-8286 or (800) 684-2405; www.auntlauras.com.

Dark Harbor Bed & Breakfast and Café, 119 Derby Road, Islesboro, ME; (207) 734-9772. There are a wide variety of motel options on the mainland, from Belfast to Camden. An example is the **Comfort Inn Ocean's Edge,** 159 Searsport Avenue, US 1, Belfast, ME; (207) 338-2528. Rates are typical of coastal areas.

Bike Shops

Belfast Bicycles, 158 High Street, Belfast, ME; (207) 338-0008; www.belfastbicycles.com.

Birgfeld's Bike Shop, 184 East Main Street, Searsport, ME; (207) 548-2916.

Ragged Mountain Sports, 46 Elm Street, Camden, ME; (207) 236-6664.

Map

DeLorme: Maine Atlas and Gazetteer: Pages 14, 15.

35 Cape Rosier Ramble

Take your time, stop for all the sights, immerse yourself in an atmosphere that seems far removed from the present. Or just pedal hard and enjoy a great exercise loop. Cyclists with mountain bikes should consult the DeLorme atlas and take advantage of dirt roads on the peninsula, especially in the Holbrook Island Sanctuary.

Start: Parking lot of the Brooksville Town Offices and Public Library, on Maine Highway 176.
Length: 15.8 miles.
Terrain: Hilly.

Traffic and hazards: Some traffic and no shoulders on ME 176. Otherwise, traffic will be minimal. Some roads are very narrow—really a single lane. About 1.5 miles of unpaved road shouldn't be a problem for road bikes.

Getting there: Cape Rosier is part of the Blue Hill Peninsula. On the map, it's due south of Castine but is not directly accessible by road from Castine. From Bucksport, go about 1.7 miles east on U.S. Highway 1. Turn right off US 1 onto Maine Highway 175 South. Stay on ME 175 for about 18 miles, to the intersection with ME 176, just west of Bagaduce Falls. Bear right onto ME 176 and proceed about 5 miles to the Brooksville Town Offices, Public Library, and Fire Station, on the left. Park in the parking area for the town offices and library, to the left of the building.

Cape Rosier is the sort of coastal area that you almost don't want to mention. It's kind of a dreamy place: beautiful and unspoiled, and you just hope it doesn't fall into the hands of developers. It's named after James Rosier, who accompanied Captain George Waymouth on a voyage of exploration in 1605, and who wrote *A True Relation of the Most Prosperous Voyage Made this Year, 1605, by Captain George Waymouth In the Discovery of the North Part of Virginia*. There are spots along the ride that look much the same today as they did when James Rosier first saw them in 1605. Even the most prosaic of cyclists may find themselves wondering if this is the coastline Rosier saw when he waxed poetic over a land that's "woody, grouen with Firre, Birch, Oke and Beech as farre as we saw along the shore . . . On the verge grow Gooseberries, Strawberries, Wild pease, and Wild rose bushes. The water issued foorth down the Rocky cliffs in many places; and much fowle of divers kinds breed upon the shore and rocks."

James Rosier had high hopes for the land he described. Four hundred years later, his hopes for the New World live on—albeit in a different form—at the Good Life Center on Orr Cove, at 7.9 miles. This is the home built by Helen and Scott Nearing in the early 1950s. Pay attention, or you'll miss it; the only indicator is the Nearing mailbox. The Nearings were pacifists, authors, and nonconformists who moved from New York City to Vermont and then on to this idyllic spot. They devoted themselves to "sustainable living" at a time when that concept wasn't the buzzword it is today. There's a shop that stocks the Nearings' books, and visitors can take a self-guided tour of the homestead.

Sailboat on Orr Cove

Another recommended stop—just before the Good Life Center—is Four Season Farm, a large organic farm and farm stand. Admire fields of eggplant and kale, then buy a tomato and some carrots to supplement that candy bar in your pocket.

Be sure to make the turn onto Cape Rosier Road at 9.6 miles. Continuing on Goose Falls Road, straight ahead, looks tempting. It goes through the Holbrook Island Sanctuary, a rugged, mostly forested preserve that is being allowed to flourish untouched by human intervention. The road, however, turns to a loose, unimproved dirt surface soon after the Cape Rosier intersection. Check the map, but try it only if you have real fat tires. Note that although you can bike on the road, only walking is permitted on sanctuary trails.

Miles and Directions

- **0.0** Parking area at Brooksville Town Offices and Public Library. Turn left out of parking area entrance onto ME 176, heading south.
- **0.3** Turn right (west) off ME 176 onto Cape Rosier Road, following signs for Cape Rosier and Holbrook Island Sanctuary.
- **2.0** Holbrook Island Sanctuary is to the right. Continue straight on Cape Rosier Road.

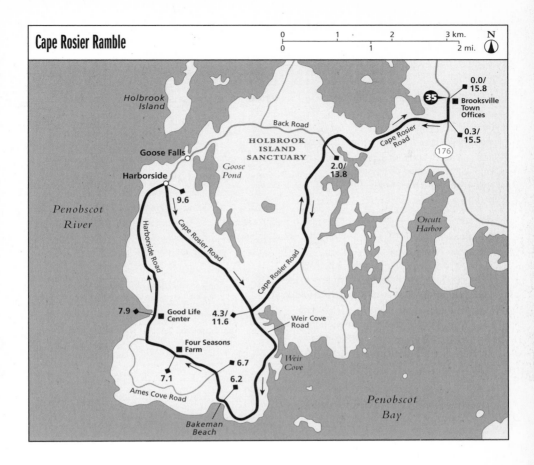

Cape Rosier Ramble

4.3 Cape Rosier Road bears right. Turn left (south) off Cape Rosier Road onto Weir Cove Road, following signs for Four Seasons Farm and Good Life Center.

6.2 Bakeman Beach is on the left. Good swim/picnic stop.

6.7 Ames Cove Road (dirt) to left. Continue straight on Weir Cove Road, which turns to dirt.

7.1 Four Seasons Farm on right.

7.9 Good Life Center on right. Road surface returns to pavement just after the Good Life Center and is now called Harborside Road.

9.6 Turn right (south) onto Cape Rosier Road.

11.6 Turn left (east) with Cape Rosier Road. Weir Cove Road is straight ahead. (You have now completed a loop.)

13.8 Junction with Back Road to left. Continue straight on Cape Rosier Road.

15.5 Junction with ME 176. Turn left onto ME 176, heading north.

15.8 Turn right off ME 176 into parking area.

Local Information

Blue Hill Peninsula Chamber of Commerce, 28 Water Street, Blue Hill, ME; (207) 374-3242; www.bluehillpeninsula.org.

Local Events/Attractions

Good Life Center, 372 Harborside Road, Harborside, ME; (207) 326-8211; www.goodlife .org. Open daily 1:00 to 5:00 p.m., closed Wednesday in summer, closed Tuesday and Wednesday the rest of the year.

Holbrook Island Sanctuary, 172 Indian Bar Point, Harborside, ME; (207) 326-4012.

Food

Four Season Farm, 609 Weir Cove Road, Cape Rosier, ME; www.fourseasonfarm.com. The farm stand is open during the "precise summer" (June 21 through September 21), 1:00 to 5:00 p.m., Monday through Saturday.

Morning Moon Café, 1 Bay Road, Brooklin, ME; (207) 359-2373. Open for breakfast and lunch. Sit at the big table in the middle for local news and socializing.

Accommodations

The Blue Hill Peninsula is attractive for cycling because it doesn't have the high volume of tourist traffic that plagues much of coastal Maine. There are accommodations—mostly inns—that are best found by using the chamber of commerce Web site.

Blue Hill Inn, 40 Union Street, P.O. Box 403, Blue Hill, ME 04614; (207) 374-2844 or (800) 826-7415; www.bluehillinn.com.

The Lookout Inn, 455 Flye Point Road, Brooklin, ME; (207) 359-2188; www.thelookout inn.biz.

Ellsworth, about 14 miles northeast of Blue Hill, is the best option for motel lodging. Check the **Ellsworth Area Chamber of Commerce,** P.O. Box 267, 163 High Street, Ellsworth, ME 04605; (207) 667-5584; www.ellsworthchamber.org.

Bike Shops

Bar Harbor Bicycle Shop, 193 Main Street, Ellsworth, ME; (207) 667-6886; www.bar harborbike.com.

Cadillac Mountain Sports, 32 High Street, Ellsworth, ME; (207) 667-7819; www.cadillac sports.com.

Map

DeLorme: Maine Atlas & Gazetteer: Page 15.

36 Blue Hill Challenge

Thanks to Joe Thompson—master sailor, boatbuilder, biker, and brewer—for this ride. Biking in Maine doesn't get any better than this.

Start: Parking area for the municipal park at the end of Water Street in Blue Hill.
Length: 44.3 miles.
Terrain: Flat to gently hilly.

Traffic and hazards: Most roads have no paved shoulders. The route is designed to avoid traffic as much as possible, but the usual care should be taken, especially during busier summer months.

Getting there: Blue Hill is on the peninsula due west of Mount Desert Island and Acadia National Park. From Ellsworth, take Maine Highway 172 South about 12.5 miles to the junction with Maine Highway 176 in Blue Hill. Turn right onto ME 172 South/ME 176 West. Proceed about 0.3 mile and turn left onto Water Street, following signs for the hospital. Continue about 0.2 mile to the end of Water Street, where there is a municipal park. Park in the public lot.

Brooklin, the tiny village near the southern end of the peninsula, posts a sign welcoming visitors to the "boatbuilding capital of the world." Visitors sometimes ask whether the folks in Bath (home of Bath Ironworks) might dispute that title. Visitors are solemnly assured that Brooklin is indeed a more important center for boat building. "They build ships in Bath. In Brooklin, we build boats"—wooden sailboats and yachts for customers worldwide. There will be plenty of opportunities to see examples of these magnificent sailboats, as much of this ride is close to the water and there are stops at harbors where examples of the Brooklin boatbuilders' craft are proudly moored.

The town of Blue Hill, our starting point, is a bustling center of cultural as well as economic activity. Plan to spend time before or after the ride exploring some of the shops, galleries, and cafes. This is a peninsula where the natives and the people "from away" generally seem to have found common ground. There are still frictions—mostly rooted in the enormous wealth of some outsiders—but the lines between them and us seem more blurred here than in some coastal communities. Everybody on the peninsula is particularly proud of an assortment of famous residents, many of whom have so immersed themselves in the community that they're fondly viewed as hometown heroes. An example is E. B. White, known to most of us as the author of *Charlotte's Web* and *Stuart Little*. They're even prouder of his son Joel, a renowned wooden boat designer.

Parker Point Road, the left off Main Street in Blue Hill, gets the ride off to a fine start. Traffic is light, and views of Blue Hill Harbor are magnificent. This is the kind of road cyclists hope to find in coastal Maine. The good news is that there will be more roads like it on this trip. The turn onto Maine Highway 175 South, at 3.4 miles, signals an increase in traffic for the next few miles, especially during summer

Naskeag Point Harbor

months. Just after the turn onto ME 175, cross a little stone bridge over an inlet, then another bridge over a second inlet. This is a reversing falls, so the direction of the falls will change with the tide.

Notice the blueberry barrens on the left after the turn onto Flye Point Road. From mid-July through August, you can stop and pick a snack. This is the first of the route's three short side-trips. The Lookout Inn, at the end of Flye Point, was reputedly one of Julia Child's favorite restaurants. This probably isn't the place for cyclist snacks—that's coming up in just a few miles, in Brooklin.

The second side-trip is south from Brooklin to Naskeag Point and Harbor. In Brooklin, either on the way out or on the return, stop at the Morning Moon Café or the Brooklin General Store. Both supply friendly local gossip and good food. The publishing headquarters of *Wooden Boat Magazine* is another recommended stop on the Naskeag Peninsula. The magazine has grown into a whole complex of wooden boat activities, including a school where you can watch students working, a store, and beautiful grounds overlooking Eggemoggin Reach. There's a small harbor at the end of Naskeag Point, with a beach, more photo opportunities, and a picnic area.

The third side-trip passes by another harbor on yet another lovely, lightly

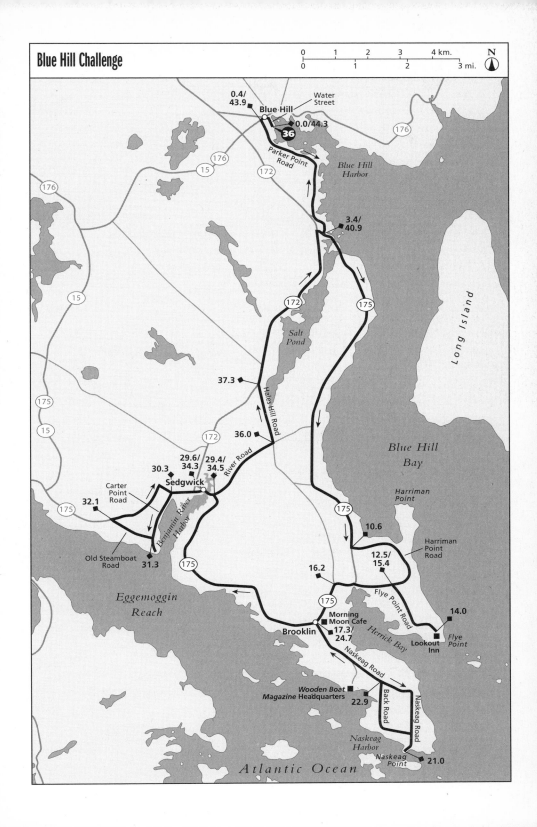

Blue Hill Challenge

0   1   2   3   4 km.

0   1   2   3 mi.

N

0.4/
43.9

Water
Street

176

Blue Hill

0.0/44.3

36

176

Parker Point
Road

172

15

176

Blue Hill
Harbor

176

3.4/
40.9

172

175

Salt
Pond

Long Island

37.3

Hales Hill Road

36.0

Blue Hill
Bay

River Road

29.6/
34.3

29.4/
34.5

172

30.3

Sedgwick

Carter
Point
Road

32.1

175

Harriman
Point

175

Harriman
Point
Road

10.6

Benjamin River Harbor

Old Steamboat
Road

31.3

175

12.5/
15.4

16.2

175

Flye Point Road

14.0

Eggemoggin
Reach

175

Morning
Moon Cafe

Brooklin

17.3/
24.7

Herrick Bay

Lookout
Inn

Flye
Point

Naskeag Road

Wooden Boat
Magazine Headquarters

22.9

Back Road

Naskeag Road

Naskeag
Harbor

Naskeag
Point

21.0

Atlantic Ocean

traveled side road. This is Sedgwick's town harbor, where some of those handcrafted wooden boats are moored.

River Road and Hales Hill Road are two more delightful rural cycling roads, but traffic will be heavier on ME 172 North, heading back toward Blue Hill. Stay focused on the road in spite of the views of Salt Pond to the right and the blueberry barrens all around. Be sure to make the right off ME 172 onto ME 175 South (which seems like the wrong direction), then an immediate left onto Parker Point Road for a shady, nearly traffic-free return to Blue Hill.

Miles and Directions

0.0   Parking area at the end of Water Street. Proceed west, back toward Main Street.

0.2   Junction with Main Street. Turn left onto Main Street (Maine Highway 15/172/176), heading south.

0.4   Turn left off Main Street onto Parker Point Road.

3.4   Junction with ME 175. Turn left onto ME 175 South.

3.9   Bridge over reversing falls.

10.6   Turn left (east) off ME 175 onto Harriman Point Road.

12.5   Junction with Flye Point Road. Turn left off Harriman Point Road onto Flye Point Road, heading south.

14.0   Flye Point Harbor and Lookout Inn. Turn around and return north on Flye Point Road.

15.4   Junction with Harriman Point Road. Bear left, continuing on Flye Point Road.

16.2   Junction with ME 175. Turn left onto ME 175, heading west toward Brooklin.

17.3   Village of Brooklin. Turn left (south) off ME 175 onto Naskeag Road. The Morning Moon Café and the Brooklin General Store are on opposite corners.

18.5   *Wooden Boat Magazine* headquarters, school, and store are to the right. Continue straight (south) on Naskeag Road.

21.0   Naskeag Point Harbor, boat launch, and picnic area. Turn around and return north on Naskeag Road.

21.4   Turn left (west) off Naskeag Road onto Back Road.

22.9   Junction of Back Road and Naskeag Road. Turn left onto Naskeag Road, heading north.

24.7   Return to intersection of Naskeag Road and ME 175 in Brooklin. Turn left (west) onto ME 175, heading toward Sedgwick.

29.4   Junction with River Road. Stay left on ME 175.

29.6   ME 175 crosses a causeway, then makes a sharp left. Continue on ME 175.

30.3   Turn left (south) off ME 175 onto Carter Point Road.

30.8   Sedgwick town landing on Benjamin River Harbor.

31.3   Road forks. Bear right (west) on what is now called Old Steamboat Road.

32.1   Junction with ME 175. Turn right onto ME 175, heading east back toward Sedgwick.

34.3   Cross the causeway in Sedgwick, continuing east on ME 175.

34.5   Turn left off ME 175 onto River Road, heading north. (Watch for this turn—the sign is hard to spot.)

36.0 At the four-way intersection, turn left (north) onto Hales Hill Road. (No road signs at all here, but this is the first intersection of four paved roads.)

37.3 At the junction of Hales Hill Road and ME 172, turn right onto ME 172 North.

40.8 ME 172 joins ME 175. Turn right onto ME 175 South.

40.9 Turn left off ME 175 onto Parker Point Road, heading north.

43.9 Junction with Main Street in Blue Hill. Turn right onto Main Street.

44.0 Turn right off Main Street onto Water Street.

44.3 Return to parking area at end of Water Street.

Local Information

Blue Hill Peninsula Chamber of Commerce, 28 Water Street, Blue Hill, ME; (207) 374-3242; www.bluehillpeninsula.org.

Local Events/Attractions

Blue Hill Peninsula Arts, *Lodging & Business* Web site, www.bluehillme.com.

***Wooden Boat* Publications,** 41 Wooden Boat Lane, P.O. Box 78, Brooklin, ME 04616; (207) 359-4651; www.woodenboat.com or www.woodenboatstore.com.

Eggemoggin Reach Regatta, annual wooden boat race, held in early August; www.erregatta .com.

The Blue Hill area has a full calendar of cultural and social events. The area is particularly known for high-quality musical performances. Check with the chamber of commerce (www.bluehillpeninsula.org) for details.

Food

Pain de Famille, 9 Main Street, Blue Hill, ME; (207) 374-2565. It's between Water Street and Parker Point Road, along the route. Stop for a muffin or a scone to take along.

Morning Moon Café, 1 Bay Road, Brooklin, ME; (207) 359-2373. Open for breakfast and lunch. Sit at the big table in the middle for local news and socializing.

Brooklin General Store, 2 Reach Road, Brooklin, ME; (207) 359-8817.

There are many cafes and restaurants in Blue Hill. They range from the natural food co-op to elegant dining.

Accommodations

One of the reasons that the Blue Hill Peninsula is so attractive for cycling is that it doesn't have the high volume of tourist traffic that plagues much of coastal Maine. There are accommodations—mostly inns—that are best located using the chamber of commerce site.

Blue Hill Inn, 40 Union Street, P.O. Box 403, Blue Hill, ME 04614; (207) 374-2844 or (800) 826-7415; www.bluehillinn.com.

The Lookout Inn, 455 Flye Point Road, Brooklin, ME; (207) 359-2188; www.thelookout inn.biz.

Ellsworth, about 14 miles northeast of Blue Hill, is the best option for motel lodging. Check the **Ellsworth Area Chamber of Commerce,** P.O. Box 267, 163 High Street, Ellsworth, ME 04605; (207) 667-5584; www.ellsworthchamber.org.

Bike Shops

Bar Harbor Bicycle Shop, 193 Main Street, Ellsworth, ME; (207) 667-6886; www.bar harborbike.com.

Cadillac Mountain Sports, 32 High Street, Ellsworth, ME; (207) 667-7819; www.cadillac sports.com.

Map

DeLorme: Maine Atlas & Gazetteer: Page 15.

37 Mount Desert Island Cruise

No guide to Maine cycling would be complete without a chapter on Mount Desert Island and Acadia National Park—the place that comes to mind when almost anyone talks about biking in Maine. Acadia is the second most visited national park on the East Coast (Great Smoky Mountains Park is first). That means a lot of tourist traffic. This is a spectacular ride anytime but is most enjoyable in early spring or fall, when crowds are lighter. If summer is the only choice, try to do it early in the morning, before most visitors are on the road.

Start: Rear of the parking area at Hulls Cove Visitor Center, Acadia National Park.
Length: 25.6 miles.
Terrain: Hilly.

Traffic and hazards: Significant tourist traffic, but slow moving, mostly on a one-way road. Bring a lock, as you'll almost certainly want to walk to a few sights along the way.

Getting there: From Ellsworth, take Maine Highway 3 South, following signs for Acadia National Park. Hulls Cove Visitor Center is on the right, about 15 miles south of Ellsworth.

Having issued the above warning about traffic, I must confess that the last time I did this ride was in the middle of the afternoon, on a hot day in July. The visitor center was packed, and there was a steady stream of cars on the Park Loop Road. In spite of the crowds, I stopped at all the sights (a short walk from the road, and you're alone), breathed the salt air, and simply had a great ride. Whenever I go to Acadia, I applaud the foresighted people—public and private—who worked to preserve this area. Without the 1929 national park designation, the island would have succumbed to development, and most of us would never have an opportunity to visit this national treasure.

Although the total mileage is relatively short, this ride has been labeled a "cruise" rather than a "ramble." That categorization is based on both traffic and terrain. Don't be misled by the fact that this is a coastal ride: It's very hilly. Readers who are looking for an easy "ramble" will be happier with the Schoodic Peninsula ride or with one of the shorter carriage road loops on Mount Desert Island.

Be careful during the first 3 miles of the ride, where traffic is two-way and shoulders are narrow. During the first couple of miles, there will be views of Frenchman Bay and the town of Bar Harbor. If your timing is right, you'll watch the Nova Scotia ferry leaving, or returning to, its Bar Harbor port.

The Park Loop Road offers observation points, geologic features, and other natural sights too numerous to mention here. The basic map of the park, available at the visitor center, points out the most popular stops along the Park Loop Road. It also indicates where restrooms are located. Additionally, an inexpensive booklet called "Motorist Guide, Park Loop Road" contains fascinating details about most stops along the route.

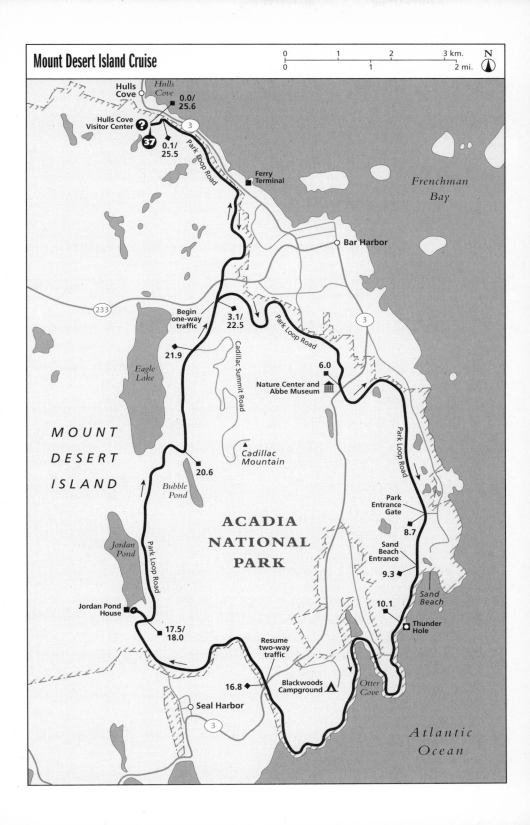

Mount Desert Island Cruise

0 1 2 3 km.

0 1 2 mi.

N

Hulls Cove

Hulls Cove

0.0/ 25.6

Hulls Cove Visitor Center

37

0.1/ 25.5

Park Loop Road

Ferry Terminal

Frenchman Bay

Bar Harbor

233

Begin one-way traffic

3.1/ 22.5

21.9

Park Loop Road

3

Cadillac Summit Road

Eagle Lake

Nature Center and Abbe Museum

6.0

MOUNT DESERT ISLAND

20.6

Cadillac Mountain

Park Loop Road

Bubble Pond

ACADIA NATIONAL PARK

Park Entrance Gate

8.7

Jordan Pond

Park Loop Road

Sand Beach Entrance

9.3

Sand Beach

Jordan Pond House

17.5/ 18.0

10.1

Thunder Hole

Resume two-way traffic

16.8

Blackwoods Campground

Otter Cove

Seal Harbor

3

Atlantic Ocean

A couple of stops are especially recommended. The first is Sand Beach, at 9.3 miles. Visitors traveling by car find that the parking lot here fills up fast. But parking a bike is easy. Although the southern Maine coast has a number of long, sandy beaches, this is one of just a handful along the northern part of the coast. There are restrooms and changing areas. If you've been hankering for an invigorating swim, this is the spot.

Thunder Hole, at 10.1 miles, might be another important stop. On a calm day at low tide it's interesting, but not memorable. If the tide is right and the seas are running rough, however, you'll definitely want to witness the boom made as each wave compresses air in the back of the chasm.

At 16.8 miles traffic becomes two-way again. Be especially careful. Most traffic will still be traveling in the same direction, so cars can easily get around cyclists. But it's easy for drivers to forget that the one-way rules are over, and that there may be oncoming cars and trucks. Stay right and be ready to get off the road if necessary.

The route as written makes a short side-trip to the parking area at Jordan Pond House. This is the best opportunity on the route to visit one of the freshwater ponds on Mount Desert, and there are some fine short hiking trails that start here. For over a century the Jordan Pond House restaurant has been famous for its popovers and tea.

And finally, there's the Cadillac Summit Road, a thigh-burning side-trip recommended only for the very ambitious. On a clear day, the view from the 1,530-foot summit is just as lovely as you'd expect. Be sure brakes are in good order before the descent.

This ride is spectacular, but, really, it's just the beginning of biking on Mount Desert Island. There are also 44 miles of interior gravel carriage roads—with their famous stone bridges—where vehicular traffic is prohibited. Most people use mountain or hybrid bikes on these roads, but I have happily ridden them on a road bike with 28mm tires. The carriage roads are well maintained and offer a wide variety of terrain and scenery, including several freshwater ponds. Stop at the visitor center for a special "Carriage Road User's Map."

Miles and Directions

0.0 Rear of parking area at Hulls Cove Visitor Center. Proceed to visitor center entrance.

0.1 Exit visitor center and proceed onto Park Loop Road, directly opposite.

3.1 Turn left with Park Loop Road, which becomes one-way here.

6.0 Entrance to Nature Center and Abbe Museum is on the right. Continue straight.

6.5 Bear Brook picnic area is to the left.

7.9 Precipice Rock trailheads to right.

8.7 Park entrance gate. You must show pass or pay.

9.3 Entrance to Sand Beach is to the left. Continue straight on Park Loop Road.

10.1 Thunder Hole is on the left.

11.1 Southern end of Otter Point. Continue on Park Loop Road.

16.8 Road to the left goes south to Seal Harbor. Bear right, continuing on Park Loop Road. Note that two-way traffic resumes here.

17.5 Turn left off Park Loop Road to Jordan Pond House picnic area, beach, etc.

17.7 Turn around and head back to Park Loop Road.

18.0 Turn left onto Park Loop Road, heading north. Remember, traffic is two-way.

20.6 Bubble Pond to the right. Continue straight on Park Loop Road.

21.9 Cadillac Summit Road is to the right. Continue straight on Park Loop Road.

22.5 Road forks. Route has now completed the Park Loop. Bear left, heading north toward the visitor center.

25.5 Turn into entrance to Hulls Cove Visitor Center.

25.6 Return to rear of parking area.

Local Information

Bar Harbor Chamber of Commerce, P.O. Box 158, 93 Cottage Street, Bar Harbor, ME 04609; (207) 288-5103 or (800) 288-5103; www.barharborinfo.com.

Ellsworth Area Chamber of Commerce, P.O. Box 267, 163 High Street, Ellsworth, ME 04605; (207) 667-5584; www.ellsworthchamber.org.

Local Events/Attractions

Acadia National Park, P.O. Box 177, Bar Harbor, ME 04609; (207) 288-3338; www.nps .gov/acad. A seven-day parking permit is $20 during summer months ($10 before mid-June or in the fall). If you leave a vehicle elsewhere (for example, at a motel), the fee is $5 per person.

Food

Jordan Pond House, Park Loop Road, P.O. Box 24, Acadia National Park, Bar Harbor, ME 04609; (207) 276-3316; www.jordan pond.com. Reservations are recommended during peak summer months.

Tourism is the major industry in Bar Harbor, so restaurants are abundant. The Bar Harbor Chamber of Commerce Web site has a comprehensive list.

Accommodations

See the Bar Harbor Chamber of Commerce Web site for a comprehensive list of lodging possibilities. Prices are predictably high, and advance reservations may be necessary during the summer months. Prices may be a little lower in Ellsworth.

Two campgrounds, **Blackwoods and Seawall,** are located in Acadia National Park. Blackwoods accepts reservations, Seawall does not. Both are mostly tent sites, with limited amenities. See www.acadia.national-park.com /camping.htm for details. For Blackwoods reservations, call (800) 365-2267.

Bike Shops

Acadia Bike, 48 Cottage Street, Bar Harbor, ME; (207) 288-9605; www.acadiabike.com. Rentals available.

Bar Harbor Bicycle Shop, 141 Cottage Street, Bar Harbor, ME; (207) 288-3886; www.barharborbike.com. Rentals available.

Southwest Cycle, 370 Main Street, Southwest Harbor, ME; (207) 244-5856; www.southwest cycle.com. A good place to inquire about bike routes on the western half of the island.

Map

DeLorme: Maine Atlas & Gazetteer: Page 16.

38 Schoodic Ramble

This is an easy ramble in one of the lesser known sections of Acadia National Park. It's a good choice for riders looking to escape crowds and traffic during the busy summer season on neighboring Mount Desert Island.

Start: Frazer Point Picnic Area, at entrance to Acadia National Park, Schoodic Point Section.
Length: 12.1 miles.
Terrain: Gently hilly.

Traffic and hazards: Tourist traffic is one-way and slow moving for almost half the ride. Regular traffic resumes on Maine Highway 186, where shoulders are narrow.

Getting there: From Ellsworth, take U.S. Highway 1 east about 18 miles. Turn right onto ME 186 South and proceed a little over 16 miles to the town of Winter Harbor, where ME 186 makes a sharp left. Continue 1.5 miles to a right turn onto Moore Road, following signs for Acadia National Park, Schoodic Point Section. The entrance to Frazer Point Picnic Area is in 1.6 miles, on the right.

To most of the two million annual visitors to Acadia National Park, the Schoodic Peninsula is the land you see across Frenchman Bay as you stand at a Park Road overlook on Mount Desert Island. Few people realize that the Schoodic Peninsula is also part of the national park—in fact, it's the only part that isn't on an island. Views of rocky headlands, Frenchman Bay, and the general natural beauty of the downeast coast are pretty much the same on Schoodic as on Mount Desert Island. The crowds are the missing element. This short ride could be done very quickly, or better yet, you could bring a picnic for a stop at Schoodic Point. As with all coastal cycling, be prepared for fog that rolls in fast.

Winter Harbor, the small town near the park entrance on the Schoodic Peninsula, was so named because it typically didn't freeze and could be used all winter. An earlier name, "Mosquito Harbor," was less appealing but may provide a warning about bringing bug spray for spring rides. The name "Schoodic" is apparently something of a mystery. Various sources list "point of land," "trout place," and "opened by fire" as possible Abenaki or Malecite derivations.

A stop at the Schoodic Education and Research Center, at 3.3 miles (or at 4.1 miles on the return from Schoodic Point) is recommended. It's located on the grounds of a former naval base and is currently administered by the National Park Service in cooperation with Acadia Partners for Science and Learning, a nonprofit organization. There's a small visitor center where you can learn about the area and about projects and research that take place here.

Geologists will be delighted with the rocky headland at Schoodic Point. The pinkish granite is punctuated by black, north/south, basalt dikes. Waves surge into the trenches that form where the basalt erodes more quickly than the harder granite. You don't have to be a geologist to enjoy rock hopping here. It's also a great spot

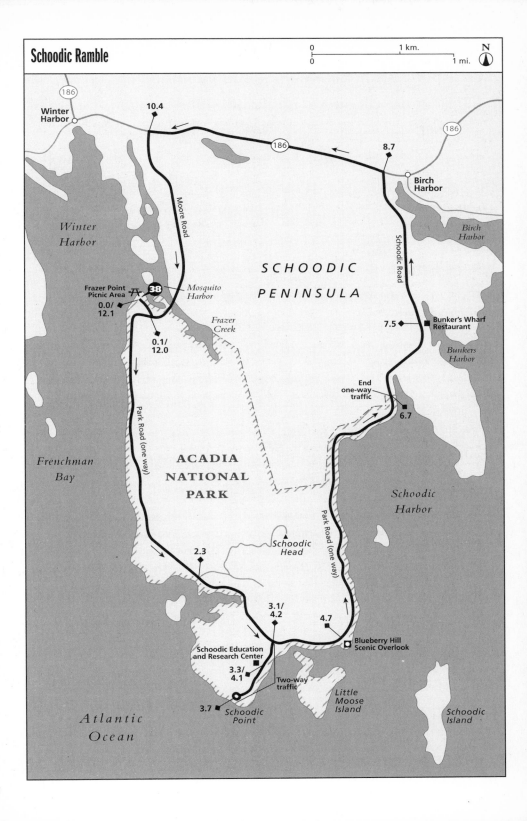

Schoodic Ramble

0 — 1 km.
0 — 1 mi.

N

186
Winter Harbor

10.4

186

8.7

Birch Harbor

186

Moore Road

Winter Harbor

SCHOODIC PENINSULA

Schoodic Road

Birch Harbor

Frazer Point Picnic Area

38

Mosquito Harbor

0.0/ 12.1

0.1/ 12.0

Frazer Creek

7.5

Bunker's Wharf Restaurant

Bunkers Harbor

End one-way traffic

6.7

Park Road (one way)

Frenchman Bay

ACADIA NATIONAL PARK

Schoodic Head

Schoodic Harbor

2.3

Park Road (one way)

3.1/ 4.2

4.7

Blueberry Hill Scenic Overlook

Schoodic Education and Research Center

3.3/ 4.1

Two-way traffic

3.7

Schoodic Point

Little Moose Island

Schoodic Island

Atlantic Ocean

for watching coastal birds or just for sitting on a rock and watching lobster boats in Frenchman Bay.

Blueberry Hill Scenic Overlook, at 4.7 miles, is another fine picnic/observation stop. If you've got walking shoes along, you might want to lock your bike and take the Alder or the Anvil hiking trail (no bikes), which both go to Schoodic Head, the highest point on the peninsula.

The views of Schoodic Harbor, to the right as you head north on the east side of the peninsula, are spectacular. Note that traffic becomes two-way at 6.7 miles, and remember to stay right.

The final part of the ride, west on ME 186 and then south on Moore Road, are a little hillier. A short side-trip into the village of Winter Harbor would be a pleasant way to end the ride.

Miles and Directions

0.0 Parking lot at Frazer Point Picnic Area. Head back to entrance.

0.1 Entrance to Frazer Point Picnic Area. Turn right (south) onto Park Road, following signs for Schoodic Point. Road becomes one-way.

2.3 Gravel road to left leads to Schoodic Head (mountain). Continue straight on Park Road.

3.1 Road forks. Bear right (south), following signs for Schoodic Point. Traffic becomes two-way.

3.3 Entrance to Schoodic Education and Research Center on right. Continue straight on Park Road.

3.7 Schoodic Point. Turn around and head back north.

4.1 Entrance to Schoodic Education and Research Center on left. Continue straight.

4.2 Road forks. Bear right on Park Road, now called Schoodic Road. Traffic becomes one-way.

4.7 Blueberry Hill Scenic Overlook is to the right.

6.7 Traffic becomes two-way.

7.5 Bunker's Wharf Restaurant is on the right.

8.7 At junction with ME 186 in Birch Harbor, turn left onto ME 186 West. Mc's Marketplace is on the right.

10.4 Turn left (south) off ME 186 onto Moore Road, following signs for Acadia National Park, Schoodic Point Section.

12.0 Turn right off Moore Road at entrance to Frazer Point Picnic Area.

12.1 Return to parking lot.

Local Information

Schoodic Area Chamber of Commerce, P.O. Box 381, Winter Harbor, ME 04693; (207) 963-7658 or (800) 231-3008; www.acadia-schoodic.org.

Ellsworth Area Chamber of Commerce, P.O. Box 267, 163 High Street, Ellsworth, ME 04605; (207) 667-5584; www.ellsworthchamber.org.

Local Events/Attractions

Acadia National Park, P.O. Box 177, Bar Harbor, ME 04609; (207) 288-3338; www.nps.gov/acad. A seven-day parking permit is $20 during summer months ($10 before mid-June or in the fall). If you leave a vehicle elsewhere (for example, at a motel), the fee is $5 per person.

Food

Bunker's Wharf Restaurant, 260 East Schoodic Drive, Birch Harbor, ME; (207) 963-2244; www.bunkerswharfrestaurant.com.

Accommodations

Main Stay Inn & Cottages, 66 Sargent Street, P.O. Box 459, Winter Harbor, ME 04693; (207) 963-2601; www.awa-web.com/stayinn.

Pines Motel & Cottages, 17 Main Street, Winter Harbor, ME; (207) 963-2296.

Ocean Wood Campground, 1 Ocean Wood Way, Birch Harbor, ME; (207) 963-7194. Large oceanfront sites.

Bike Shops

Bar Harbor Bicycle Shop, 193 Main Street, Ellsworth, ME; (207) 667-6886; www.bar harborbike.com.

Cadillac Mountain Sports, 32 High Street, Ellsworth, ME; (207) 667-7819; www.cadillac sports.com.

Map

DeLorme: Maine Atlas & Gazetteer: Page 17.

39 Way Downeast Classic

Maine doesn't get any better than this. Gaze out over the Atlantic from the easternmost point in the United States, stop for a snack at wild blueberry barrens, and visit a fishing village that hardly ever sees a tourist. Even in peak summer months, traffic on most of the route won't be a problem. Although serious cyclists can do it in a day, two days are recommended, as you'll want time to enjoy the sights and flavors. A sensible overnight is at the motel in Lubec or the campground at Quoddy Head State Park. A side-trip to Campobello is also recommended: Take a third day, and make it an international adventure!

Start: Parking area at Washington Academy, on Maine Highway 191 in East Machias. Stop in or call (207) 255-8301 to let the Academy know you're leaving a vehicle, and they'll direct you to the best parking lot to use. Overnight parking is okay.

Length: 80.6 miles.

Terrain: Gently rolling. A few moderate hills.

Traffic and hazards: Maine Highway 189 west of Lubec carries the most traffic, including Canadian-bound truck traffic. As of this writing, shoulders are narrow and pavement is choppy. Exercise extreme caution on ME 189.

U.S. Highway 1 is also heavily traveled, although volume here is light compared to more westerly sections of the road. This area of Maine is prone to dense fogs that roll in quickly. The sun may be shining in East Machias while a pea-soup fog engulfs Cutler. Carry rain gear and reflective clothing or, preferably, a light. This is a remote area with no stores between East Machias and Lubec (about 36 miles) or between Whiting and East Machias (about 31 miles), so carry water, food, and basic tools for repairs.

Getting there: Take US 1 east from Machias about 4.3 miles to the intersection with ME 191 in East Machias. Turn right onto ME 191 South. Proceed 0.4 mile to Washington Academy. Ask Academy personnel which parking lot to use.

Tenting at Cobscook Bay State Park

As you head south from the parking area, along the Machias River, you'll immediately notice two important features of the downeast coastal landscape: beach roses and blueberry bushes. For years to come, the smell of roses or the taste of wild blueberries will bring back memories of this ride. There aren't many places to buy food along the route, but during July and August you won't go hungry, even if you've neglected to pack snacks. Most blueberries along the roadside are free for the taking, and they're delicious.

The village of Cutler is about as picturesque, and certainly as authentic, a Maine fishing village as you'll find. There's a post office and firehouse, but no stores or postcards for tourists. The piles of lobster traps in yards are a clue to the area's main industry. There's a range of as much as 28 feet between high and low tides in Cutler's well-protected harbor. If you happen to arrive at low tide, you'll see boats perched patiently on the sand, awaiting the incoming tide.

The sparse traffic you saw between East Machias and Cutler will diminish even more after Cutler. The stretch between Cutler and the West Quoddy Head Light is especially remote. Forests and blueberry barrens are about all you'll see. If you've brought along a pair of hiking shoes, you might want to lock your bike and walk the trails to the sea cliffs (3 or 4 miles one way) from the trailhead at 20.0 miles. There are also camping spots.

One might expect a sign pointing visitors to what is arguably the most famous lighthouse in the United States. But no, there's no sign. You don't want to miss an opportunity to stand on the easternmost point in America, so watch carefully for the turn onto Boot Cove Road at 24.1 miles. Boot Cove Road is recently paved (it used to be dirt), and you almost have to wonder why they bothered. There's nothing on it. You may travel the entire distance of the road (over 5 miles) without seeing a car or truck.

The famous red and white striped West Quoddy Head Light is well worth a short side-trip, and so has been included in the route and mileages. On my last visit, it was completely socked in by fog. I couldn't see the ocean (or the other side of the picnic table) but was able to witness the foghorn in action. They've got a fine little visitor center, museum, and gift shop.

At the junction with ME 189, at 36.5 miles, many cyclists will want to make an optional side-trip to Lubec, where there are stores, restaurants, and an information center. Lubec was once a hub for herring fishing and sardine canneries. The herring industry has given way to aquaculture (mostly salmon), and they're experimenting with various uses of the cannery buildings. You can buy a jar of "Quoddy Mist," sea salt that's now processed in Lubec. Lubec is also where you cross the border for an extended side-trip to Campobello Island, Canada. It would be easy to spend a day on Campobello. Cycling is good, and a tour of the Roosevelt Campobello International Park is inspiring. Jointly administered by the United States and Canada, it's the only such international park in the world. As of spring 2008, a government issued photo I.D. (driver's license) and proof of citizenship (birth certificate), or a green card, is sufficient for a North American land or sea border crossing. However, beginning in June 2009 a passport, "passport card," or green card will be required (unless the law is changed).

Be especially cautious on ME 189, where there's a significant amount of truck traffic. A little relief from the traffic is provided by the jag onto the delightful Crow Neck and Timber Cove Roads.

The Whiting Village Store, at the intersection of ME 189 and US 1, is the last chance to stock up on food and fluids for the next 30-plus miles, so a stop is probably wise. On my last trip, I camped at Cobscook Bay State Park (entrance at 54.0 miles). It may be the most beautiful campground I've stayed in. It's certainly one of Maine's hidden gems, but it's becoming better known. If you want a waterfront campsite, you'll probably need a reservation.

On a map, Maine Highway 86 west of Dennysville looks like a major road. It even looks like a major road up close as you're pedaling along it—except for the absence of traffic. There are cars and trucks, but you can happily pedal long distances without much vehicular competition. And once again, blueberries are abundant in July and August. There are a couple of possible lake stops along ME 86. The first is at 62.8 miles, where a paved road to the left leads to Great Works Pond. The pavement turns to unimproved dirt, and you may need to walk the final stretch to the water. The second lake stop is at Patrick Lake, at 68.5 miles.

Way Downeast Classic

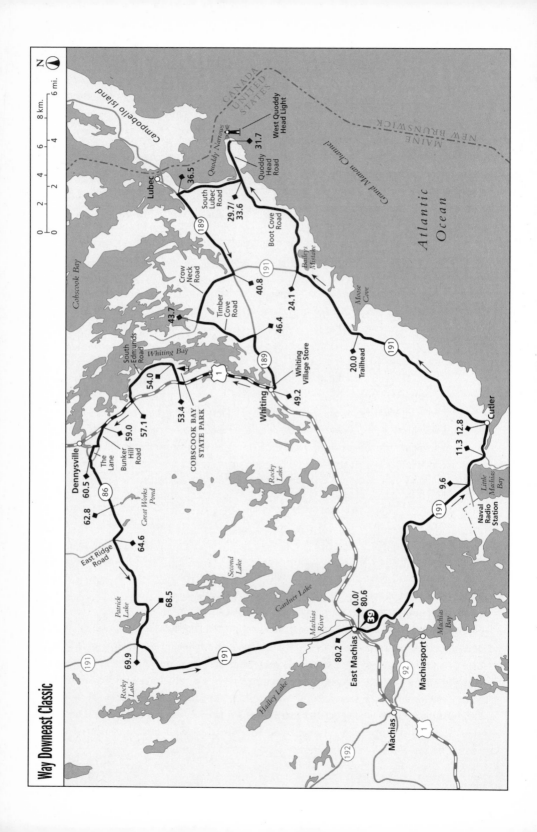

The turn off ME 86 onto ME 191 signals a slight increase in traffic. It's a straight road, however, with good visibility, at least a small shoulder, some fine views, and more blueberry barrens. Cross US 1 carefully. Then it's just a short uphill to the parking area and, alas, the ride is over.

Miles and Directions

0.0 Parking area at Washington Academy. Turn right onto ME 191 South.

9.6 Road to Naval Station is to the right. Continue straight on ME 191 (Cutler Road).

11.3 Road to Little Machias to the right. Bear left (east), continuing on ME 191 (Cutler Road).

12.8 Village of Cutler. Continue straight on ME 191 as it bears left (north).

20.0 Trailhead and parking area are to the right. Trails lead to camping areas and sea cliffs.

24.1 Turn right (east) off ME 191 onto Boot Cove Road.

29.7 At the junction with South Lubec Road and Quoddy Head Road, turn right onto Quoddy Head Road, heading east toward the West Quoddy Head Light.

31.7 West Quoddy Head Light. Turn around and return west on Quoddy Head Road.

33.6 At the junction with South Lubec Road, bear right onto South Lubec Road, heading north.

36.5 At the junction with ME 189, turn left onto ME 189 West. **Option:** Turn right onto ME 189 East for side-trip to Lubec and/or Campobello Island.

40.8 Turn right (north) off ME 189 onto Crow Neck Road.

43.7 Turn left off Crow Neck Road onto Timber Cove Road, heading south.

46.4 At the junction with ME 189, turn right onto ME 189 West.

49.2 At the junction with US 1, turn right onto US 1 North. The Whiting Village Store is on the corner.

53.4 Turn right (east) off US 1 onto South Edmunds Road, following signs for Cobscook Bay State Park.

54.0 Entrance to Cobscook Bay State Park on right. Continue straight on South Edmunds Road.

57.1 At the junction with US 1, turn right onto US 1 North.

59.0 Turn left (west) off US 1 onto Bunker Hill Road, following signs for Dennysville.

59.8 Cross Dennys River. Bear right, then make an immediate left onto The Lane.

60.5 At the junction with ME 86, turn left onto ME 86 West.

62.8 Road to Great Works Pond is on the left. Continue straight on ME 86.

64.6 East Ridge Road is to the right. Bear left (west), continuing on ME 86.

68.5 Boat launch and public access on Patrick Lake to the right. Continue straight on ME 86.

69.9 At the junction with ME 191, turn left onto ME 191 South.

80.2 At the junction with US 1. Turn left onto US 1 East., then immediately turn right off US 1 onto ME 191 South.

80.6 Return to parking area at Washington Academy.

Local Information

Machias Bay Area Chamber of Commerce, 12 East Main Street, Machias, ME; (207) 255-4402; www.machiaschamber.org (click "Visitor Guide" for comprehensive lists of restaurants, accommodations, and services in the Machias area).

Cobscook Bay Area Chamber of Commerce, P.O. Box 42, Whiting, ME 04691; (207) 733-2201; www.cobscookbay.com.

Local Events/Attractions

Lubec Historical Society Museum and Tourist Information, 135 Main Street (ME 189), Lubec, ME; (207) 733-4696.

Machias Maine Wild Blueberry Festival, annual mid-August celebration with parade, arts and crafts, food, and more. Visit www.machiasblueberry.com.

West Quoddy Head Light, Quoddy Head State Park, Lubec, ME; (207) 733-0911; www.maine.gov/doc/parks. Free admission to the museum and visitor center. Open daily Memorial Day to mid-October. Hiking trails and picnic areas.

Roosevelt Campobello International Park, Campobello Island, New Brunswick, Canada. Send for information: P.O. Box 129 Lubec, ME 04652; www.fdr.net. The Canadian Visitor Center, on the right just after the bridge onto the island, provides a variety of maps, lodging information, etc.

Food

Murphy's Village Restaurant, 122 Main Street (ME 189), Lubec, ME; (207) 733-4440. Good biker stop. Hearty portions of home-cooked downeast favorites.

Whiting Village Store, US 1, Whiting, ME; (207) 733-4432. Located at the junction of ME 189 and US 1. Large general store with deli and indoor seating.

Helen's Restaurant, 28 East Main Street, Machias, ME; (207) 255-8423; www.helenspies.com. A favorite with locals for family dining. Prize-winning blueberry pie.

Accommodations

Eastland Motel, 385 County Road (ME 189), Lubec, ME; (207) 733-5501; www.eastlandmotel.com.

Cobscook Bay State Park, RR 1, Box 127, Dennysville, ME 04628; (207) 726-4412. For information and reservations, use www.state.me.us/doc/parks.

Machias Motor Inn, 26 East Main Street (US 1), Machias, ME; (207) 255-4861/4862; www.machiasmotorinn.com.

Bike Shops

Bar Harbor Bicycle Shop, 193 Main Street, Ellsworth, ME; (207) 667-6886; www.barharborbike.com.

Cadillac Mountain Sports, 32 High Street, Ellsworth, ME; (207) 667-7819; www.cadillacsports.com.

Map

DeLorme: Maine Atlas & Gazetteer: Pages 26, 27.

40 Passamaquoddy Bay Ramble

This is what coastal New England cycling should be: great views, rolling terrain, minimal traffic. Take your pick of salt or fresh water, or make stops at both. This ride is guaranteed to send you back to the trusty DeLorme atlas for more rides in the area. You may even find yourself checking local real estate listings.

Start: Gleason Point Boat Launch, east of Perry and north of Eastport.

Length: 18.9 miles.

Terrain: Flat to hilly.

Traffic and hazards: Traffic will be minimal, even in summer. Be careful crossing U.S. Highway 1, especially in Perry, and especially during local morning and evening commutes.

Getting there: Take US 1 north from Machias, about 36 miles, to Perry. Turn right off US 1 onto Shore Road, following signs for Gleason Cove. Proceed 0.3 mile to a right turn onto Gleason Cove Road, following signs for the public boat access. The public access parking area is at the end of the road (about 0.8 mile).

"Passamaquoddy" probably means "plenty pollock jumping" or "plenty pollock jumping place." The Passamaquoddy Bay separates Maine and New Brunswick, Canada, and fishing is still the livelihood for many residents. That's Deer Island (New Brunswick) across the water at the beginning of the ride. Only the most dedicated Maine tourists make it this far "downeast," so tourist traffic won't be much of an issue here.

For most of the first 6 miles, views of Passamaquoddy Bay are spectacular. The descent from the plateau to sea level, at about 1.5 miles, is especially memorable. Then the road climbs a bit, so you get a panoramic view of the bay and Canada to the east. On a clear day, you'll want to make some photo stops along this stretch of the ride.

Don't miss the right turn at 3.9 miles. It isn't surprising to learn that Gin Cove Road is so named for the liquor smuggling that took place here during Prohibition.

After crossing US 1, it's a gradual climb to Boyden Lake, a beautiful freshwater lake where waterfowl, loons, moose, and assorted other wildlife clearly outnumber the human inhabitants. "This is what New England lakes *should* be like," is the comment from admiring visitors. There are a few summer cottages, and there are plenty of pull-offs along the north side of the lake. But even on a hot day in July, the boat launch may be empty and the few cars and trucks on the road are local.

The remainder of the ride back to US 1 is pleasantly rolling back-road cycling. Although caution is advised when crossing US 1, the short stretch of pedaling on US 1 is safe, as shoulders are wide.

A side-trip south on Maine Highway 190 is an interesting option for another day or for an extension to this ride. ME 190 passes through the Passamaquoddy

Descent to Passamaquoddy Bay with New Brunswick, Canada, in the distance

Indian Reservation and ends in Eastport. Traffic is heavier on ME 190, but there are substantial shoulders for much of the 7 miles to the end of the peninsula.

Miles and Directions

0.0 Parking area at Gleason Point Boat Launch. Head inland on what is, according to the sign, Gleason Cove Road, but is labeled on maps as Gleason Point Road.

0.8 At the junction with Shore Road, turn right onto Shore Road, heading north.

3.9 Turn right off Shore Road onto Gin Cove Road.

6.3 Cross US 1 onto Lake Road, heading west.

7.6 Golding Road is to the left. Continue straight on Lake Road.

9.9 At the junction with Ridge Road (unmarked here), turn left onto Ridge Road.

10.7 Boat launch on Boyden Lake, to the left.

11.2 At the four-way intersection, turn left onto South Meadow Road, heading southeast toward Perry.

16.9 Golding Road is to the left. Continue straight on South Meadow Road.

17.5 Junction with US 1. Perry Farmers' Union General Store is on the left. Turn left onto US 1 North.

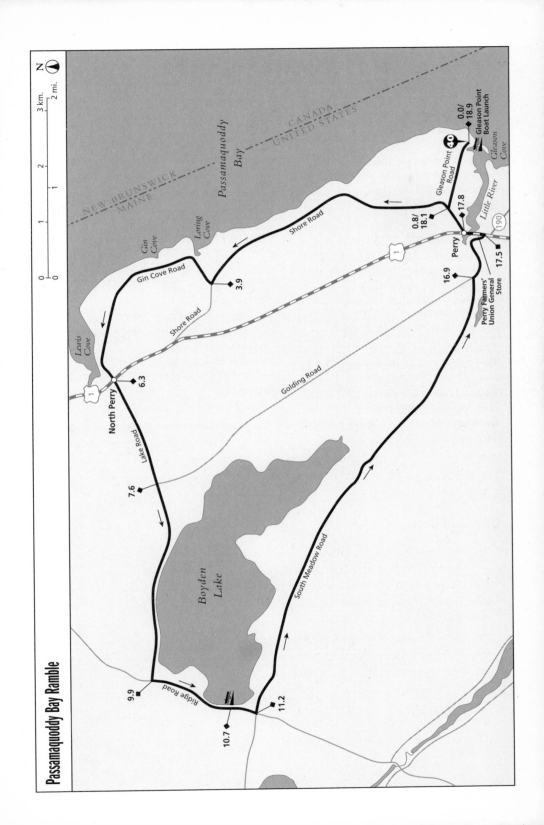

Passamaquoddy Bay Ramble

N

0 1 2 3 km.
0   1   2 mi.

New Brunswick
Maine

Passamaquoddy Bay

Canada
United States

Lewis Cove

Gin Cove

Loring Cove

Gin Cove Road

Shore Road

Shore Road

North Perry

6.3

7.6

Lake Road

Golding Road

Boyden Lake

Ridge Road

9.9

10.7

11.2

South Meadow Road

3.9

16.9

Perry

Perry Farmers'
Union General
Store

17.5

190

Little River

Gleason Point Road

0.8/
18.1

17.8

0.0/
18.9

Gleason Point Boat Launch

Gleason Cove

17.8 Turn right (east) off US 1 onto Shore Road, following signs for Gleason Cove.

18.1 Turn right off Shore Road onto Gleason Cove (Point) Road, following signs for public boat access.

18.9 Return to parking area.

Local Information

Eastport Chamber of Commerce, P.O. Box 254, Eastport, ME 04631; (207) 853-4644.

Eastport Maine Area Information Directory, www.eastportme.info.

Local Events/Attractions

New Brunswick Ferry, (506) 747-2159; www.eastcoastferries.nb.ca. Leaves from 167 Water Street in Eastport and goes to Deer Island and Campobello.

Waponahki Museum, 59 Passamaquoddy Road, Pleasant Point, ME; (207) 853-4001; www.wabanaki.com/museum.htm.

Food

Perry Farmers' Union General Store, US 1, Perry, ME; (207) 853-2891.

The New Friendly Restaurant, 1014 US 1, Perry, ME; (207) 853-6610.

The Happy Crab, 35 Water Street, Eastport, ME; (207) 853-9400.

Accommodations

For motels, see the Eastport Maine Area Information Directory.

The Motel East, 23A Water Street, Eastport, ME; (207) 853-4747; www.eastportme.info/moteleast.html.

Cobscook Bay State Park, RR 1, Box 127, Dennysville, ME 04628; (207) 726-4412. The park has a campground. For information and reservations, use www.state.me.us/doc/parks.

Bike Shops

Bar Harbor Bicycle Shop, 193 Main Street, Ellsworth, ME; (207) 667-6886; www.barharborbike.com.

Cadillac Mountain Sports, 32 High Street, Ellsworth, ME; (207) 667-7819; www.cadillacsports.com.

Map

DeLorme: Maine Atlas & Gazetteer: Page 37.

Ride Index

About the Author

The people of Rutland County, Vermont, know Sandy Duling as an avid cyclist, an explorer of the New England countryside, and as the library director at Castleton State College. When not pedaling, she enjoys cross-country skiing and canoeing, and plays the tin whistle in a traditional Irish band. Her other publications include *Short Bike Rides in Vermont* (second edition, Globe Pequot Press, 2000) and articles in *Adventure Cyclist* and *American Libraries*. She recently returned from five months in Rovaniemi, Finland, where, she reports, bicycle commuters are undaunted by arctic weather. She lives with her husband, Ennis, in East Poultney, Vermont.

Help Us Keep This Guide Up to Date

Every effort has been made by the author and editors to make this guide as accurate and useful as possible. However, many things can change after a guide is published—roads are closed for repairs, regulations change, techniques evolve, facilities come under new management, and so forth.

We would love to hear from you concerning your experiences with this guide and how you feel it could be improved and kept up to date. While we may not be able to respond to all comments and suggestions, we'll take them to heart, and we'll also make certain to share them with the authors. Please send your comments and suggestions to the following address:

> The Globe Pequot Press
> Reader Response/Editorial Department
> P.O. Box 480
> Guilford, CT 06437

Or you may e-mail us at:

> editorial@GlobePequot.com

Thanks for your input, and happy travels!